Slavery and the Commerce Power

DAVID L. LIGHTNER

Slavery and the Commerce Power

HOW THE STRUGGLE AGAINST THE INTERSTATE SLAVE TRADE LED TO THE CIVIL WAR

Yale University Press
New Haven &
London

Set in Sabon by Keystone Typesetting, Inc.
Printed in the United States of America by Sheridan Books, Chelsea, Michigan.

Library of Congress Cataloging-in-Publication Data
Lightner, David L., 1942–
Slavery and the commerce power : how the struggle against the interstate slave trade led to the Civil War / David L. Lightner.
p. cm.
Includes bibliographical references and index.
ISBN-13: 978-0-300-11470-6 (cloth : alk. paper)
ISBN-10: 0-300-11470-2 (cloth : alk. paper)
1. Slave trade—United States—History—19th century. 2. Antislavery movements—United States—History—19th century. 3. Interstate commerce—United States—History—19th century. 4. Slavery—Political aspects—United States—History—19th century. 5. United States—History—Civil War, 1861–1865—Causes. I. Title.
E442.L54 2006
973.7′112—dc22

2006007377

A catalogue record for this book is available from the British Library.

The paper in this book meets the guidelines for permanence and durability of the Committee on Production Guidelines for Book Longevity of the Council on Library Resources.

10 9 8 7 6 5 4 3 2 1

The internal slave trade is the great jugular vein of slavery; and if Congress will take the same weapon with which they cut off the foreign trade, and cut this vein, slavery would die of starvation in the southern, and of apoplexy in the northern slave states.

—Henry B. Stanton
7 May 1839

Contents

Preface

This is the story of a constitutional loophole and of a law that never was. When the founding fathers met at Philadelphia in 1787, delegates from the South tried to ensure that it would be impossible for the new national government to interfere with slavery. The southerners overlooked a possible opportunity for such interference, however, when they agreed to give Congress the power to regulate interstate commerce. That much became clear in the nineteenth century when the great cotton boom took hold in the South. As vast amounts of new land were brought under cultivation, it became necessary to transfer great numbers of slaves southward and westward from the upper South to the booming new frontier regions of the lower South. Consequently, the interstate slave trade swelled to vast proportions. It also became one of the ugliest features of slavery, as traders ruthlessly separated African Americans from their loved ones and carried them off in chains to be sold in distant markets. Opponents of slavery were shocked by the cruelty of the slave trade, and many of them began insisting that it was an evil that could and should be curbed by the federal government. For forty years, from the 1820s to the 1860s, antislavery activists struggled to persuade Congress to use its authority over interstate commerce to outlaw the interstate slave trade. The story of that long struggle is here told fully for the first time.

Although it failed to achieve its goal, the crusade for congressional action against the slave trade is important because of its impact upon southern consciousness. The crusade reached its zenith in the 1830s and 1840s but then lost momentum. Ironically, it was only after the agitation had peaked and was on the wane that southern fears of the threat to the slave trade waxed strong in the 1850s and reached their climax in the secession crisis of 1860–61. Some historians have found it puzzling that the South should have reacted so violently to the election of Abraham Lincoln to the presidency in 1860. Lincoln opposed any further territorial expansion of slavery, but he had no intention of interfering with slavery where it was already established. Why then should southerners have become so unhinged by his mere election that they plunged the nation into the catastrophe of secession and civil war? The answer, I think, is that by 1860 many influential southerners had lost confidence that slavery was safe within the existing American constitutional framework. They had become convinced that a Lincoln presidency, although perhaps endurable in itself, would be the first link in an inexorable chain of developments that must culminate in the destruction of slavery. One of the most injurious of those inexorable links would be the suppression of the interstate slave trade.

The book begins with an introductory chapter describing the nature and extent of the interstate slave trade. Chapter 2 then grapples with the thorny question of what the founding fathers at Philadelphia actually intended when they embodied into the Constitution two key clauses, one of them giving Congress authority over both foreign and interstate commerce, and the other specifying that Congress could not outlaw the importation of slaves into the United States until the year 1808. The third chapter traces the slow emergence from the 1790s through the 1820s of the idea of using the commerce power as an antislavery weapon. Chapter 4 tells how the Supreme Court dealt with cases involving the commerce power and the slave trade throughout the antebellum decades. Chapter 5 describes how in the 1830s the radical abolitionist movement mounted a massive campaign for federal action against the slave trade through an avalanche of publications, speeches, and petitions. Here I challenge the prevailing view that the abolitionists were at first apolitical. I argue that, on the contrary, their movement was intensely political from the start, and lobbying for congressional action against the slave trade was a core facet of their politics. Chapter 6 focuses on the antislavery political parties that arose in the 1840s and 1850s. It explains why the initially clamorous calls for suppression of the interstate slave trade faded to a whisper as the Liberty men yielded pride of place first to the Free-Soilers and then to the Republicans. I argue that southerners feared that Abraham Lincoln and his fellow Republicans harbored a secret radical agenda and that there were some grounds for such suspicion. Chapter 7 is about the election of 1860 and the crisis that followed. It is here that I make my key argument that southern anxiety over the threat to the interstate slave trade was an important element in precipitating the secession crisis and the Civil War. The final chapter focuses on the war years. It describes the last efforts to secure congressional action against the slave trade, the futile attempts by some southern reformers to curb the worst abuses of the trade, the role of the slave trade issue in the British debate over whether to support the Union or the Confederacy, and, finally, the demise of the interstate slave trade, not as a consequence of the long struggle against it, but as a byproduct of Confederate defeat and the collapse of slavery itself.

This book has been a long time coming. I can trace its inspiration back to the academic year 1963–64, when I was in my first year of graduate study. The United States was then convulsed by the civil rights revolution. One day I was surprised to see in the *New York Times* a large advertisement sponsored by a white supremacist organization. The advertisement featured a series of quotations from Abraham Lincoln, in which he said that he did not regard Negroes as equals and did not favor granting them civil rights. Unable to believe that Lincoln could have said such terrible things, I began reading some of the scholarly literature about him as well as his own speeches and writings. I soon discovered that he had indeed said those terrible things. But I discovered also that he had, on other occasions, said very different things. After much further thought and reading—all of it in moments snatched from the utterly different topics that constituted my research agenda both in graduate school and for many years afterward—I became convinced that if one took into account the historical context of each of Lincoln's conflicting statements, it was possible to discern a core of egalitarian idealism that was ever present in his mind but that he sometimes concealed for reasons of political expediency, carefully choosing his words in order to avoid outright lying and yet conveying to his white audiences the racist messages that they often wanted to hear. It would be many years before I worked up the courage to publish my thoughts on Lincoln—not until 1982, to be precise—but in the meantime my study of his words had awakened my interest in the subject that was to become the focus of the present book. I noticed that early on in the famous debates of 1858, Stephen A. Douglas asked whether Lincoln was pledged to the prohibition of the slave trade among the states. It seemed curious that Douglas should have asked that question. I thought it even more curious that Lincoln avoided answering it at first, and then when he did answer it, was evasive and noncommittal. I began looking into the literature on the antislavery movement, where I learned that campaigning for a ban on the interstate slave trade had been a staple of abolitionist agitation. That explained why Douglas, who wanted to tar Lincoln with the stigma of abolitionism, had posed his question. But it did not explain why Lincoln had responded so evasively. I was left wondering about that, and also about how extensive the effort to ban the slave trade actually was, and what effect it may have had on antebellum politics and public opinion. My attempt to answer those questions led me, over the course of many years and with time out for many other projects, to unearth numerous obscure sources, to hunt for needles in a great many haystacks, to write several preliminary articles, and at long last to finish this book.

For allowing me to incorporate into the book much of the content of my earlier articles, I am obliged to the publishers of the journals in which they appeared: to Kent State University Press for "The Door to the Slave Bastille: The Abolitionist Assault upon the Interstate Slave Trade," *Civil War History* 34 (Sept. 1988): 235–52, and "The Interstate Slave Trade in Antislavery Politics," *Civil War History* 36 (June 1990): 119–36; Southern Studies Institute, Northwestern State University, for "The Interstate Slave Trade as an Issue in the Secession Crisis," *Southern Studies* 9 (Summer–Fall 1998): 1–35; University of Pennsylvania Press for "The Founders and the Interstate Slave Trade," *Journal of the Early Republic* 22 (Spring 2002): 25–51; and Blackwell Publishing for "The Supreme Court and the Interstate Slave Trade: A Study in Evasion, Anarchy, and Extremism," *Journal of Supreme Court History* 29 (Nov. 2004): 229–53.

I appreciate the tact with which Christopher Rogers, executive editor at Yale University Press, steered me over the initial bumps along the path to publication. I have benefited too from the steady hand of assistant editor Eleanor Goldberg and the eagle eye of manuscript editor Noreen O'Connor-Abel. On a more intimate note, I wish to express my gratitude to Dr. David C. Williams and his medical colleagues, without whose skill and dedication I would not be here to write these words. Most of all, I thank Ken Hara both for his help on this and other projects and for his companionship and support all through the years.

1

A Continual Torment

He trudges along a mountain trail. Perched amid the tassels of a flowering chestnut tree, a red bird sings. It is June and the woods are filled with the sweet scent of blossoming azalea and mountain laurel. He wades the frothing waters of a brook. In his free hand he carries a stick. With it he smashes every flower within his reach. As he crosses the brook, he strikes at bubbles. Discarding the stick, he reaches down to pick up a stone, then throws it with all his might at the red bird. When the bird flies away unscathed, he shakes his fist and curses. His companions chortle at his helpless rage.

He has reason to be angry. He must keep pace with the others, for he is linked to them by a handcuff and a heavy chain. He must walk twenty miles or more every day. Each step takes him farther away from his birthplace of Norfolk, Virginia. He will walk all the way to Mobile, Alabama. There he will be sold. He misses his mother. He will never see her again. He is eight years old.

She is happy when her husband is gathering his stock, for at such times he is rarely absent from their North Carolina home for more than a few days at a stretch. But she is saddened when the time comes for him to assemble his gang and march them off, for then she knows that many weeks must pass before he will return from the long, dusty journey southward and the protracted search for buyers willing to pay what he needs to turn a profit in the face of stiff competition from his many rivals in the trade. She wishes he would give it up but doubts he ever will. "I'm afraid, my dear husband," she writes to him when he is far away, "you and your friend Carson will keep up negro trading as long as you can get a negro to trade on." He replies that he has only eighteen left to sell and then he can come home. He says that he knows of another trader who has fifty that he must dispose of before he can hasten back to the bride whom he married only ten days before he left home. "We both," he declares, "are toiling for our wives and their little ones."

He has a cousin, Betsy Ann, who admires his adventurous travels. She hopes that he will bring back nice presents, and jokes that he should send suitors both for herself and for his sister Sarah. He writes back with a joke of his own. Marriage, he says, "is a long shot and a bad chance without a show of some negroes and beauty—both of which is lacking with Sarah and unfortunately for you you lack the negroes."

He describes the journey that he and a friend have made from Louisville to St. Louis aboard the steamboat Lebanon. *He says that nothing interesting happened, unless one considers it interesting to be delayed by sandbars emerging from the unusually low water. Still, he goes on to remark that the vessel's cargo had included a dozen slaves strung together in chains "like so many fish upon a trot-line." He marvels that the slaves sang songs, cracked jokes, played cards, and danced to the strains of a fiddle, despite the fact that, as he puts it, "they were being separated forever from the scenes of their childhood, their friends, their fathers and mothers, and brothers and sisters, and many of them, from their wives and children, and going into perpetual slavery where the lash of the master is proverbially more ruthless and unrelenting than any other where." It shows, he muses, that "God tempers the wind to the shorn lamb."*

Fourteen years later, he writes to the friend who had accompanied him and recalls the shackled slaves that they had seen aboard the Lebanon. *"That sight," he says, "was a continual torment to me; and I see something like it every time I touch the Ohio, or any other slave-border." He admits that his friend, who is now the owner of many slaves, has the lawful right to possess them. He recognizes, he says, "*your *rights and* my *obligations, under the constitution, in regard to your slaves. I confess I hate to see the poor creatures hunted down, and caught, and carried back to their stripes, and unrewarded toils; but I bite my lip and keep quiet." He adds, however, that it is not fair for his friend to assume "that I have no interest in a thing which has, and continually exercises, the power of making me miserable. You ought rather to appreciate how much the great body of the Northern people do crucify their feelings, in order to maintain their loyalty to the constitution and the Union."*

In these vignettes, we glimpse the reactions of three individuals to the workings of the interstate slave trade. Their responses vary sharply because each of them has an entirely different relationship to the traffic in human beings. The first vignette portrays a victim of the traffic, the second a beneficiary of it, and the third an outsider who only looked on uneasily.

The furious boy who slashed at the bubbles and blossoms was John Parker. In making the long trek from the upper South down to the booming Gulf states, he followed a path that was trod by hundreds of thousands of other enslaved boys and girls and men and women during the antebellum decades of the nineteenth century. At the end of the wretched journey, however, fortune was to smile upon John Parker far more than it did most of the African Americans whose lives were touched by the slave trade. He escaped the harsh fate of those who toiled from dawn to dark in the cotton fields, or the still harsher lot of those who grew and harvested sugarcane. Instead, he was bought by a sympathetic master, who eventually permitted him to acquire the skills of an iron molder, to hire himself out for wages, and at last to buy his freedom. He then moved to the free state of Ohio, where he established a foundry and manufactured machinery of his own invention. There he also became heavily involved in the interstate transportation of slaves. He did not carry slaves from one place of bondage to another, however, but from slavery to freedom. Time after time, in the dead of night, he rowed across the Ohio River to the Kentucky shore and returned with fugitives. He then passed them on to other conductors of the Underground Railroad who would spirit them northward toward safety in Canada.[1]

The beneficiary of the slave trade was Harriett Jarratt, the wife of a trader. Neither Harriett nor her husband Isaac saw any irony in lamenting the temporary interruptions of their domestic life that were an unavoidable part of Isaac's occupation whenever he departed for the lower South with a coffle of slaves whose closest personal ties were being sundered for ever. Although Isaac prided himself on being a hardworking entrepreneur who was doing his best to provide for his dependents, he did at last yield to his wife's pleas and promised to retire from slave trafficking. While journeying southward one last time in order to collect some monies still owed him, he wrote to reassure her, saying, "I was candid and never will make another negro trading trip without your approbation unless a kind Providence should frown upon my labors and make it actually necessary that I should leave home to make a support for my family. In that case I would resort to any Honest calling."[2]

The final vignette features a man who had no personal involvement in the interstate slave trade but merely observed it incidentally while preoccupied with his own dreams of personal betterment. His name was Abraham Lincoln. He was in his early thirties when he saw the slaves aboard the *Lebanon*. He might have marveled less at their seemingly happy demeanor had he known that traders often demanded such behavior and punished anyone who did not comply. William Wells Brown, a former slave who had once been hired out to a trader, recalled that it was his duty, before potential purchasers were allowed to enter the trader's pen at New Orleans, to see that the slaves were engaged in such activities as singing, dancing, and playing cards. "I have often set them to dancing," Wells recalled, "when their cheeks were wet with tears." Thus what Lincoln interpreted as God tempering the wind to the shorn lamb was more likely a matter of the shorn lambs being forced to gambol in the midst of a gale.[3]

But if Lincoln was not fully informed about the character of the slave trade, he certainly recognized its inhumanity. This was not his first encounter with it. Born in 1809, he had spent the first seven years of his life in Kentucky. During most of that time, his parents' cabin fronted on the Cumberland Road linking Louisville to Nashville. It is likely that among the early impressions of his boyhood was the sight of traders leading their ragged captives past the cabin door. From Kentucky his parents moved the family to Indiana and then Illinois. In his early manhood, Abraham was hired on two occasions, the first in 1828 and the second in 1831, to carry goods by flatboat down the Mississippi to New Orleans. On those journeys he must have gazed upon some of the many slaves who were being taken down the great river, and when he reached the Crescent City he may have seen some of them standing upon the auction blocks. Exactly what he saw must remain a matter of conjecture, as there is no way now of verifying the testimony of his cousin John Hanks, who, when interviewed after Lincoln's death, said that when he and Abraham were in New Orleans, "we Saw Negroes Chained—maltreated—whipt & scourged. Lincoln Saw it—his heart bled—Said nothing much—was silent from feeling—was Sad—looked bad—felt bad—was thoughtful & abstracted—I Can say Knowingly that it was on this trip that he formed his opinions of Slavery: it ran its iron in him then & there—May 1831. I have heard him say—often & often." It is apparent that well before he was anything more than a fledgling lawyer and minor politician in Illinois, Lincoln had already seen enough of slavery and the slave trade to feel an aversion to them. By 1855, when he wrote the letter saying how much he had been tormented by seeing the slaves aboard the *Lebanon,* his antislavery sentiment had hardened into firm conviction. Now he lamented that his slaveowning friend, like so many other white southerners, acknowledged that slavery was an evil yet would countenance no opposition to it. "The slave-breeders and slave-traders, are a small, odious and detested class, among you," Lincoln wrote, "and yet in politics, they dictate the course of all of you, and are completely your masters, as you are the masters of your own negroes." As to where he himself now stood, he said,

"That is a disputed point. I think I am a whig; but others say there are no whigs, and that I am an abolitionist."[4]

By the time it touched the lives of John Parker, Harriett Jarratt, and Abraham Lincoln, the interstate slave trade had swelled from minuscule beginnings into a vital feature of the southern economic system. Because a slave is by definition a human being who can be bought and sold, there was slave trading in colonial America as soon as there was slavery itself. Some of that trading transferred slaves from one colony to another. The Revolution turned the former colonies into states. As soon as there were states, there was movement of slaves across state lines. The amount of such movement increased gradually from a trickle to a torrent. In the 1780s significant numbers of slaves already were migrating from Maryland and Virginia into what were soon to become the states of Kentucky and Tennessee, and some were being taken farther southward and westward. By 1800 slaves in the Chesapeake were learning to fear the "Georgia men," who offered slaveholders ready cash in exchange for the Negroes whom they carried off to the rice swamps of Georgia and South Carolina. In later decades, Georgia and South Carolina would become net exporters rather than importers of slaves, as first the Gulf region of Alabama, Mississippi, and Louisiana, and then the still more remote frontiers of Arkansas and Texas became the principal destinations of the long-distance slave trade.[5]

In the last decade of the eighteenth century about one out of every twelve slaves of the Chesapeake was carried off to Kentucky or elsewhere, and in the first decade of the nineteenth century the proportion taken away reached one in ten. Then, in the second decade of the nineteenth century the share of Chesapeake slaves carried off across state lines leaped to one in five. One reason for the surge in out-migration from Maryland and Virginia after 1810 was the federal law banning the importation of slaves from outside the United States that went into effect in 1808. From then on, white settlers on the southern frontier could look only to the older states rather than Africa as their ultimate source of human chattels. Other factors also were important. The acquisition of the Louisiana Territory and the subsequent forced eviction of native peoples opened a vast new region to settlement. Along the lower reaches of the Mississippi River, the climate and soil conditions were suited to sugarcane, the production and processing of which employed 36,000 slaves by 1830 and more than 125,000 by 1850. Still more important, the mechanization of spinning and weaving created a ready market for raw cotton, which could be supplied cheaply once improved versions of the cotton engine or "gin" provided an efficient means of separating seed from fiber. Those technological innovations made short-staple cotton a viable cash crop throughout much of the lower South. A vast expansion of cotton cultivation began there, unleashing an immense demand both for land and for slaves. The latter demand could be met only by transferring vast numbers of African Americans from slavery's older, more northerly strongholds. Slave migration in the 1820s dwarfed that of all previous decades, and in the 1830s it reached levels that would never be matched again, not even in the renewed surge of the 1850s.[6]

Most of this mass movement of enslaved peoples went unrecorded at the time, but some idea of the scale of it can be deduced from the numbers of slaves residing in each state as reported in the federal censuses of 1790 through 1860. If it is assumed that the rate of natural increase of the slave population (that is, the excess of births over deaths) was similar throughout the South, it is apparent from a glance at the census data that the slave population of the upper South states grew more slowly than natural increase should have allowed, while that of the lower South states grew more rapidly. The deficit or surplus in each state is a rough measure of the net exportation or importation of slaves, although adjustments must be made to try to take into account both the legal importation of Africans before 1808 and the illegal smuggling in of Africans after 1808. (The latter adjustment is particularly problematic, as statistics on smuggling are hardly more than wild guesses.) This method of computation was used in a crude manner even in antebellum times. It has been refined using sophisticated quantitative techniques by modern historians, including Michael Tadman, who calculates that more than a million slaves passed from the exporting to the importing states between 1790 and 1860. Tadman estimates the slave movements out of the exporting states during each census period as follows:

1790–99	49,511
1800–09	65,791
1810–19	123,386
1820–29	154,712
1830–39	284,750
1840–49	183,902
1850–59	250,728
Total	1,112,780

It is important to realize, however, that the interstate slave trade accounted for only a part of that vast migration. It was common, especially in the earlier decades, for a planter to transfer his base of operations from the upper to the lower South, bringing with him his entire labor force. Moreover, once a planter had resided in the lower South long enough to prosper, he often made one or more return trips to the upper South in order to buy more slaves. It is impossible to know exactly what proportion of the slaves did not move with a master but instead fell into the hands of the speculators, that is, those purely commercial middlemen who bought slaves in one state, carried them away to another state, and sold them there.[7]

Tadman tried to determine the relative share of the commercial trade by analyzing the age distribution of the slaves who participated in interregional migration. He observed that a planter migrating along with his entire labor force would be likely to bring slaves of all ages. A speculator, on the other hand, was apt to be highly selective, preferring to deal mostly in slaves who were between fifteen and twenty-five years old. Given that important distinction between planter migration and the commercial trade, and given the proportion of various age groups in the makeup of interstate slave migration as a whole, Tadman concluded that 60 to 70 percent of all of the slaves who passed from the upper to the lower South moved via the commercial trade. Tadman's approach is open to question, however, as it perhaps draws too sharp a contrast between the behavior of masters and traders. Tadman presents convincing evidence that traders had virtually no regard for family ties. But masters too could be cruel. For example, when Allan Kulikoff analyzed a group of petitions from masters seeking permission to bring slaves into South Carolina in 1817, he found that more than 40 percent of that movement of slaves along with their owners resembled the commercial slave trade in that family ties had been sundered. If a planter decided to migrate to the lower South, he did not necessarily take with him a collection of intact slave families with all ages evenly represented. A young slaveholder just starting out might own only a small number of slaves, perhaps the result of a gift or an inheritance from his father. Moreover, the demanding task of clearing land and starting a new plantation called for the hard toil of hearty young men and women, not the distracting burden of tending to the very young or the very old. Finally, even if a migrating group of slaves was large and varied, it might still include a good many individuals who were leaving their loved ones behind. Slaves often had spouses who belonged to a master other than their own. Even if a migrating slaveowner was willing to buy the other partner, his offer might be rejected by the other master. And if migrating planters did not necessarily respect family ties, lower South planters who traveled northward on buying expeditions probably were even less sensitive to such matters. Thus Tadman's estimates may be too high. Perhaps the best guess currently available is that of Jonathan B. Pritchett, who believes that, overall, the commercial slave trade accounted for about one-half of the entire interregional movement of slaves.[8]

Slave trading could be a lucrative enterprise for those with the stomach for it. Only a modest amount of capital was needed to make a start. Even if a man's main livelihood came from another occupation such as horse trading or bartending, he could easily do a bit of slave dealing on the side. And if the dabbling proved remunerative, he might turn to full-time speculation. On a visit to Virginia in 1835, William H. Seward happened upon this scene at a country tavern: Ten black boys, the youngest age six and the oldest twelve, emerged in a cloud of dust from the roadway, escorted by a gaunt white man brandishing a whip. The boys were naked but tied to one another with rope. The white man led the boys up to a horse trough to drink, and then into a shed, where they lay down moaning until sleep overcame them. It is likely that the man with the whip was a relative newcomer to the business. With limited funds at his disposal, it made sense for him to deal in children. They cost less than adults, yet were just as saleable. Moreover, they were less likely to resist or run away, an important consideration to a man who could as yet afford neither to hire an assistant nor to pay for iron chains and manacles. This petty trader was on his way to Richmond. There he might sell his small captives to some larger operator in the trade, pocket the proceeds, and return to the countryside to gather another batch.[9]

From such humble beginnings, it might be possible in time to rise into the ranks of the more affluent speculators who assembled the much larger groups of slaves that made the long trek to the lucrative markets of the lower South. One then could deal not just in common field hands, but also in pricier goods like house servants, skilled tradesmen, and what the speculators called "fancies," by which they meant attractive mulatto women who were sold for purposes of sexual exploitation. One could even dream of emulating Isaac Franklin, the greatest interstate trader of them all. Together with his junior partner John Armfield, Franklin operated on a grand scale during the boom of the 1830s. The agents of Franklin and Armfield gathered up a thousand and more slaves a year in Virginia and Maryland and delivered them to Armfield at the firm's upper South headquarters, which was located in the town of Alexandria in the District of Columbia. Armfield then despatched them to Franklin, who managed the firm's lower South sales facilities at New Orleans and Natchez. A great trader like Armfield could afford to distance himself from the nastier features of the business. He cheerfully showed a northern visitor around his slave prison or "pen," so that the caller could see for himself that the slaves were housed under reasonably humane conditions. Armfield claimed that he took great pains to avoid breaking up families, and it was technically true that *he* did not separate many slaves from their loved ones. He did not need to, for the dirty work had already been done by his agents when they purchased slaves one at a time from their masters, leaving spouses and children behind. After studying

Figure 1. Breaking camp in southwestern Virginia. John Armfield (seated on a log) and his assistants oversee a coffle of three hundred slaves bound for Natchez in 1834. From George W. Featherstonhaugh, *Excursion through the Slave States, from Washington on the Potomac to the Frontier of Mexico,* 2 vols. (London: John Murray, 1844), 1: 121. Courtesy University of Alberta Libraries, Science and Technology Special Collections.

twenty-eight surviving manifests of shipments by Franklin and Armfield, Donald Sweig concluded that in its later years the firm did ship a greater proportion of mothers accompanied by their children, apparently in response both to an 1829 Louisiana law prohibiting the separate sale of children under ten years old and to criticism of the slave trade by abolitionists. Still, many women continued to be separated from their offspring, and the great majority of men were shipped alone. By 1835 Franklin and Armfield had amassed such great profits that the senior partner, Franklin, was able to retire from trading and install himself as an elite member of the planter class. When he died a decade later, he left an estate worth half a million dollars, including more than 10,600 acres of land and 700 slaves. His obituaries did not mention the original source of his fabulous wealth.[10]

The simplest way to move slaves even on the longest of journeys was merely to walk them to their destination in coffles. The adult male slaves would be lined up in pairs, with a set of handcuffs linking the right hand of one man to the left hand of another. All of the handcuffs were then connected to a long chain that passed down the center of the coffle. Behind the men marched the women and the older children, also in pairs but usually not chained. Behind them rumbled a wagon bearing the smallest children, the sick, and the infirm. Coffles varied in size from a relative handful of slaves to much larger numbers. In 1834 an English traveler passing through southwestern Virginia happened early one morning upon John Armfield and several assistants just breaking camp with three hundred slaves on their way to Natchez. Armfield and his helpers lounged about smoking cigars and directing the proceedings. Horses were being hitched to nine wagons and carriages. Two hundred shackled men were already lined up ready to set off. Women were getting up from the logs on which they had been seated. Children lingered to catch the last warmth from the fading campfires.[11]

Other methods of transport also were used. As early as 1787 a slave from Fayette County, Kentucky, was taken on a flatboat down the Kentucky, Ohio, and Mississippi rivers to be sold at New Orleans, and by the mid-1820s the great Maryland trader Austin Woolfolk was commissioning coastal vessels to carry hundreds of slaves annually from Baltimore to that same destination. As steamboats replaced flatboats on the inland rivers, it became commonplace to march slaves in coffles to a riverport like Wheeling and then ship them under steam power to a deep South trading center like Natchez. At their zenith in the mid-1830s, Franklin and Armfield not only sent a huge annual coffle overland, they also operated their own packet line of three ships, which carried slaves down the Atlantic coast and around Florida to New Orleans, then returned laden with lucrative cargoes of cotton and sugar. As canals and then railroads were built, they too were used to transport slaves. In 1856 it took one trader only thirty-six hours to move a gang by rail from Bamberg, South Carolina, to Montgomery, Alabama.[12]

No matter what means of transport they used, the traders always faced the possibility of resistance from the slaves, who greatly outnumbered their guardians. As early as 1799 a Charleston newspaper reported that a coffle had rebelled and slit the throats of two Georgia men. In 1826 seventy-five slaves being shipped by flatboat on the Ohio killed the five whites who were supervising their removal to the lower South. In 1841 nineteen individuals among a cargo of 135 slaves being shipped coastwise from Virginia to New Orleans seized control of the brig *Creole,* killed a trader who owned 39 of the slaves on board, and forced the captain to sail to the Bahamas, where British authorities, under pressure from the local population, declared the slaves free. The most common form of resistance to the slave trade was not violent rebellion, however, but the simple act of running away. That could occur before, during, or after the journey southward. As soon as he learned that he had been sold, one Virginia slave took to the woods. He managed to hide out for a whole year, returning only after a local white woman bought him from the trader and sent word through the slave community grapevine that he no longer faced the threat of separation from his family. A slave named Joe ran away from trader A. J. McElveen while the latter was gathering slaves in upcountry South Carolina. Joe made good his escape even though McElveen pursued him with dogs. When Joe was later apprehended at Charleston, McElveen asked to have him held there because, he said, "I want to Give him one hundred lashes as Soon as I come down as he has no Cause for leaving me." A slave by the name of Richard Shepard absconded only after he had been carried to Louisiana by another trader and sold to a new master at New Orleans. Shepard was retaken in Mobile, but within a few days escaped again and stowed away on a vessel bound for Liverpool. When his presence was discovered, he was landed at Savannah and jailed. Before his owner could claim him, he somehow escaped yet again. What became of him after that is unknown. Slave resistance sometimes took unusual forms. Soon after A. J. McElveen went off to sell his slaves in Louisiana, he reported that one of them, James, was "cutting up" and displaying a general contrariness, probably in the hope that he might return to the wife he had left behind. "I could Sell him like hot cakes if he would talk Right," McElveen complained, but, by telling potential purchasers that he used to wear a truss, "the Boy is trying to make himself *unsound.*" Eleven days later McElveen wrote that James had promised "to do better," but a month after that it appears that James ran away from the dealer to whom he was consigned when McElveen returned to South Carolina.[13]

No matter what form resistance took, it was only rarely successful. All slaves knew that most runaways were soon captured and punished, and that violence nearly always led to savage reprisal. Knowing that, the vast majority of the victims of the interstate slave trade met their fate with tears and wails but without offering a resistance that they knew would be futile. That was generally the case whether the slaves were young or old, male or female. Charles Ball was a small boy when his Maryland family was broken up. He was sold to a local man, while his mother passed into the hands of a Georgia trader. As his new master rode off with little Charles behind him on the saddle, Charles's mother came running after them and implored the man to buy her as well. But right on her heels came the trader, who lashed her with his cowhide whip and took her away. The journalist James Redpath, traveling through South Carolina, commiserated with an elderly male slave who had been married for twenty-four years when his wife and the couple's twelve children were sold away from him. He had later remarried, but his second wife too had been sold. Now he was alone. Redpath said it was too bad. "Yes, mass'r," the slave replied, "it *is* too bad; but we has to submit."[14]

Many white southerners were appalled by the blatant inhumanity of the interstate slave trade, and some of them actively opposed it, especially in the earlier years, when the sight of coffles was still novel and startling. Yet in the long run, the opposition by southern whites was even less effectual than that of the slaves. It is true that many of the receiving states did at one time or another pass laws that restricted or prohibited the commercial importation of slaves. Georgia, for example, repeatedly enacted and repealed such legislation. For the most part, however, the restrictive laws were not motivated by humanitarian and certainly not by antislavery intentions. Rather, they reflected the suspicion that traders were foisting dangerous and criminal slaves onto gullible customers, the fear that too disproportionate an increase in the black population might foster slave insurrection, and the calculation that the sale of slaves by traders drained away capital whereas the arrival of white settlers along with their slaves increased the net wealth of the state. Even if the motivation for the laws had been more humanitarian, it would have made little difference, for the laws proved almost impossible to enforce. The demand for slaves was so insatiable that the commercial trade flourished no matter what the law said. A visitor to Kentucky during the winter of 1826–27 reported that it was commonplace for traders to drive herds of swine from that state into Virginia, sell the animals, invest the proceeds in slaves, especially children, and return to Kentucky with their human livestock. The traders then sold the slaves in Kentucky despite the fact that the commercial importation of slaves had been prohibited there since 1798. The law was evaded, the traveler explained, "by *borrowing money* and giving the slaves in pledge, with the condition annexed, that in case the money was not repaid within a limited time, the pledge should be forfeited." Elsewhere, traders resorted to the even simpler expedient of conducting sales transactions outside the borders of the states where they were illegal. In the 1840s a group of South Carolina residents protested to the state legislature that "this State and the City of Charleston in particular, have become the common place of meeting between the Slave dealer from places north of us, and the purchaser South West of us" — "South West" meaning Alabama and Mississippi, where commercial importation was then forbidden. A British traveler riding a train in South Carolina in the 1850s fell into conversation with a trader who was on his way home after selling a lot of fifty slaves in Georgia. The trader mentioned casually that it was "against the laws of that State to import any more slaves" but that "such laws were not regarded."[15]

Instead of taking effective action to stifle the interstate slave trade, white southerners developed an elaborate myth that excused its existence by minimizing its extent and distorting its nature. The grim reality of the trade clashed dramatically with the white South's cherished belief that slavery was a paternalistic institution that was as beneficial to the slave as to the master. White southerners consequently denied that reality and replaced it with fantasy. Slave traders, it was claimed, were a small and degraded class of men who were universally despised by respectable southerners. Masters sold slaves only rarely and reluctantly, and always out of necessity rather than a desire for profit. Occasionally a slave was so evil or uncooperative that a master had no choice but to get rid of the troublemaker lest the other slaves become corrupted by the one bad apple. Or a master would go bankrupt, leaving no alternative to the selling off of his human assets. Or a master would die and the settlement of the estate would necessitate a similar dispersal. Although strenuous efforts always were made to preserve the slaves' family ties, sometimes they had to be broken. That was unfortunate, but it was not the calamity for blacks that it would be for whites. Because Negroes belonged to a primitive and inferior race, their emotional ties were ardent but transitory. Thus a husband and wife might express great sorrow at being parted, but they would soon get over it. Nehemiah Adams, a northern clergyman who visited the South in 1854, was assured by an "eminent and venerable" southern physician that the pain and grief of slave mothers when separated from their children was "peculiar" but "easily supplanted." Adams accepted the physician's explanation for the phenomenon: "The hen, and even the timid partridge, is roused when her young are in danger, and her demonstrations of affection then are unsurpassed. Yet in a few weeks she will treat her offspring as strangers. Maternal instincts in slave mothers (my friend observed) were more like this than the ordinary parental feelings of white people."[16]

Few other visitors to the South either from the North or from abroad were as credulous as Adams. Indeed, the southern myth about the slave trade was so at variance with the reality that even slaveholders often had difficulty subscribing to it in its entirety. Most visitors could see immediately that there was nothing paternalistic about the slave trade. The sheer scale of it gave the lie to the absurd notion that only lazy or wicked slaves need fear being sold, or that slave sellers were not motivated by the desire for profits, or that family separations were rare. The sight of slaves marching in chained coffles or being sold at the traders' pens or in the auction marts horrified spectators more than any other features of slavery, except perhaps for whipping and other physical brutality. When British clergyman and former missionary Ebenezer Davies strolled along a New Orleans street in the 1840s, he passed a group of slaves lined up for display to the passersby. "Looking out for a few niggers this morning?" a white attendant asked brightly. As he choked out a negative reply, Davies later recalled, "my eyes so filled with tears that I was compelled to turn my face another way. Though I anticipated such scenes, and had tried to prepare my mind for them, yet (now that they were actually before me) I was completely overcome, and was obliged to sit down while I composed my feelings." A decade earlier, the famous English writer Harriet Martineau visited the Charleston slave market, because she believed it to be "a place which the traveler ought not to avoid to spare his feelings." The bidding for a man was being completed as she arrived. She then witnessed the sale of a woman with her two children, one a babe at the breast and the other a toddler clinging to her apron. A boy aged around eight or nine was next on the block, but Martineau could not bring herself to stay any longer. "There was no bearing the child's look of helplessness and shame," she recalled, "and we went away before he was disposed of." Martineau described "the restless, jocose zeal of the auctioneer" as "the most infernal sight I ever beheld."[17]

Reactions like those to the slave trade would present a problem for the South during the Civil War, when the Confederacy desperately sought European and especially British sympathy and support. The war would also bring some renewed criticism of the worst features of the trade from within southern white society. Most important, the war would bring a vast upsurge in slave resistance, as thousands of men and women began fleeing behind Union lines. But in the antebellum decades, none of those forms of opposition represented a serious threat to the continuation of the slave trade. Slave resistance, while always a concern, was successfully contained. Southern white opposition was ineffective and foreign criticism a mere irritant. What truly worried southern slaveowners and slave traders was the opposition to the trade from northerners, especially free blacks and their white abolitionist allies. The presence of the interstate slave trade made the entire institution of slavery vulnerable to attack from the North. That was true not only because the southern myth that justified the trade was so easily exploded, but also because the interstate slave trade was the one crucial aspect of slavery that arguably was not protected by the states'-rights guarantees embedded in the federal Constitution. Northerners might dislike slavery, but they knew that the Constitution treated it as a local institution entirely under the control of the states. They might, like Abraham Lincoln, hate the thought of runaways being returned to face bloody lashings and unremitting toil, but they knew that the Constitution specifically called for the rendering up of fugitives who escaped across state lines. But the interstate slave trade was a different matter. The Constitution gave to Congress the power to regulate commerce among the several states. Was not the commercial slave trade a form of commerce? And if so, why could it not be controlled, or better yet annihilated, under the authority of Congress?

2

This Blind Mysterious Form of Words

Opponents of slavery argued throughout the antebellum period that Congress possessed the power under the Constitution to abolish the interstate slave trade. The idea horrified defenders of slavery, who denied that the framers of the Constitution had vested Congress with any such authority. It is therefore important to explore the origins of the relevant clauses in the Constitution drawn up at Philadelphia in 1787 and in that way seek to answer the question that was so fiercely debated after the Constitution had gone into effect: Did the founders intend to give to Congress the constitutional authority to regulate or even to abolish the interstate slave trade?

It must be acknowledged at the outset that to attempt to determine the intent of the founding fathers on any particular constitutional issue is to some extent to pursue a will-o'-the-wisp. About two thousand men participated in the framing and ratification of the Constitution, and oftentimes only a few of them left any clue as to the meaning that they ascribed to any specific constitutional provision. Still, as Jack Rakove observes, "It is one thing to say that few interpretations of the more ambiguous and disputable clauses of the Constitution can be established conclusively, another to treat all interpretations as equally plausible or representative of the prevailing ideas of the time." Furthermore, as Rakove also says, historians "can rest content with—even revel in—the ambiguities of the evidentiary record, recognizing that behind the textual brevity of any clause there once lay a spectrum of complex views and different shadings of opinion."[1] In the case of the interstate slave trade issue, views were complex and opinions shaded indeed.

When representatives of the several states met at Philadelphia in 1787 to construct a more perfect union, they readily agreed that the new national government should have the power to regulate commerce. They disagreed, however, on the details. New Englanders, heavily involved in the carrying trade and eager for regulations that would benefit their mercantile and shipping interests, wanted the federal commerce power to be broadly defined and easily wielded. Southerners, dependent upon their cash crops of tobacco, rice, and indigo, wanted export taxes prohibited altogether and a two-thirds majority of Congress required for the adoption of other commercial legislation. In addition, the two southernmost states, South Carolina and Georgia, sought to protect from federal interference their right to import African slaves. Many delegates from the other states, even the other southern states, viewed the continued importation of captive Africans as an embarrassment to a nation that had justified its birth on the noble theory that all men are created equal and with an inalienable right to liberty. But the delegates from South Carolina and Georgia insisted that their states needed more slaves. If the new constitution banned the importation of Africans, they said, then their states would never accept it. When Luther Martin of Maryland protested that allowing the importation of Africans was "inconsistent with the principles of the revolution and dishonorable to the American character," John Rutledge of South Carolina replied that "Religion & humanity had nothing to do with this question —Interest alone is the governing principle with Nations—The true question at present is whether the Southn. States shall or shall not be parties to the Union."[2]

That clash of interests and values resulted in the last of the important compromises agreed upon by the founding fathers. Whatever their scruples about slavery, the New Englanders were more concerned about their own economic well-being. In exchange for South Carolina's conceding that only a simple majority rather than a two-thirds vote of Congress would be required for navigation acts, New England joined the deep South in voting to prohibit export taxes and to allow the continued importation of African slaves for another two decades. In the final draft of the Constitution, the "commerce clause" (Article 1, Section 8, Clause 3) declared that Congress should have the power to "regulate Commerce with foreign Nations, and among the several States, and with the Indian Tribes." But to prevent Congress from using its broad power over commerce to attack the slave trade, the Constitution also contained the "1808 clause" (Article 1, Section 9, Clause 1), which stated,

"The Migration or Importation of such Persons as any of the States now existing shall think proper to admit, shall not be prohibited by the Congress prior to the Year one thousand eight hundred and eight, but a tax or duty may be imposed on such Importation, not exceeding ten dollars for each Person."

That the 1808 clause was the result of a deal between the most northerly and the most southerly states is obvious from the vote by which it was adopted, on 24 August 1787. New Hampshire, Massachusetts, and Connecticut joined with Maryland, North Carolina, South Carolina, and Georgia in supporting the measure. Pennsylvania, New Jersey, Delaware, and Virginia were opposed. Thus both New England and the deep South voted "yes," while the Middle Atlantic and upper South states voted "no." The only exception to the sectional pattern was Maryland, which backed the measure despite being located in the upper South.[3]

Abundant evidence testifies to the bargain that was made. In his record of the discussions that resulted in the commerce clause, James Madison inserted a note explaining that an "understanding on the two subjects of *navigation* and *slavery,* had taken place between those parts of the Union." Luther Martin wrote that "the *eastern* [i.e., New England] States, notwithstanding their *aversion* to *slavery,* were very willing to indulge the southern States, at least with a temporary liberty to prosecute the *slave trade,* provided the southern States would in their turn gratify them, by laying no *restriction on navigation acts.*" Both Charles Cotesworth Pinckney of South Carolina, who approved of the deal, and George Mason of Virginia, who detested it, agreed that it had been made. Pinckney said at the convention that it was because of the "liberal conduct" of the New Englanders toward his state that he "thought it proper that no fetters should be imposed on the power of making commercial regulations." Mason refused to sign the Constitution and complained bitterly to Thomas Jefferson about the "precipitate, & intemperate, not to say indecent Manner, in which the Business was conducted, during the last week of the Convention, after the Patrons of this new plan found they had a decided Majority in their Favour; which was obtained by a Compromise between the Eastern, & the two Southern States, to permit the latter to continue the Importation of Slaves for twenty odd Years; a more favourite Object with them, than the Liberty and Happiness of the People."[4]

Like all of the Constitution's provisions relating to human chattels, the 1808 clause avoided any explicit use of the word "slavery," but everybody knew that the clause meant that Congress could not use its power over commerce to prohibit before 1808 the bringing in of African slaves. Indeed, just after the convention voted in favor of the clause, Gouverneur Morris of Pennsylvania moved to replace it with a simple statement that the importation of slaves into North Carolina, South Carolina, and Georgia could not be prohibited. Roger Sherman of Connecticut pointed out that being so explicit was "not pleasing to some people," however, and so Morris withdrew his motion.[5] Consequently, the 1808 clause retained its clumsy and obscure phrasing. That phrasing would give rise to arguments over its meaning that would continue throughout the antebellum period. Even though everyone at the Constitutional Convention understood that the clause forbade Congress temporarily from halting the importation of slaves, a few antislavery extremists would later challenge even that understanding. Far more important than the question of whether the 1808 clause applied to the importation of slaves, however—for in all of the decades down to the Civil War, it was really only a handful of cranks who ever doubted that it did—was whether the clause also had a further implication. Did the clause perhaps mean that Congress could prohibit after 1808 not only the importation of slaves but also the internal movement of slaves across state lines?

There seems some logical basis for supposing that the 1808 clause did give Congress authority over the interstate slave trade as well as over the importation of slaves from outside the country. Since the commerce clause gave Congress power over interstate as well as foreign commerce, it would seem perfectly appropriate for the 1808 clause to delimit both those aspects of the commerce power as it applied to the commerce in slaves. Also, it is worth noting that the temporary bar against congressional action in the 1808 clause applied only to "the states now existing." That wording obviously meant that Congress could prohibit any new states admitted to the Union after the adoption of the Constitution from importing African slaves even *before* the year 1808. But what would be the point of imposing that prohibition if the new states could readily get round it simply by bringing in all the slaves they wanted from the older states that still were allowed to import Africans? Therefore, it might be inferred that the framers of the 1808 clause intended to give Congress authority over the interstate as well as the foreign slave trade. Moreover, the wording of the clause seems consistent with that inference. The clause defined the power of Congress over "migration or importation." Were those words perhaps intended to differentiate between, on the one hand, the "migration" of those slaves who moved from place to place within the United States, and, on the other hand, the "importation" of those slaves who entered the United States from abroad?

Reasoning along those lines, political scientist Walter Berns argues that the founding fathers indeed intended to vest Congress with the authority not only to ban slave imports in 1808 but also to prohibit the interstate transfer of slaves into new states before 1808 and among all of the states after 1808.

Furthermore, according to Berns, the expectation that Congress would do just that explains why, during the struggle over the ratification of the Constitution, there was talk in some quarters of Congress possessing the power to suppress not just the external slave trade but the entire institution of slavery after 1808. It is hardly likely that anybody could have anticipated that merely halting slave imports would be enough to destroy slavery, Berns reasons, but it is understandable that some people might have supposed that suppressing both the internal and the external slave trade would do the trick. Berns maintains that it was only later on, after the Constitution had gone into effect, that southern politicians succeeded in thwarting the original intent of the founders by convincing most Americans that the word "migration" in the 1808 clause had naught to do with the interstate movement of slaves and instead referred to the voluntary influx of white immigrants into the United States. Thus, according to that bogus southern interpretation, Congress could prohibit the importation of African slaves after 1808, and it could also regulate free white immigration after 1808, but it would never possess any license ever to interfere in any way with the domestic slave trade.[6]

Berns's thesis has won approval from his fellow political scientists John Alvis and Richard G. Stevens, both of whom accept his article on the topic as a conclusive demonstration that the Constitution gave Congress the power to prohibit the interstate movement of slaves. Historians, in contrast, have mostly ignored the Berns thesis, and the few who have paid cursory attention to it have found it wanting. David Brion Davis lists a number of objections to the thesis and concludes that there is "no reason to believe that the framers intended or could have agreed upon" giving Congress the power to interdict the interstate slave trade. William Wiecek acknowledges that the Constitution is ambiguous on the issue but treats that ambiguity as the unintentional result of the founders' resort to euphemisms when referring to slavery. Paul Finkelman forcefully rejects the Berns thesis, declaring, "This analysis defies all understanding of the Convention. Berns, moreover, provides no evidence that anyone at the Constitutional Convention or in any of the state ratifying conventions believed this." Because no historian has ever considered Berns's arguments in detail, however, a careful assessment of his contentions is appropriate here.[7]

Berns's research was admirably thorough and wide ranging, but his article has the attributes of a brilliant brief by a lawyer who is hell-bent on winning his case, rather than those of a cautious essay by a historian who is grinding no particular axe and is content with uncertainty where evidence is inconclusive. Consequently, Berns's thesis is vulnerable in several respects. One weakness is that in his discussion of the meaning of the words "migration or importation" Berns posits a false dichotomy. Berns takes it as a given that those words can only have been intended either to differentiate between the carrying of slaves from state to state ("migration") and the bringing in of slaves from outside the country ("importation")—which Berns believes to be their true meaning—or to draw a distinction between the immigration of free whites ("migration") and the bringing in of slaves ("importation")—which is what Berns calls the southern interpretation. Berns fails to consider a third possibility, which is that *both* "migration" and "importation" may have been intended to refer to the bringing in of slaves. Why might the founders have used two words for the same thing? There may have been a good reason for the redundancy. At the Constitutional Convention, in an early draft of the 1808 clause, as it was being developed by the Committee of Detail, only the word "importation" was used. But by the time the committee reported the clause to the entire convention, it contained the dual wording "migration or importation." The change could have been an effort to accommodate those delegates who insisted that the Constitution, as the fundamental law for the entire nation, should not recognize property in slaves; instead, the Constitution should leave it entirely to the individual states to sanction slavery, if they wished to do so, through their own laws. If the 1808 clause had used only the word "importation" to refer to the bringing in of slaves, it would have carried a strong implication that property was involved. By speaking instead of the "Migration or Importation of such Persons as any of the states now existing shall think proper to admit," the clause became ambiguous as to whether or not "such Persons" were property. Finally, to add a further complication that escaped Berns, it should be recognized that the three interpretations of the word "migration" are not necessarily mutually exclusive. It is conceivable that "migration" could have been intended by the founders to encompass slaves moving over state lines, *and* whites immigrating into the United States, *and* slaves coming into the United States, all at the same time.[8]

Berns argues that because it made no sense to give Congress the power to control immigration into the existing states beginning in 1808 but not before then, the word "migration" cannot have been intended to refer to white immigration. Here Berns is correct in his premise, but not in the conclusion that he draws from it. If Congress was to be given the power to control immigration, there was indeed no rational reason for the founders to deny it that power before 1808. But Berns fails to recognize that the founders did the latter anyway. They did so because, while they were deeply concerned with how the 1808 clause would affect the importation of African slaves, none of them was much worried about what Congress might or might not do in regard to white immigration. They expected that Congress might enact reasonable regulations, but they were confident that it would not dream of obstructing the flow of ordinary white immigrants into America. We know that was their attitude because of the way they handled the matter at the Constitutional Convention. In an early version of what became the 1808 clause, the second part of the clause allowed the levying of a tax or duty on both migration and importation. Therefore, Gouverneur Morris pointed out, "as the clause now stands it implies that the Legislature may tax freemen imported." George Mason replied that such provision was necessary in order to prevent the introduction of convicts. The Convention then agreed unanimously to amend the clause so as to allow a tax or duty to be levied on importation but not on migration. Everyone involved must have realized that the first part of the 1808 clause—the part allowing Congress to prohibit migration or importation after 1808—had not been changed. Therefore they must also have known that they were giving Congress the power to prohibit white immigration after 1808 but not before, however absurd that was.[9]

Two of the delegates who were present later acknowledged what had occurred. James Wilson told the Pennsylvania ratification convention that white immigrants could not be taxed because of "the care that the Convention took in selecting their language." Luther Martin of Maryland realized that the founders wanted to tax only the importation of slaves, but thought that the clause, even in its amended form, did not make that clear. He said that "the clause is so worded, as really to authorize the general government to impose a duty of ten dollars on every foreigner who comes into a State to become a citizen, whether he comes *absolutely free*, or *qualifiedly* so as a servant—although this is contrary to the design of the framers, and the duty was only meant to extend to the importation of *slaves*."[10]

The ambiguity of the phrase "migration or importation" also received criticism from others. The author of a letter published in a Connecticut newspaper protested "this *blind mysterious form of words*" and said that the "*seeming care* taken to cover the true intent and meaning of this and some other parts" of the Constitution was "sufficient reason, in my mind, not to vote for one single paragraph it contains." At the North Carolina ratification convention, delegate James Galloway said, "I do not wish to see the tax on the importation extended to all persons whatsoever. Our situation is different from the people to the north. We want citizens; they do not. Instead of levying a tax, we ought to give a bounty to encourage foreigners to come among us." He was then reassured by James Iredell, who explained, "The first part of the clause will extend to persons who come into this country as free people, or are brought as slaves. But the last part extends to slaves only. The word *migration* refers to free persons; but the word *importation* refers to slaves, because free people cannot be said to be imported. The tax, therefore, is only to be laid on slaves who are imported, and not on free persons who migrate." Implicit in the comments by Wilson, Martin, and Iredell was the assumption that the word "migration," whatever else it may or may not have encompassed, did embody the immigration of white people into the United States.[11]

Another conceptual weakness in Berns's argument is his belief that the issue of Congress's power over the internal slave trade turns entirely upon the meaning accorded to the word "migration" in the 1808 clause. That is not necessarily the case. It is true that if "migration" embodies the domestic movement of slaves, then it follows that Congress has power over the interstate slave trade. However, if the word "migration" does not refer to the domestic movement of slaves, it does not necessarily follow that Congress lacks that power. For if "migration" does not refer to the domestic movement of slaves, then the 1808 clause neither affirms nor denies the existence of congressional power over the interstate slave trade, it simply says nothing about it. If the 1808 clause is silent on the issue, then the only provision of the Constitution that does speak to it is the commerce clause. And the commerce clause gives Congress power over all interstate commerce, including the interstate slave trade. Indeed, the power of Congress to regulate the interstate slave trade is actually greater if only the commerce clause applies to the issue than it is if both the commerce clause and the 1808 clause apply to it. If the 1808 clause is relevant —that is, if "migration" in the 1808 clause encompasses the interstate movement of slaves—then the power of Congress over the internal slave trade is limited in that it cannot be exercised until 1808 except in the case of new states. But if the 1808 clause is not relevant and only the commerce clause applies, then Congress has an unrestricted power to prohibit the interstate slave trade, both before and after 1808, in old states as well as new.

Having thrown much darkness on the conceptual issues, let us consider more of the surviving historical evidence and the use Berns makes of it. A pervasive weakness in Berns's argument is that his interpretations of evidence are not preemptive. Again and again, he reads evidence in the manner that supports his thesis, when it can be read just as plausibly, and often more so, in other ways. Take, first of all, Berns's contention that people who spoke of Congress having the power to end slavery after 1808 did so because they expected Congress to outlaw the interstate slave trade. There were people here and there who talked of the coming demise of slavery. In most cases, however, there is not the slightest clue that they had any conception of employing the interstate commerce power as a means toward that end. Often there is rather clear indication that they did not. Some of them, through careless reading of the Constitution, political opportunism, or wishful thinking, simply confused the power to end slave importations with the power to end slavery itself.

Thus at the Pennsylvania ratification convention, delegate Thomas McKean rejoiced that in the 1808 clause "there is a provision made for an event which must gratify the feelings of every friend to humanity. The abolition of slavery is put within the reach of the federal government." Nobody made any immediate answer to McKean, but elsewhere similar comments met with swift rebuttal. At the North Carolina ratification convention, James Galloway said of the 1808 clause, "I apprehend it means to bring forward manumission. If we must manumit our slaves, what country shall we send them to? It is impossible for us to be happy, if, after manumission, they are to stay among us." Galloway was once again put right by James Iredell, who replied, "the gentleman is mistaken. . . . He seems to say that this extends to the abolition of slavery. Is there any thing in this Constitution which says that Congress shall have it in their power to abolish the slavery of those slaves who are now in the country? Is it not the plain meaning of it, that after twenty years they may prevent the future importation of slaves? It does not extend to those now in the country." Similarly, at the New Hampshire convention, Joshua Atherton challenged an earlier speaker by saying, in regard to the 1808 clause, "The idea that strikes those, who are opposed to this clause, so disagreeably and so forcibly, is, . . . that we become *consenters to,* and *partakers in,* the sin and guilt of this abominable traffic, at least for a certain period, without any positive stipulation that it should even then be brought to an end. We do not behold in it that valuable acquisition so much boasted of by the honorable member from Portsmouth, '*that an end is then to be put to slavery.*' Congress may be as much, or more, puzzled to put a stop to it then, than we are now. The clause has not secured its abolition." It is uncertain whether the word "it" in Atherton's last two sentences refers to the importation of slaves or to slavery itself. Berns takes Atherton's meaning to be that Congress will have the power to abolish slavery in 1808 but will not necessarily exercise it. It seems at least as likely that Atherton intended to say that Congress will have the power to end the importation of slaves in 1808, but that it may be "puzzled" to do so, and that in any case ending the importation of slaves is not to be equated with abolition.[12]

Other people who talked about eliminating slavery realized that the immediate impact of the 1808 clause would be modest but hoped that it would have greater effect in the long run. At the Massachusetts convention, Thomas Dawes, Jr., said, "It would not do to abolish slavery, by an act of Congress, in a moment, and so destroy what our Southern brethren consider as property. But we may say, that although slavery is not smitten by an apoplexy, yet it has received a mortal wound, and will die of a consumption." Berns presumes that Dawes expected Congress to use the 1808 clause to ban the interstate as well as the external slave trade, but there really is no evidence to back that speculation. Given Dawes's choice of metaphor, it is more likely that he merely voiced a naive expectation that banning slave importations alone would cause slavery to die out eventually.[13]

Other optimists rested their hopes on the more realistic notion that the 1808 clause, by tacitly recognizing the evil of slavery, would encourage state emancipation laws, private manumissions, and perhaps someday an amendment to the Constitution that would abolish slavery throughout the nation. That was the view of Tench Coxe of Pennsylvania, who wrote, "The importation of slaves from any foreign country is, by a clear implication, held up to the world as equally inconsistent with the dispositions and the duties of the people of America. A solid foundation is laid for exploding the principles of negro slavery." It was also the perspective of a writer using the name "Plain Truth," who, in a Pennsylvania newspaper, claimed that by giving Congress the power to prohibit the importation of slaves, "The constitution says, by implication," to the states that have taken steps toward abolition, " 'well done ye good and faithful servants, continue your endeavors to compleat the glorious work — our assistance is not very far distant; for, ere the child now born, shall arrive to an age of manhood, the supreme power of the United States shall abolish slavery altogether, and in the mean time they will oppose it as much as they can.' "[14]

Similar reasoning probably explains why Benjamin Rush described most Pennsylvania Quakers as believing "that the Abolition of slavery in our country must be gradual in order to be effectual, and that the Section of the Constitution which will put it in the power of Congress twenty years hence to restrain it altogether, was a great point obtained from the Southern States." Because he takes Rush to be saying that the 1808 clause will allow Congress to abolish slavery, Berns thinks Rush must have expected Congress to outlaw the interstate slave trade. But when he speaks of restraining "it" altogether, does Rush mean slavery or just slave importation? And is restraining it, whatever it is, the same thing as abolishing it? Other evidence contradicts the notion that the Quakers expected the 1808 clause to bring about abolition all by itself. Just days after Rush made his comment, a spokesman for the Quaker-dominated Pennsylvania Abolition Society said in making public a memorial that the Society had hoped to present to the Constitutional Convention, "While we rejoice in the step which has been taken by the convention to put a total stop to the commerce and slavery of the negroes one and twenty years hence, it is to be hoped the publication of the memorial may have some weight with individual states, to pass laws to prohibit that inhuman traffic, before the power of Congress over that part of the commerce of the states shall take place." Although that comment did suggest a linkage between the ending of slave importations and the abolition of slavery, it was not inconsistent with earlier statements by other Quakers who had made it clear that the 1808 clause was, at best, just one step in the direction of ending slavery, rather than a guarantee that abolition would be achieved. One Massachusetts Friend said, "I understand, some of the Southern members utterly refused doing any thing unless this horid part was admitted, which occasions me to say that its very foundation was on Slavery & Blood. . . . I much fear it will be taken for an implicit encouragement, to pursue the trade. . . . [Y]et as the work is on the wheels I fully believe it is the determination of Heaven that Slavery shall be abolished, though it may be through some sore judgments." James Pemberton, an influential Pennsylvania Quaker, said of the men who made up the Constitutional Convention,

> Charity leads me to conclude that they have done the best they could under the circumstances attending their deliberations, and Some of the Delegates apologize for its imperfections particularly in respect to that part which appears to give countenance to the Slave trade for twenty one years. . . . However should the plan be adopted, which seems not to be improbable; it will be requisite for the Advocates for the Enslaved Negroes to consider, whether consistent with their laudable desire for their emancipation, and the Suppression of the iniquitous Commerce to Africa for Slaves, they ought not firmly to remonstrate against those very exceptionable parts of a Constitution said to be intended to hold up a Standard of impartial Liberty.[15]

The most intriguing example of a person who predicted the demise of slavery after 1808 is James Wilson of Pennsylvania. Not only was Wilson a delegate to the Constitutional Convention, he also served on the committee that formulated the 1808 clause. Wilson later told the Pennsylvania ratification convention that the clause presented "the pleasing prospect" that after "the lapse of a few years" Congress would have the power "to exterminate slavery from within our borders." Berns thinks that because ending slave imports obviously could not have brought about such a rapid and extreme change, Wilson must have expected Congress to kill slavery by banning the internal as well as the external slave trade. But that is an unjustified inference from Wilson's vague assertion. Only the day before, Wilson had made a similar comment, describing the 1808 clause as "laying the foundation for banishing slavery out of this country," but on that occasion he added that it would "produce the same kind, gradual change, which was pursued in Pennsylvania." The latter words do not sound like a clarion call for the federal government to abolish the interstate slave trade. Perhaps all Wilson had in mind was that when Congress banned the importation of Africans in 1808, it would set a good example that would encourage more states to adopt schemes of gradual emancipation and more individual slaveowners to manumit their slaves.[16]

Another difficulty for Berns is that in that same speech Wilson treated the word "migration" in the 1808 clause as applying to white immigrants coming into the United States. He did so after another delegate, William Findley, had complained that "Migration, etc. is unintelligible. It is unfortunate if this guarantees the importation of slaves or if it lays a duty on the importation of other persons." In reply, Wilson first explained that Congress could prohibit the importation of slaves after 1808 and then added:

> The gentleman says, that it is unfortunate in another point of view; it means to prohibit the introduction of white people from Europe, as this tax may deter them from coming amongst us. A little impartiality and attention will discover the care that the Convention took in selecting their language. The words are, the *migration or* IMPORTATION of such persons, etc. shall not be prohibited by Congress prior to the year 1808, but a tax or duty may be imposed on such IMPORTATION; it is observable here, that the term migration is dropped when a tax or duty is mentioned; so that Congress have power to impose the tax only on those imported.

Berns appears to be flummoxed by Wilson's applying "migration" to white immigrants, but he should not be. Wilson did not say that "migration" applied *only* to white immigrants, so it is possible that in his mind it encompassed also the slaves moving in the interstate slave trade. And even if he did not see the 1808 clause as allowing congressional interference in the domestic slave trade, Wilson may have thought that the commerce clause did so.[17]

In the same speech in which he applied "migration" to whites, Wilson expressed his hope that the importation of slaves would be ended in 1808 and said that "in the meantime, the new states which are to be formed will be under the control of Congress in this particular; and slaves will never be introduced amongst them." The latter statement certainly suggested that Congress had the power to prevent the movement of slaves across some state lines, so Wilson may have contemplated a limited use by Congress of some kind of authority over the domestic commerce in slaves. On the other hand, maybe not. A decision by Congress to keep slaves out of the new states would not necessarily be an exercise of the interstate commerce power. Wilson may have thought that Congress would derive its authority to keep slaves out of the new states not from either the 1808 clause or the commerce clause of the Constitution, but rather from the Northwest Ordinance, a measure enacted originally by the Articles of Confederation Congress in 1787 and soon to be reenacted by the new government under the Constitution in 1789. And the Northwest Ordinance, Berns admits, was regarded as a contractual arrangement between the national government and the new states in the region to which the Ordinance applied. It was not an exercise of any power to control commerce, for the national government under the Articles of Confederation lacked such power.[18]

Isolated scraps of evidence suggest that a few other individuals may have entertained ideas similar to Wilson's except that they did not anticipate the demise of slavery. Berns points out that at the Massachusetts ratifying convention, General William Heath defended the 1808 clause by saying, "The federal Convention went as far as they could. The migration or importation, &c., is confined to the states now *existing only;* new states cannot claim it. Congress, by their ordinance for erecting new states, some time since, declared that the new states shall be republican, and that there shall be no slavery in them. But whether those in slavery in the Southern States will be emancipated after the year 1808, I do not pretend to determine. I rather doubt it."[19] As the new states would be located inland and so would not have direct access to the foreign slave trade, Heath perhaps thought that Congress by virtue of the 1808 clause would have the power to block the interstate movement of slaves into them. Either that or else he thought that the contractual nature of the Northwest Ordinance (which is, of course, the "ordinance for erecting new states" that he mentions) would prevent those states from ever allowing slavery to penetrate their borders. Thus Heath's views were similar to Wilson's—and were similarly ambiguous.

An interesting case that Berns does not consider is that of George Mason of Virginia. At the Constitutional Convention, Mason vigorously opposed what was to become the 1808 clause in a comment recorded as follows: "Maryland & Virginia he said had already prohibited the importation of slaves expressly. N. Carolina had done the same thing in substance. All this would be in vain if S. Carolina & Georgia be at liberty to import. The Western people are already calling out for slaves for their new lands; and will fill that Country with slaves if they can be got thro' S. Carolina & Georgia." Mason possibly believed that forbidding Congress to interfere with "migration or importation" would rule out any congressional interference in the interstate slave trade as well as in the bringing in of Africans, for he appears to have assumed that slaves imported by South Carolina or Georgia would necessarily pass freely across state lines into Virginia, Maryland, North Carolina, and the West. That could explain why later on, after the 1808 clause had been accepted by the convention, Mason contemplated proposing a constitutional clause guaranteeing the right of citizens to move their property from one state to another. By that time he was becoming so disenchanted with the work of the convention, however, that he never introduced his motion.[20]

Of all of the men who had a hand in the creation of the 1808 clause, the one about whom there exists the most extensive and intriguing evidence is James

Madison. Berns admits that twenty years after the Constitution was adopted, Madison supported the southern interpretation of the 1808 clause. But Berns claims that in 1787 and for some years after that, Madison had a different view. Berns points out that in his "Federalist 42" essay, Madison said that although it was too bad that the power to ban the importation of slaves had been postponed until 1808, it was still "a great point gained in favor of humanity, that a period of twenty years may terminate forever, within these States, a traffic which has so long and so loudly upbraided the barbarism of modern policy." From Madison's use of the phrase "within these States," Berns infers that Madison believed Congress could ban the interstate slave trade as well as the importation of Africans after 1808. That is, however, an exceedingly dubious inference, based as it is upon a mere verbal technicality. Madison in this context mentioned explicitly only "the importation of slaves," and that is likely the only slave trade he had in mind, even if it would have been more verbally accurate for him to have spoken of importing Africans *into* rather than *within* the United States.[21]

Berns also thinks it significant that in "Federalist 42," Madison dismissed as unworthy of comment the suggestion by some opponents of the Constitution that the 1808 clause could prevent "voluntary and beneficial emigrations from Europe to America." Berns thinks that shows that for Madison the word "migration" in the 1808 clause did not refer to white immigration—and consequently that it *did* refer to the interstate movement of slaves. Here again, however, Berns infers too much. Madison was just scorning as ridiculous the idea that Congress would ever choose to interfere with desirable immigration from Europe; he was not saying Congress would never have constitutional authority over it.[22]

Curiously, Berns buries in a footnote what is in fact his most salient evidence that in these early years Madison may have contemplated the possibility of some kind of federal interference in the movement of slaves across state lines. The evidence is a speech Madison made in the first federal Congress under the Constitution. The speech was reported as follows:

> He then entered into a critical review of the circumstances respecting the adoption of the Constitution; the ideas upon the limitation of the powers of Congress to interfere in the regulation of the commerce in slaves, and showing that they undeniably were not precluded from interposing in their importation; and generally, to regulate the mode in which every species of business shall be transacted. He adverted to the western country, and the cession of Georgia, in which Congress have certainly the power to regulate the subject of slavery; which shows that gentlemen are mistaken in supposing that Congress cannot constitutionally interfere in the business in any degree whatever.

When Madison said that Congress could use its commerce power to touch not just the importation of slaves but also "every species of business," he may have hinted that the commerce power also extended to the domestic slave trade. But we cannot be sure. Perhaps he was merely arguing for a fulsome view of the authority of Congress over foreign commerce. His subsequent comments about the western country and the Georgia cession do nothing to lift the fog of ambiguity, for there he may have been alluding to the constitutional power of Congress to regulate territories rather than trade.[23]

When Berns discusses what Madison said in later years, when the latter had become defensive of the South and its peculiar institution, he is almost too busy damning Madison's statements to notice how curiously ambiguous some of them continued to be. It is true that in the midst of the Missouri controversy in 1819, Madison stated unequivocally that the 1808 clause did not give Congress the constitutional right to interfere in the domestic slave trade. When the authors of the 1808 clause used the words "migration or importation," Madison said, "it is most certain, that they referred, exclusively, to a migration or importation from other countries into the U. States; and not to a removal, voluntary or involuntary, of Slaves or freemen, from one to another part of the U. States." But for Madison to insist that the 1808 clause did not give Congress power to interfere in the interstate slave trade did not foreclose the possibility that the commerce clause gave Congress that same power. And in an 1829 letter, Madison made this revealing comment about the authority of Congress over interstate commerce:

> I always foresaw that difficulties might be started in relation to that power. . . . Being in the same terms with the power over foreign commerce, the same extent, if taken literally, would belong to it. Yet it is very certain that it grew out of the abuse of the power by the importing States, in taxing the non-importing; and was intended as a negative & preventive provision agst. injustice among the States themselves; rather than as a power to be used for the positive purposes of the General Gov^{t}. in which alone however the remedial power could be lodged, and it will be safer to leave the power with this key to it, than to extend to it all the qualities & incidental means belonging to the power over foreign commerce.[24]

Here Madison said that it was "safer" to take a narrow view of the power of Congress over interstate commerce—which, from his by then resolutely southern point of view, it certainly was—but admitted that the power is broad indeed if the commerce clause is taken to mean exactly what it says. There is a hint here that Madison realized (as Walter Berns does not) that even if the 1808 clause gave Congress no power over the interstate slave trade, the commerce clause did.

Berns missed one last, tantalizing piece of evidence. In 1835, the year before Madison died, the English writer Harriet Martineau visited the old statesman and talked with him at length about the slavery question. In *Retrospect of Western Travel,* a memoir of her American tour, Martineau summarized their discussion. Sandwiched in between Madison's opinion that the South could not win an uprising against the North and an anecdote showing that he treated his slaves well, she threw in the bare sentence "He believed that Congress has power to prohibit the internal slavetrade." There is nothing ambiguous about that statement. The difficulty is that it is just one person's uncorroborated account of what someone else said in a private conversation, and it is possible that Martineau's abolitionist sympathies led her to hear what she wanted to hear. But if Martineau is to be believed, then the aged, world-weary Madison of 1835 admitted to her what the youthful, idealistic Madison of 1787 may have known but the cautious, states'-rights Madison of 1819 preferred to forget: that the commerce clause of the Constitution did give Congress the power to abolish the interstate slave trade.[25]

Although evidence on the matter is spotty and difficult to interpret, Madison and perhaps some other individuals among the founding fathers may have envisioned using the commerce power, at least in a circumscribed way, to inhibit the domestic slave trade. But if it is possible that some of the men who participated in the framing and ratification of the Constitution had that idea in mind, it is dead certain that others did not. Both at the Constitutional Convention and in the state ratification debates, some participants made comments from which we can safely infer that it had never entered their heads that either the 1808 clause or the commerce clause conferred any power on Congress to interfere in the interstate movement of slaves.

At the Constitutional Convention, when Charles Cotesworth Pinckney sought to protect "migration or importation" from federal interference, he said, "S. Carolina & Georgia cannot do without slaves. As to Virginia she will gain by stopping the importations. Her slaves will rise in value, & she has more than she wants. It would be unequal to require S. C. & Georgia to confederate on such unequal terms."[26] Pinckney assumed that if the constitutional protection he wanted was not provided and Congress subsequently used its commerce power to end slave importation, the domestic slave trade would continue nevertheless. We know Pinckney made that assumption, because Virginia's surplus slaves would not increase in value unless they could be transferred across state borders into those markets where there was greater demand for them. Therefore, it evidently had not occurred to Pinckney that Congress might use its commerce power to ban the interstate as well as the foreign slave trade.

A remark that another South Carolinian, David Ramsay, made during the ratification contest in his state is more ambiguous but perhaps carries the same implication. Arguing that New England shipping interests might not want slave importations to end even in 1808, Ramsay said, "Though Congress may forbid the importation of negroes after 21 years, it does not follow that they will. On the other hand, it is probable that they will not. The more rice we make, the more business will be for their shipping: their interest will therefore coincide with our's. Besides, we have other sources of supply—the importations of the ensuing 20 years, added to the natural increase of those we already have, and the influx from our northern neighbours, who are desirous of getting rid of their slaves, will afford a sufficient number for cultivating all the lands in this state."[27] In expecting an influx of slaves from the more northerly states, Ramsay obviously assumed that the slaves would move without hindrance across state lines, but it is unclear whether he referred to their doing so only until 1808 or afterward as well. If the latter, then he too had no thought that Congress could ever interfere with the interstate trade.

The most conclusive proof that most southerners did not think the Constitution gave the federal government the right to interfere with the domestic slave trade lies not in what supporters of the Constitution like Pinckney and Ramsay said, however, but rather in what their Antifederalist opponents did *not* say during the ratification debates. Although the Antifederalists racked their brains to conjure up every possible objection to the Constitution, not one of them ever suggested that it opened the way for Congress to restrict the interstate movement of slaves. At the Virginia ratification convention, Patrick Henry insisted that slavery would be insecure under the Constitution, but he pointed to the powers of Congress to tax, make war, and provide for the general welfare as the ones that endangered it. Henry did criticize the 1808 clause, but only by making the specious argument that the clause showed that Congress would have implied powers exceeding those explicitly given it by the Constitution. Other delegates readily answered Henry by pointing out that the 1808 clause did no such thing: it merely set out an exception to the power granted to Congress by the commerce clause. One of the replies came from George Nicholas, whose response was reported as follows: "He endeavoured to obviate the objection of Gentlemen, that the restriction on Congress was a proof that they would have power not given them, by remarking, that they would only have had a general superintendency of trade, if the restriction had not been inserted. But the Southern States insisted on this exception to that general superintendency for twenty years. It could not therefore have been a power by implication, as the restriction was an exception from a delegated power." It is interesting to observe that although Nicholas recognized that the federal commerce power was vast, its scope limited only by the 1808 clause, he nevertheless had no more inkling than Henry that Congress might have power to attack the domestic slave trade by virtue of either the 1808 clause (if the word "migration" in the 1808 clause encompassed the interstate movement of slaves) or just the commerce clause (if the 1808 clause had no bearing on the domestic slave trade).[28]

We can conclude then, that during both the drawing up of the Constitution and the battle over ratification, it never entered the minds of most southerners that the Constitution gave Congress the authority to outlaw the interstate slave trade. But how can the southerners have failed to notice so obvious a threat to their interests? They knew that the commerce clause gave Congress authority over domestic as well as foreign commerce. They knew that the 1808 clause limited the latter power by forbidding Congress to prohibit the external slave trade until 1808. They knew that after 1808 Congress would have power to prohibit the external slave trade. How could they not see that under the same provisions of the Constitution, Congress could claim the power to outlaw the interstate slave trade, at least after 1808 and possibly even before then?

The eagerness of the exhausted delegates to the Constitutional Convention to strike one last deal, conclude their business, and go home might explain why the southerners among them overlooked the danger to the domestic slave trade, but it cannot account for the failure of the southern Antifederalists to raise the alarm during the ratification debates. The silence of the latter probably resulted from the fact that the interstate slave trade was of minor significance in 1787 and slaveholders had no inkling of how it would burgeon in the next century. They did not foresee the technological developments that would spur the great cotton boom of the antebellum decades, nor did they know that the Louisiana Purchase and other territorial acquisitions would open up vast new lands for cotton—and for slavery.[29]

That the slaveholders did not anticipate the future importance of interstate slave trafficking is hardly surprising, for the opponents of slavery were no better at gazing into their crystal balls. Those few persons active in the fledgling antislavery organizations at the time of the Constitutional Convention gave little attention to the internal slave trade. Even the Quakers and other Pennsylvanians who spearheaded the only attempt to interest the founding fathers in curbing slavery focused their attention on the foreign slave trade and on the institution of slavery itself, not the domestic trade. When the Pennsylvania Abolition Society drew up its June 1787 petition to the Constitutional Convention, it implored the founders to end the importation of Africans but made no mention of the interstate trade. To the extent that there was concern with the movement of slaves across state lines, it was focused on keeping slaves within the borders of a particular state in the hope that they might eventually be emancipated. In May 1786 the New-York Manumission Society presented to the state legislature of New York a petition written by the society's president, John Jay, which included these paragraphs:

> That your memorialists being deeply affected by the situation of those who, altho free by the Laws of God are held in Slavery by the Laws of this State, view with Pain & Regret the additional miseries wh[ich] those unhappy people experience from the Practice of exporting them like cattle and other articles of Commerce to the West Indies and the Southern States.
>
> That in the course of this Inhuman commerce there have been frequent and very affecting Instances of Husbands being torn from their wives, wives from their Husbands, Parents from their children, children from their Parents.

The petition ended by praying that the New York State legislature would "pass an act to prevent the further exportation of negroes or slaves from this State." Despite their concern for the slaves being removed from New York, it evidently did not occur to Jay and his associates to ask the framers of the new national government to impose a nationwide ban on the interstate slave trade. Either that or else they were realistic enough to surmise that the men gathered at Philadelphia would have spurned any such appeal.[30]

Many of the delegates to the Constitutional Convention did regard slavery as an evil institution that was incompatible with the human rights ideals of the American Revolution. They hoped that someday, somehow, the time would come when there would be no slavery in the United States. It was to humor them that the convention as a whole agreed to use tortured circumlocutions rather than mention slaves explicitly in the 1808 clause and elsewhere in the Constitution. But acknowledging that slavery was an evil was one thing, doing something about it was something else. The key obstacle for the founders was that, to them, the right to property was as fundamental as the right to liberty. Although Thomas Jefferson in his formulation of the rights of mankind had substituted the right to pursue happiness for the right to hold property, nobody at the Constitutional Convention disagreed when Pierce Butler of South Carolina declared that the national government "was instituted principally for the protection of property." The result was a dilemma. On the one hand, slavery violated the sacred right of the slave to liberty. On the other hand, ending slavery by any coercive means violated the sacred right of the slaveowner to property.[31]

That the founding fathers could not cut the Gordian knot may strike the modern reader as ludicrous, but it should not. The founders lived in their time, not ours. As they strolled to and from their sessions at Independence Hall, they

Figure 2. Philadelphia street scene. Both slaves and free blacks were routine participants in the daily life of eighteenth-century Philadelphia. Here a white servant girl has dropped a pie in the street, much to the amusement of some black chimney sweeps. *The Accident in Lombard Street,* etching by Charles Willson Peale, 1787. Courtesy Winterthur Museum.

would have thought it unremarkable to glimpse one of the hundreds of slaves who then resided in Philadelphia. In their eyes, slavery was a widespread and ancient institution sanctioned by custom, law, and religion. As Charles Cotesworth Pinckney put it at the Constitutional Convention, "If slavery be wrong, it is justified by the example of all the world. He cited the case of Greece Rome & other antient States; the sanction given by France England, Holland & other modern States. In all ages one half of mankind have been slaves." Ending slavery in the United States by riding roughshod over the property rights of the slavemasters was unthinkable. True, many of the northern states were already taking steps toward extinguishing slavery within their borders, but they were doing so only slowly and painfully, usually through schemes that freed only the slaves born after a specified date, thus ensuring that the slaveowners lost only their expected capital gains of the future rather than the human chattels they actually possessed in the here and now. Yet even that exceedingly modest invasion of property rights met vehement objection from those who maintained, like one New Jersey slaveholder, that gradual abolition was "publick ROBBERY." The emancipation programs ultimately succeeded in the North only because they were exceedingly gradual and because northern slaveholders were a small minority interest group in a region where slavery was of lesser economic importance.[32]

Given their reverence for property rights and their lack of awareness of the future importance of the domestic slave trade, it is highly unlikely that any delegates to the Constitutional Convention or to the state ratification conventions consciously set out to destroy slavery by giving Congress the power to crush that trade. The most that can be said for Walter Berns's thesis is that a relatively few participants did make statements that imply that either the commerce clause alone or the commerce clause in combination with the 1808 clause gave Congress authority over the interstate slave trade. Unfortunately for Berns, however, those same statements also imply that those delegates thought of the power as a relatively minor one that would be used only to stop the movement of slaves across state lines into the territories and states where slavery was prohibited. When conceived of in that limited way, the power merely provided some extra constitutional backing for federal actions that were already sanctioned by other means. For in 1787 nobody doubted that the power of Congress to regulate the territories included the power to prohibit slavery in them, or that the Northwest Ordinance established a contractual arrangement under which slavery was barred for ever from the new states to be created northwest of the Ohio River. The one possible exception to this blanket conclusion is James Madison. Although the evidence is ambiguous, Berns may be right in believing that briefly, in the period of the Constitutional Convention and the first Congress, Madison did envision Congress someday using its interstate commerce power to outlaw the entire interstate slave trade. But if the youthful Madison ever harbored such a dream, it became a nightmare to him in his later years.

The preponderance of evidence is against the Berns thesis that the founding fathers intended to give Congress the power to destroy slavery by abolishing the interstate slave trade. Both at Philadelphia and in the ratifying conventions, the vast majority of white southerners would never have accepted the Constitution if they had thought that it granted such power, and the vast majority of white northerners were too respectful of property rights to have embraced such a purpose. And yet, the fact remains that no matter what was in the minds of the delegates to the Constitutional Convention when they drew up the commerce clause and the 1808 clause, and in the minds of the men who ratified the Constitution at the several state conventions, those clauses were so worded that they could be read as giving Congress the power to prohibit the interstate slave trade. The founding fathers had, however inadvertently, created a constitutional loophole with huge potential as an antislavery weapon.

3

Are They Not the Lord's Enemies?

For many years following the adoption of the Constitution, the question of federal control over the interstate slave trade did not arise. In 1790 the first Congress pondered what it might do about slavery, but nobody suggested that it could attack domestic slave trafficking. In 1798 there was a vigorous congressional debate about the meaning of the 1808 clause, yet remarkably even then no one suggested that the clause empowered Congress to interfere with the interstate slave trade. There may have been isolated individuals here and there who glimpsed the potential of the federal commerce power as a mechanism for undermining slavery, but most people, even those for whom slavery was a central concern, remained oblivious to the concept. Not until 1807, when Congress moved toward exercising its acknowledged power to ban the importation of slaves from abroad beginning in 1808, did it dawn upon some southern representatives in Congress that there was a danger of federal interference in the domestic slave trade. The outcry of the southern few was not taken seriously by their congressional colleagues, however, and the issue subsided into its usual somnambulance for another decade. Then, abruptly, in the Missouri Debates of 1819–1820, the issue burst into prominence. It would never again disappear from view. In the arena of public debate between opponents and defenders of slavery, on the floors of the House and the Senate, and in cases contested before the Supreme Court of the United States, the question would arise again and again: Did Congress have the constitutional power to attack the interstate slave trade?

In February 1790 a yearly meeting of Quakers from the mid-Atlantic region submitted to Congress a petition calling attention to "the licentious wickedness of the African trade for slaves, and the inhuman tyranny and blood guiltiness inseparable from it." Another petition was submitted on behalf of the Pennsylvania Abolition Society by its president, Benjamin Franklin. It pointed out that the Constitution had vested Congress with its "many important and salutary powers" for the express purpose of promoting the general welfare and securing the blessings of liberty. On the grounds that such blessings "ought rightfully to be administered, without distinction of color, to all descriptions of people," the petitioners urged Congress to "step to the very verge of the power vested in you for discouraging every species of traffic in the persons of our fellow-men." The principal aim of both petitions was to persuade Congress to levy the ten-dollar-per-capita tax on the importation of Africans that was permitted by the 1808 clause of the Constitution. In discussing among themselves that and other possible antislavery measures, the Quaker lobbyists at one point pondered whether Congress perhaps might also impose a ten-dollar tax on slaves that were sent from one state to another. While that could be regarded as the first recorded case of anyone contemplating the use of the interstate commerce power against the domestic slave trade, it is uncertain that the individuals involved consciously viewed it as such. At any rate, they did not convince anyone in Congress to pursue the idea.[1]

In the House of Representatives, James Madison defended the antislavery petitions, saying that there were "a variety of ways" in which Congress could "countenance the abolition" of the slave trade, including making regulations about the introduction of slaves into the new states to be created in the West. Exactly what Madison had in mind is unclear. It is possible that he was thinking of combating the domestic as well as the external slave trade and so was suggesting that the interstate commerce power could be used to restrict the entry of slaves into new states. That he referred specifically to the *new* states may indicate that he thought the 1808 clause temporarily prevented Congress from interfering with the interstate trade (as well as slave importations from Africa) into the existing states. On the other hand, however, he may have been thinking only of the external slave trade and of mechanisms for keeping only those slaves newly imported from Africa from being carried into the western territories that would eventually become new states.[2]

Unlike Madison, the representatives of the deep South vehemently opposed even formally receiving the antislavery petitions, much less acting upon them. A South Carolina delegate said that the Quakers had come to the Capitol "to meddle in business with which they had nothing to do," and declared, "The rights of the Southern States ought not to be threatened, and their property endangered, to please people who would be unaffected by the consequences." In denouncing the petitioners and their aims, the southerners voiced virtually every proslavery argument that would be heard over the course of the next seventy years: Slavery is the exclusive concern of the slave states. If slavery is an evil, it is one for which there is no remedy. Even to discuss it is harmful, as it undermines the value of slaves. Such talk also may buoy up the slaves with false hopes for freedom, which will make them unruly and their masters proportionately more harsh in their discipline. Slaves are treated humanely, and, because they belong to an inferior race, are happy with their lot. (That these happy people might nevertheless be tempted to rebel was explained by their inability to "reason on the subject, as more enlightened men would.") Slavery has existed throughout history. It is sanctioned by the Bible. Slaves are essential to the economy of the South. The South will not accept emancipation without a bloody civil war.[3]

Despite all of this bluster, the House voted by a large majority to refer the petitions to a special committee. The committee was intended to have a member from each state, but every southern delegation except Virginia's refused to name a participant. That bit of southern obstinacy proved to be a tactical blunder, for it explains why the committee subsequently brought in a report that was strikingly sympathetic to the aims of the petitioners. The report began by stating the obvious fact that until 1808 Congress could not prohibit the importation of slaves into any of the existing states. But then it went on to declare that "Congress, by a fair construction of the Constitution, are equally restrained from interfering in the emancipation of slaves, who already are, or who may, within the period mentioned, be imported into, or born within any of the said States." That statement horrified the spokesmen for the deep South. William L. Smith of South Carolina pointed out that it "appeared to hold out the idea that Congress might exercise the power of emancipation after 1808." He argued vehemently and at length that Congress possessed no such power.[4]

While Smith's reaction to the ambiguous statement by the select committee is understandable, it is unlikely that the committee had intended to assert that Congress would be able to pursue a general policy of emancipation after 1808. More likely the committee had in mind that if Congress should decide to exercise its power to outlaw the foreign slave trade in 1808, then it would have the power thereafter to emancipate those slaves who were imported into the country illegally. Still, it is curious that the statement of the select committee referred to slaves "born within" as well as "imported into" the states, which does seem to imply some broader aim than just freeing any Africans smuggled in after importations were banned. Be that as it may, there is no hint that anybody on the committee viewed the interstate commerce power as a possible mechanism to achieve emancipation. On the contrary, in the next section of the report, which set out a long list of matters concerning the treatment of slaves that were said to fall under exclusively state rather than federal jurisdiction, the committee included "the seizure, transportation, or sale of free negroes." Apparently it had not occurred to the committee that the forced movement of kidnaped free blacks across state lines in order to sell them into bondage was a matter that might well be regarded as falling squarely within the power of the federal government to regulate interstate commerce.[5]

The deep South condemnation of the select committee report prompted one northern congressman to present his own understanding of the 1808 clause, based on his own novel theory of constitutional interpretation. Thomas Scott of Pennsylvania refused to acknowledge that the "persons" mentioned in the 1808 clause were slaves, because, he said, "When we are considering our constitutional powers, we must judge of them by the face of the instrument . . . and not by the certain understandings that the framers of that instrument may be supposed to have had of each other . . . and at any rate, the constitution was in no degree obligatory until ratified by a certain number of state conventions, who I presume cannot be supposed to be acquainted with this understanding in the national convention, and consequently must have ratified it upon its own merits, as apparent on its face. I had the honor of a seat in one of those conventions, and gave my assent to its ratification on those principles." Scott went on to claim that Congress could outlaw the foreign slave trade even before 1808 and also that it could, whenever it pleased, "declare (by law) that every person, whether black, white, blue or red, who from foreign parts can get his or her foot on the American shore . . . shall to all intents and purposes be not only free persons, but free citizens." Scott made no mention of the interstate slave trade, but his remarks leave little doubt that he would have upheld the power of Congress to ban it, had anyone put the proposition to him. His approach to the Constitution does not appear to have impressed his colleagues, many of whom, like himself, had participated in the drawing up or ratification of the document only a few years earlier. It was an approach that would have more appeal in the future, however, as time passed and a new generation of political leaders emerged that had not been party to the bargains and deliberations of 1787–1789.[6]

Paying no heed to Scott or to the handful of other northerners who spoke up in defense of the Quakers and their aims, the proslavery southern representatives lambasted the committee report and set about emasculating it with deletions and amendments. Eventually they got their way, in part because many congressmen were eager to put the fractious slavery issue aside in order to concentrate upon the more pressing matter of Alexander Hamilton's program for restoring the national credit. In the end, the House voted to insert in its journal *both* the original report of the special committee *and* the remnant of it that had survived from the deliberations of the House sitting as a committee of the whole, a remnant that discarded everything of substance in the original report. There the matter rested. Nothing of consequence had been decided, other than what everybody had already known at the outset: that Congress was prohibited from interfering in the importation of Africans until the year 1808. Whether Congress could take action of any kind against domestic slavery, either before or after 1808, was unresolved.[7]

In 1793 the national government enacted the first federal fugitive slave act. The law not only helped masters to recover slaves who escaped across state lines; it also led to the widespread seizure of free blacks, who were misrepresented as fugitives and sold into bondage by unscrupulous whites. The Pennsylvania Abolition Society publicized and protested against that abuse as well as all slave trading. In 1796 the Society received a report that "a bill to prevent the trade in slaves being carried on from one part to another of the United States, and for protecting free blacks from being carried into slavery," was about to be introduced in Congress. The Society responded by appointing a committee to render all possible assistance in pushing the bill forward. The report appears to have been a false alarm, however, for nothing came of the matter. The Pennsylvania Abolition Society was not alone in attempting to influence Congress. Free blacks, who were excluded from membership in the elitist Pennsylvania Abolition Society, took independent action on their own. In January 1797 four African Americans originally from North Carolina who were living in precarious freedom in Philadelphia appealed to a free black clergyman, Absalom Jones, to help them avoid falling prey to slave catchers. Jones drew up a petition asking Congress to protect free Negroes from "kidnappers and man-stealers." When a Pennsylvania representative presented the petition to the House, a North Carolina colleague protested that the petitioners were not free men because the laws of his state did not permit manumission. The House voted 50 to 33 to refuse even to receive the petition much less respond to it. In December 1799 Absalom Jones composed and submitted to Congress another petition, this one signed by seventy black residents of Philadelphia, but again without result. That petition complained about both the slave trade to Africa and another "equally wicked" trade that was "practised openly by Citizens of some of the Southern States upon the waters of Maryland and Delaware." The latter complaint referred to whites who kidnaped free blacks and smuggled them southward: "thus these poor helpless victims like droves of Cattle are seized, fettered, and hurried into places provided for this most horrid traffic, such as dark cellars and garrets" and subsequently are "forced on board vessels, crouded under hatches, and without the least commiseration, left to deplore the sad separation of the dearest ties in nature, husband from wife, and Parents from children[;] thus pocket'd together they are transported to Georgia and other places and there inhumanely exposed to sale: Can any Commerce, trade, or transaction, so detestably shock the feelings of Man, or degrade the dignity of his nature equal to this[?]" Although its wording sounds like an appeal to Congress to exercise its interstate commerce power to end the abuse complained of, the petition made no explicit reference to the commerce clause. Instead, it simply noted that the declared purpose of the Constitution was to establish justice and secure the blessings of liberty, and contended that slave trading was incompatible with those objectives.[8]

In the meantime, and in a rather curious way, the 1808 clause had become the focus of close congressional scrutiny. By 1798 the dominant Federalists were becoming worried by the increasing strength of their political opposition, clustered around Thomas Jefferson and James Madison, which was coalescing into an organized party known as the Republicans. Ostensibly to combat espionage and intrigue by agents of revolutionary France, but also with the rather transparent intent of hobbling their domestic political rivals, the Federalists in 1798 enacted the infamous Alien and Sedition Acts, repressive laws which, among other things, authorized the President of the United States to order the summary deportation of any alien whom he regarded as subversive. In the congressional debate over the latter measure, Albert Gallatin led the attack of the Republicans, and he seized upon the 1808 clause as his constitutional weapon. A member of the Pennsylvania Abolition Society, Gallatin had strong antislavery convictions. While serving in the Pennsylvania legislature in 1793 he had written a committee report denouncing slavery and calling for the state to abolish it. In the U.S. House of Representatives in 1798 he supported an attempt to ban slavery from the Mississippi Territory west of Georgia. It does not appear, however, that Gallatin had ever considered the possibility that "migration" in the 1808 clause referred to the domestic movement of slaves. If such a thought occurred to him now, he suppressed any mention of it. Instead, he contended that the word "migration" referred to the entry of free white immigrants into the United States. If the 1808 clause had been intended to refer only to slaves, he said, then it would have used only the one word "importation." After all, as another Republican asked rhetorically, "who ever heard of a migration of slaves?" Furthermore, said the Republicans, if Congress had the power to banish white immigrants who were perceived as dangerous, then it would also have the power to remove "all that species of property (slaves,) which may well be looked upon as an evil and dangerous to society, not only at present, but in the most peaceable times."[9]

The Federalists replied that the 1808 clause referred only to slaves and not white immigrants. That was "pretty evident," according to one Federalist, from the fact that the limitation on congressional power expired in 1808: "If it had related to emigrants, it would have been without any limitation of time." For surely no one wanted Congress to prohibit white immigration after 1808 any more than before then. The Federalists did not attempt to explain why if the 1808 clause encompassed only slaves it nevertheless used the term "migration." They could have strengthened their argument that the clause referred only to slaves and not white immigrants by claiming that "migration" referred to the interstate movement of slaves. They made no such assertion, however, either because the idea did not occur to them, or perhaps because the idea *did* occur to them, but they knew better than to introduce another incendiary issue into a debate that was already overheated. Instead, the Federalists simply said that giving the president the power to remove aliens would not interfere with the right of the states to admit them in the first place, even if it were true that the 1808 clause guaranteed to the states the right of admission. The right to admit immigrants and the right subsequently to banish them were, the Federalists said, entirely different powers.[10]

An interesting incident of the 1798 debate was a sharp dispute over historical memory. The ranks of the founding fathers still active in public life were dwindling. Although the Constitution had been drawn up little more than a decade before, already there were only two current members of the House of Representatives who had been delegates to the 1787 Constitutional Convention. They were Abraham Baldwin of Georgia and Jonathan Dayton of New Jersey. Dayton was now Speaker of the House. In arguing against the Federalist claim that the 1808 clause referred only to slaves and not also to white immigrants, Baldwin said that when the wording of the clause was under discussion at the Convention in 1787, it was pointed out that it could encompass other persons as well as slaves, "which was not denied, but this did not produce any alteration of it." Baldwin's recollection was vehemently disputed by Dayton, who declared that Baldwin was either suffering from "absolute forgetfulness" or indulging in "wilful misrepresentation." Dayton insisted that in the entire discussion at Philadelphia "no question arose, or was agitated respecting the admission of foreigners, but, on the contrary, that it was confined simply to slaves." Baldwin tried to be conciliatory without yielding his ground. He said that he had "more confidence than common in his recollection on this point" and gave it "as the result of his very clear recollection" of what had occurred at the Constitutional Convention. "Any other member of that body was doubtless at liberty to say he did not recollect it," Baldwin added, but "that would not diminish the confidence" he himself had in his own memory of what had occurred.[11]

Dayton exploded. According to the *Annals of Congress,* as soon as Baldwin sat down "The SPEAKER rose from the Chair and said, that there was something so unmanly and improper in the opportunity which had been sought by the member from Georgia of replying to the observations he had made yesterday, that he felt himself irresistibly impelled to break through the rigid form, and to express, in a single word, his sense of it." He charged that Baldwin had deliberately withheld his reply until Dayton was presiding as Speaker and so could not join in the debate. But as to the substance of Baldwin's remarks, "it was not of such importance, nor so worthy of notice, the Speaker said, as to justify his requesting the House to go again into a committee [of the whole], merely to give him an opportunity of directly and positively contradicting the member from Georgia, as he should most assuredly and positively do, so far as respected the proceedings of the Federal Convention in 1787." Here was one clash between a northerner and a southerner in which the southerner was entirely civil in his manner and entirely correct in what he said, whereas the northerner was both hot-headed and wrong-headed. For it was Dayton, not Baldwin, whose memory had failed him. Clearly neither Dayton nor Baldwin agreed with Gallatin, who said that the discussions of 1787 no longer mattered, for "whatever might have been the intention of the framers of the Constitution, it must be taken as it now stands." Actually, even Gallatin knew that the question of original intent could not be cast aside so easily, for he went on to quote remarks by James Wilson at the Pennsylvania ratifying convention in order to support his own insistence that the 1808 clause applied to white immigrants as well as to imported slaves.[12]

It was a foregone conclusion that the Alien Act would become law, not because the Federalists won the constitutional argument over the 1808 clause, but simply because the Federalists were in firm control of the House, the Senate, the Presidency, and the Supreme Court. All that the Republicans could then do was to appeal to those states in which they were dominant and to the general public for support in their struggle to overturn the obnoxious statute. Jefferson himself wrote the famous Kentucky Resolutions of 16 November 1798, in which the bluegrass state declared the Alien and Sedition Acts to be unconstitutional. The resolutions took it for granted that "migration" in the 1808 clause referred to white immigrants, and consequently declared that since "this Commonwealth does admit the migration of alien friends," the federal government cannot deport them, because "to remove them when migrated is equivalent to a prohibition of their migration, and is therefore contrary to the said provision of the Constitution, and void."[13]

In the national elections of 1800 the Republicans triumphed over the Federalists. With Jefferson as president and their party in control of Congress, the Republicans repealed the Alien and Sedition Acts. They also shifted national policy in new directions, including the acquisition via the Louisiana Purchase of 1803 of a vast territory west of the Mississippi River, doubling the size of the United States at a stroke. In 1804 Congress approved legislation that for a time allowed only bona fide settlers to bring slaves into the new territory. Even the settlers were forbidden to bring in slaves that had been imported into the United States since 1798, which gently censured South Carolina for its recent decision to resume importations from Africa. The debate over the 1804 bill focused almost entirely upon moral and practical rather than constitutional concerns, but it appears that everybody involved was operating on the assumption that it was the authority of Congress over the territories that was the basis for the proposed law. No one made any reference to the interstate commerce power.[14]

As the year 1808 loomed closer, the clause of the Constitution that would then permit action against slave importations drew renewed attention. In January 1806 the House of Representatives discussed the possibility of enacting a law that would impose a tax of ten dollars per capita on every slave brought into the United States—which really meant into South Carolina, because that was the only state that allowed such importation. The levying of such a tax—permissible under the 1808 clause—had been somctimes talked about but never implemented. There arose a brief debate over whether the law should apply the tax explicitly to slaves or should instead use the same obscure wording as the 1808 clause itself and thus apply the tax to all "persons" imported. Some congressmen feared that the latter wording would mean that white immigrants would be taxed. Others replied that only persons bound to service could be said to be imported and therefore the only whites to whom the tax could apply would be convicts and indentured servants, not free immigrants. In the end, no action was taken, partly because the lawmakers were preoccupied with the threat posed by the growing possibility of American entanglement in the Napoleonic wars. As one member put it, "Shall a man spend time in adjusting the tie of his cravat when the hangman's noose is at his neck?"[15]

Almost a year later, the House returned to the subject, this time dropping the idea of a tax and instead concentrating on a bill that would prohibit the importation of slaves as of the first of January 1808. In arguing for such a bill, some of its warmest advocates adopted a novel constitutional position. They denied that the power of Congress to ban slave importations derived from the commerce clause of the Constitution. Such a notion, they said, "was of the most dangerous complexion, as it went to sanction the principle that it was lawful for Congress to deal in human beings as an article of commerce—a principle abhorrent to humanity, and at war with our fundamental institutions." Instead, they argued, when Congress banned slave importations it would be an exercise not of the commerce power but of the power to punish offenses against the law of nations.[16] Why these congressmen chose to adopt that position is uncertain. If they were trying to head off southern fears that banning slave importations as an exercise of the congressional power to regulate foreign commerce might become a precedent for prohibiting the interstate slave trade as an exercise of the congressional power to regulate interstate commerce, then they were remarkably prescient, for no southerners had as yet expressed any such fears. But they were about to.

When the House started hammering out the details of the bill to end slave importations, it was realized that measures would be needed to prevent smuggling once the ban took effect. For if slaves could continue to be shipped domestically from one location to another in any vessel of any size, then it would be virtually impossible to prevent illegally imported slaves from being surreptitiously mixed in among them. Moreover, even if the number of vessels carrying domestic slaves could be reduced to a manageable level, it still might be all too easy for the captain of a ship landing slaves at, say, New Orleans to claim that he had brought his human cargo from one of the upper South ports, when in reality the slaves on board had come illegally from Africa or Cuba. To prevent such chicanery, the bill outlawing the importation of slaves from abroad also provided that only vessels with a carrying capacity of at least forty tons could transport slaves domestically and that before any such ship embarked upon a domestic voyage it must prepare duplicate manifests specifying the name, sex, age, and height of each slave taken on board. One copy of the manifest would be left with port officials and the other copy taken along by the ship's captain. When the vessel arrived at its destination, it could not unload until the port officials there had checked the cargo against the manifest and confirmed that the slaves on board were the same ones who had begun the voyage.[17]

Peter Early of Georgia tried to weaken the bill by proposing an amendment declaring that slaves being conveyed from one place to another within the United States could be carried "in any vessel or species of craft whatever." The House accepted Early's amendment but the Senate refused to go along with it. When the House then considered whether to surrender the point, some southerners spoke out forcefully, declaring that it must not. Here was a defining moment in the long story of the struggle over the interstate slave trade. For the first time, some southern spokesmen clearly grasped the enormity of the potential danger to slavery that lurked in the federal power to regulate interstate commerce. Two whose remarks were recorded were David R. Williams of South Carolina and John Randolph of Virginia. Williams moved that the House insist on retaining the amendment, protesting that without it the bill "would provide that no negroes shall be transported from one State to another to be sold or held in service." Randolph sounded the alarm even more strongly. If the bill passed without Early's amendment, Randolph said, then "the Southern people would set the law at defiance," and he himself "would begin the example."[18]

Randolph is a fascinating figure, a bridge between the fading eighteenth-century southern values of George Washington and the emerging nineteenth-century southern values of John C. Calhoun. Like Washington, Randolph regarded slavery as a moral evil. He accepted responsibility for the slaves that he had inherited, but he never bought or sold a slave. He abhorred commercial slave trading. In 1816 he tried unsuccessfully to persuade Congress to abolish the commercial slave trade in the District of Columbia, where he thought there was no question that the federal government had the constitutional authority to act. (Later on, southern leaders would vigorously disagree, largely because they came to fear that to abolish the slave trade in Washington would be to enter upon a slippery slope that might lead to the abolition of the interstate trade.) In 1818 Randolph wrote, "Avarice alone could have produced the slave trade; avarice alone can drive, as it does drive, this infernal traffic, and the wretched victims of it, like so many post-horses, whipped to death in a mail coach." When he died in 1833, his will provided for the emancipation and resettlement of every one of his several hundred slaves. But despite his sincere antislavery beliefs, and his call for federal action in the District of Columbia, Randolph was adamantly opposed to any federal interference in the right of the southern states to deal with their peculiar institution as they saw fit. Thus he pioneered in advancing the extreme states'-rights doctrine that would be championed later on by Calhoun and others. Randolph realized that allowing the federal government to restrict the domestic slave trade even in so minor a way as by limiting the size of the vessels that were allowed to carry slaves would set a fearful precedent. "The next step," he declared, "would be to forbid the slaveholder himself going from one State to another."[19]

The House voted to insist upon Early's amendment. A conference committee of the House and Senate then worked out a compromise that permitted slaves to be carried on vessels of any size but only on inland waterways and not along the coasts, where the forty-ton rule remained in effect. Thus the compromise measure moved some way to accommodate the southern concerns but preserved the regulation of coastwise shipping that was essential to protect against the smuggling in of slaves from abroad. Probably the conference committee thought that in retaining the rules governing the coastal trade it was not exercising a power to regulate the interstate slave trade. Rather, it was merely providing for a mechanism that was necessary and proper for carrying out the unquestioned right of Congress to suppress slave importations. But Early, Williams, and Randolph would have none of it. Randolph declared that the new provision invaded property rights and at some future time might be made the pretext for complete emancipation. "He had rather lose the bill," he exclaimed, "he had rather lose all the bills of the session, he had rather lose every bill passed since the establishment of the Government, than agree to the provision. . . . It went to blow up the Constitution in ruins." Randolph predicted that if the Union were ever to dissolve, "the line of severance would be between the slaveholding and the non-slaveholding States." He declared that men like himself bore no blame for having inherited the institution of slavery. "It was a thing with which they had no more to do than with their own procreation." All that he asked of northerners was that they remain neutral about slavery and not "erect themselves into an abolition society."[20]

Despite Randolph's fulminations, the House approved the bill incorporating the conference committee's amendment. So did the Senate. Randolph then made a last-ditch effort to head off what he still insisted was a disastrous precedent. Claiming that the bill as amended "involved the exercise of a power not possessed by Congress, which was subversive of the rights of property of the holders of slaves, and which might eventuate in their general emancipation," he proposed a bill supplementing and explaining the one already approved. In Randolph's new bill, Congress would explicitly disavow any authority to abridge the property rights of slavemasters and would declare that nothing in the law banning slave importations should be construed in such a way as to penalize slaveowners who transported slaves from one port to another within the United States in vessels with a capacity of less than forty tons. Randolph threatened that if his supplementary bill was not approved, he and the other representatives from Virginia would ask President Jefferson to veto the main bill imposing the ban on slave importations.[21] The session ended without action on Randolph's supplementary bill, however, and Jefferson signed the main bill into law on 3 March 1807.

At that time only a handful of southerners shared Randolph's fear of the potential for federal aggression against domestic slavery and slave trading. It was a different story a decade later, however, when the nation experienced its first great sectional crisis. In December 1818 Henry Clay presented to the House of Representatives the request of the territory of Missouri to be admitted to the Union as a state. What seemed at first to be a routine matter was thrown into confusion when James Tallmadge, Jr., of New York surprised the House by moving an amendment to the Missouri enabling act prohibiting the further entry of slaves into Missouri and providing for the gradual extinction of slavery there. Delegates from North and South immediately locked horns over whether or not Congress had the power to impose such conditions on Missouri. Because Tallmadge was ill, the first extended speech on behalf of his amendment to be recorded in the *Annals of Congress* was presented by his fellow New Yorker John W. Taylor. Although Taylor apologized for being unable to do full justice to his subject, owing to its having been introduced so unexpectedly, he argued that since Congress had the powers under the Constitution both to admit new states and to make all needful regulations for the territories, it could demand anything it liked from a territory before consenting to admit it as a state. He also emphasized that Congress was about to set a precedent for the whole region west of the Mississippi River and thus to decide the destiny of millions of human beings.[22]

The argument was then taken up by Timothy Fuller of Massachusetts. Fuller repeated Taylor's claim that Congress could impose conditions on new states but raised it a notch by declaring that the national legislature had not only the right but also the duty to prohibit slavery in them. He pointed out that the Constitution says that the United States shall guarantee to each state a republican form of government, and contended that slavery is inconsistent with republicanism. He conceded that at the time the Constitution was drawn up, necessity had required that republican principles be sacrificed to the extent of allowing the continued existence of bondage in the original states. But he insisted that to permit it when admitting new states was to violate the Constitution. Southerners here interrupted Fuller to protest against the suggestion that their states were not republican in character and to warn that there might be slaves in the gallery listening to Fuller's shocking assertions. But they were about to hear worse. Fuller now introduced an entirely new constitutional point. He said that under the authority of the 1808 clause, Congress had prohibited the further importation of slaves. But that clause gave Congress the power to prohibit not just importation but also migration. Now was the time, he said, to move against the latter evil: "Hitherto it has not been found necessary for congress to prohibit the migration or transportation from State to State. But now it becomes the right and duty of congress to guard against the further extension of the intolerable evil and the crying enormity of slavery."[23] Here was another watershed in the emergence of the interstate slave trade as an issue in American life. For the first time, a congressman had publicly declared that the national legislature could prohibit the interstate slave trade.

In the Senate, the effort to make Missouri a free state was led by Rufus King of New York. King delivered major speeches on the subject on 26 and 27 February 1819. The speeches were not recorded at the time, but he later published a summary of their content. According to that summary, King argued that Congress had the power both to regulate territories and to impose conditions on the admission of new states. He also alluded to the 1808 clause, saying, "Since the year 1808 congress have possessed power to prohibit and have prohibited the further emigration or importation of slaves into any of the old thirteen states, and at all times under the constitution have had power to prohibit such migration or importation into any of the new states, or territories of the United States." He pointed out that "so long as markets are open for the purchase of slaves so long they will be supplied; and so long as we permit the existence of slavery in our new and frontier states, so long slave markets will exist." He dismissed the notion that interstate migration benefitted the slaves, declaring that "no one who has ever witnessed the experiment, will believe, that the condition of slaves is made better by the breaking up, and separation of their families, nor by their removal from the old states to the new ones."[24]

Southern representatives were aghast at the proposed Tallmadge amendment and the constitutional arguments voiced in support of it. They declared that if such a policy and such arguments were to prevail, disunion and civil war would ensue. But the advocates of the amendment would not easily be dissuaded, as Tallmadge himself made clear. He noted that Thomas W. Cobb of Georgia, with his gaze fixed on Tallmadge, had declared that the New Yorker had "kindled a fire which all the waters of the ocean cannot put out, which seas of blood only can extinguish." To which Tallmadge replied, "Sir, language of this sort has no effect on me; my purpose is fixed, it is interwoven with my existence." Tallmadge insisted that the 1808 clause unquestionably gave Congress the power to prohibit the entry of slaves into any new state, "probably as a matter of legislation, but more certainly as a right, to prescribe the time and the condition upon which any new State may be admitted into the family of the union." He pointed out that even as the current discussion had gone on, a slave trader, "a trafficker in human flesh, as if sent by Providence, has passed the door of your Capitol, on his way to the West, driving before him about fifteen of these wretched victims of his power," the men in handcuffs and chains, the women and children bringing up the rear "under the guidance of the driver's whip!" To Tallmadge the scene was a disgrace to the republic. "Sir," he said, "if the western country cannot be settled without slaves, gladly would I prevent its settlement till time shall be no more."[25]

The fifteenth Congress ended with no decision on Missouri. A majority of the House supported the Tallmadge amendment, but southern strength in the Senate ensured its rejection there. Supporters of the amendment now sought to stir up grass-roots interest in a debate that had been, up to now, of more concern to the members of Congress than to the public at large. Most Americans were preoccupied with the economic hard times that had set in with the Panic of 1819 and so gave little thought to the Missouri question. The most important figure who stepped forward to change that was Elias Boudinot, an elderly New Jersey philanthropist and long-time foe of slavery. Boudinot began organizing public meetings to oppose the admission of Missouri as a slave state. He also scored a major propaganda coup by securing the endorsement of the almost equally elderly John Jay, one of the most eminent among the survivors of the founding generation. In a letter that Boudinot made sure was widely publicized, Jay agreed that slavery ought not to be permitted in any new states and should be gradually abolished everywhere. Jay said, "To me the constitutional authority of the Congress to prohibit the migration and importation of slaves into any of the States, does not appear questionable." After quoting the 1808 clause, he said, "I understand the sense and meaning of this clause to be, that the power of the Congress, although competent to prohibit such migration and importation, was not to be exercised with respect to the *then existing* States (and them only) until the year 1808; but that the Congress were at liberty to make such prohibition as to any new State, which might, in the *mean* time, be established, and further, that from and after *that period,* they were authorized to make such prohibition, as to all the States, whether new or old." Interestingly, no one seems to have taken any notice of the fact that Jay had not participated in the creation of the Constitution. In the 1780s he had done such a good job of promoting the need for a stronger national government that the New York state legislature had refused to name him as a delegate to the Constitutional Convention. Jay now declined on grounds of ill health to take an active role in the anti-Missouri movement, but his son Peter A. Jay joined with newspaper editor Theodore Dwight and others in spearheading the campaign within New York State.[26]

By December 1819 the movement had spread to Boston, where a public meeting endorsed a memorial that vigorously upheld the power of Congress to prohibit the interstate slave trade. The memorial said that just as the federal power to regulate foreign commerce had allowed Congress, once the constraint imposed by the 1808 clause had expired, to prohibit the importation of slaves from abroad, so the federal power to regulate interstate commerce allowed Congress to interfere similarly in domestic slave trafficking. "Commerce in Slaves, since the year 1808, being as much subject to the regulation of Congress as any other commerce," the memorial declared, "if it should see fit to enact that no Slave shall ever be sold from one State to another, it is not perceived how its Constitutional right to make such provision should be questioned." To open up Missouri as a destination for slaves would make the federal government a collaborator in a traffic that it had condemned as "impolitic, unchristian, inhuman." To punish the smuggling of slaves into the nation from abroad and yet "at the same time to tempt cupidity and avarice by the allurements of an insatiable market, is inconsistent and irreconcilable." Daniel Webster signed the Boston memorial and may have been its principal author.[27]

Another key figure in the effort to arouse public opinion was the Philadelphia journalist Robert Walsh. Walsh published a pamphlet in which he provided a much lengthier and more substantial argument in support of the power of Congress to attack the interstate slave trade than it had ever before received. Walsh pointed out that the 1808 clause was unique in that it was the only place in the Constitution where a provision was made that applied only to the states that were already in existence as of 1787. It was only in those states, and not in newer states and territories, that Congress was forbidden to interfere with migration or importation prior to 1808. The clause therefore "bespeaks a compromise in which, on the one hand, the privilege of multiplying the race of slaves within their limits, either by importations from abroad or domestic migration, is reluctantly yielded for a term to those southern states who made this compliance a *sine qua non* of their accession to the union; while, on the other hand, the power is conceded, by implication, to the federal government, of preventing at once the extension of slavery beyond the limits of the old states — of keeping the territory of the union, and the new states, free from the pestilence; and ultimately, of suppressing altogether the diabolical trade in human flesh, whether *internal* or external." The founders chose every word of the Constitution with care. Each phrase in it "was weighed with a view to the utmost precision, by members who were thought especially qualified to decide. I have this fact upon the authority of one of them, and not the least distinguished." If the founders had wanted to halt only the importation of slaves in 1808, then they would have used only the one word "importation." Their meaning would have been clear. Instead they elected to use two words. "We are then left to understand by the word *migration* in the clause, the transportation or removal of slaves from one state to another, or from a state to a territory." While it is true that the word "migration" implies an independent, voluntary action that would not normally be ascribed to slaves, the founders applied it to them because it was consonant with the word "persons," a euphemism which "belongs to that policy of virtuous shame which sought to shadow our internal condition, in a constitution destined for the study and admiration of the world, and for indefinite duration."[28]

Walsh said that given their determination to end the importation of Africans, the founders could not have avoided giving Congress the power to prohibit the movement of slaves into new states. Otherwise it would have been futile to ban the importation of slaves from abroad, for the foreign origin of smuggled slaves could easily be concealed beyond detection if they could be quickly transported from the old states along the coast into the new states of the interior. Moreover, the founders surely wanted to discourage "that *internal trading* in human flesh, *the negro-driving,* which is among the most odious and disgraceful incidents of the institution of slavery . . . and its twin practice —kidnapping." The founders could not have failed to realize that the continuation of those evils would obstruct emancipation in the older states and so ensure that slaves who might have been "liberated from their shackles" would instead be "offered as victims upon the new altars raised to remorseless and insatiable avarice." Finally, Walsh argued that Congress had already exercised its power over the interstate slave trade on two occasions. In 1804 it had prohibited the bringing into the territory of Orleans from any other place within the United States of slaves that had been imported from abroad since 1798, and in 1807 it had imposed regulations upon the coastwise transport of slaves at the same time that it had ended importations from abroad.[29]

Walsh cited remarks by both John Jay and James Madison as proof that Congress had power over the interstate slave trade. Jay had of course said exactly that in his recent letter to Elias Boudinot, which Walsh quoted. Madison had never said anything so unequivocal, but in one of the "Federalist" essays that he wrote during the struggle to win ratification of the Constitution he had ridiculed the idea that the 1808 clause might be used to inhibit white immigration. Walsh presented that statement as proof that the word "migration" in the 1808 clause referred not to white immigration but to the domestic movement of slaves. Jay was no doubt happy to have his words put to good use by Walsh, but Madison was not. While researching his essay, Walsh had in fact written to Madison, who wrote back declaring in no uncertain terms that however the words "migration or importation" in the 1808 clause might be construed, it was quite certain that they referred only to the influx of people from other countries into the United States and not to any kind of internal population movement. Madison pointed out that none of the opponents of the Constitution, despite their painstaking efforts to find objections to it no matter how far-fetched, had ever suggested that the 1808 clause could be used to prohibit interior movement of any sort. Had anyone ever made such a suggestion, there would have been an immediate demand to amend the Constitution so as to eliminate any such possibility. In writing his pamphlet, however, Walsh simply ignored Madison's hostile response.[30]

By the time the sixteenth Congress convened on 6 December 1819, public opinion North and South had been considerably aroused. There ensued a prolonged debate in both the House and the Senate over the proposed admission of Missouri and the constitutional questions that had been raised. Although the surviving record occupies more than a thousand pages of fine print in the *Annals of Congress,* it is far from complete. Many important orations, including key ones lasting several hours by both John Randolph and Henry Clay, went unrecorded. Other important developments took place offstage. For example, because John Quincy Adams was then serving as Secretary of State, he took no public role in the controversy. But in private he did. He recorded in his diary that when some congressmen called upon him to sound out his views, he told them that although he thought that slavery generally was subject to state rather than federal control, he nevertheless had "no doubt that Congress have Constitutional powers to prohibit any internal traffic in slaves between one State and another."[31] Still, the main theater of action was Congress, where the essentials of a great many speeches were preserved, and dozens of them addressed the question of whether the national legislature had authority over the interstate slave trade. Those on either side of the question presented almost every conceivable argument that could support their position, as well as some that were so strange as to be almost inconceivable.

Many of the speakers who sought to prohibit the movement of slaves into Missouri repeated one or more of Walsh's arguments in support of the notion that the 1808 clause allowed Congress to block the movement of slaves from one state to another. Some of the speakers may have read Walsh's pamphlet, but others probably either arrived at the same ideas on their own or picked them up from colleagues who had already spoken. They often argued, as had Walsh, that the fact that the 1808 clause had temporarily prohibited Congress from interfering in the importation of slaves into the states that existed in 1787 but not into any new ones created even before 1808 showed that the founders had intended to halt the spread of slavery. It had made sense to allow the interstate slave trade to go on among the existing states for as long as those states were permitted to import Africans, but no longer. Many speakers also echoed Walsh's claim that the two words "migration" and "importation" necessarily had distinct meanings, for otherwise the authors of the Constitution would have used only one word. The founders were careful writers who could never have committed the "sin of tautology." Some speakers added to that last point an additional bit of evidence that had escaped Walsh. They pointed out that according to the 1808 clause, a tax of ten dollars per person could be levied prior to 1808 upon importation but not upon migration. That was a clear indication, they said, that migration and importation were not the same thing. The reason migration was not taxed was that the Constitution prohibited the levying of taxes on articles exported from any state. Finally, like Walsh, the anti-Missourians often cited as precedents for interfering in the interstate slave trade the laws by which Congress had regulated the entry of slaves into Orleans territory in 1804 and the coastwise carrying of slaves in 1807.[32]

Only one southerner, Samuel Smith of Maryland, agreed with the northerners that the word "migration" in the 1808 clause referred to the interstate movement of slaves. But unlike the northerners, Smith claimed that it referred to the interstate movement of only those slaves who had been imported into the United States. The word "migration" was, he claimed, put into the 1808 clause in order to ensure that slaves that were imported into South Carolina would be allowed to pass into the neighboring states of Georgia and North Carolina. It did not, he said, apply to any slaves who had been born within the United States. Thus according to Smith's unique interpretation, Congress did have the power to control the interstate movement of some but not all slaves, and it was a power that would whither and eventually disappear as the last of the foreign-born slaves died out. All other southerners disagreed with Smith and held that "migration" did not refer to the interstate movement of any slaves, no matter where they were born. However, while these southerners were all agreed that "migration" did not mean that, they were not unanimous on what it *did* mean. Most of them claimed that it referred to the entry of white immigrants into the United States—that is, that whites migrated into the country whereas slaves were imported into it. Slaves could not migrate because the word implied volition, which slaves lacked. And the reason the 1808 clause provided that only importation and not migration could be taxed was that the founders wanted to discourage the importation of slaves but not the immigration of whites. But some southern speakers suggested other interpretations. Benjamin Hardin, Jr., of Kentucky thought that "importation" referred to slaves who were imported through the regular process supervised by customs officials, whereas "migration" referred to slaves who entered the United States in some other way. Robert Reid of Georgia presented a more elaborate version of the same, or at least a similar, idea when he said that the word "migration" was included in the 1808 clause in order to ensure that someone who was caught smuggling slaves into the United States after their importation had been banned could not escape prosecution by claiming that the blacks in his possession were being brought into the country as free people rather than slaves. Thus Congress was empowered to outlaw not only the importation of slaves but also the (im)migration of free blacks in order to thwart such "frauds, shifts, and artifices."[33]

A still more fanciful explanation of "migration" was offered by Freeman

Walker of Georgia. Walker said that he had been inclined at first to think that "migration" and "importation" were synonymous and that both referred to bringing slaves into the United States. (Many of his southern colleagues probably wished that his thinking had stopped there.) "But," said Walker, "on more mature reflection, my mind came to the conclusion that the words were entitled to be considered separately." And what were their separate meanings? Well, he still thought that both terms referred to bringing slaves into the United States, but he had decided that "importation" meant bringing slaves in by water from Africa or elsewhere, whereas "migration" meant bringing them in by land from areas contiguous to the United States and owned by foreign powers. As if that suggestion were not in itself bizarre enough, Walker also claimed that Congress had acted in a manner consistent with his peculiar interpretation. He said that in the act of 1807 that ended slave importations as of 1 January 1808, Congress had prohibited the bringing in of slaves both by sea and by land. "But so far from attempting to prohibit the removing of slaves from one State to another, they have by the same act regulated coastwise the manner of this intercourse. So far, then, as the experience of Government reflects light upon this subject, its tendency is to illumine the path I have taken in the exposition of this section of the Constitution."[34] Thus for Walker the fact that Congress had regulated the coastwise carrying of slaves from state to state somehow proved that it did *not* have authority over the interstate slave trade. With friends like Walker, the southern cause scarcely needed enemies.

By the time James Johnson of Virginia addressed the House on 16 February 1820, the meaning of the terms "migration" and "importation" had been debated for more than two months. Congressmen on both sides of the question probably breathed a sigh of relief when Johnson announced that he would not dwell on those words, because, he said, they had been uttered so often "as to cause them to grate on the ear as harshly and disagreeably as the chains of the convict." Fortunately for Johnson and his cohorts, the southerners displayed more solidarity as well as better logic on other points. They said that when a planter moved with his slaves to a new state, the slaves were members of his family rather than articles of commerce. But even when commercial slave traders moved slaves across state boundaries with the intention of selling them, Congress still had no right to interfere, because the purpose of the interstate commerce clause of the Constitution was to promote free trade among the states rather than to shackle it. If anybody had suggested in 1787 that Congress had the power to prohibit the interstate slave trade, then the southern states would never have ratified the Constitution. Indeed, at that time even the northern states would have opposed giving Congress any such power, because they were moving toward the gradual abolition of slavery within their borders and so were in the process of selling off their slaves to the South. Finally, the southerners argued that even if—perish the thought—Congress did possess the power to interfere with the interstate slave trade, it would have to do it by passing a law that was applicable to all of the states and not just to Missouri, because the Constitution prohibited the preferential treatment of one state over another in the regulation of trade.[35]

In March 1820 the Missouri crisis culminated in a great sectional compromise. Maine was split off from Massachusetts and admitted as a free state, Missouri was admitted without any restriction as to slavery and the slave trade, and slavery was prohibited in the remainder of the Louisiana Purchase northward of the southern boundary of Missouri. The compromise was accepted easily by the Senate, but in the House it took skillful and even unethical maneuvering by Henry Clay to win approval of the individual compromise measures on a piecemeal basis, for even Clay could not obtain a majority vote in favor of the unified package. John Randolph tried at the last minute to derail the compromise but was tricked by Clay into postponing his motion until it was too late. Looking back on it all seven weeks later, Thomas Jefferson said that the Missouri crisis, "like a fire-bell in the night, awakened and filled me with terror. I considered it at once as the knell of the Union."[36]

The nation had weathered its first profound sectional confrontation between the North and the South, but the constitutional issues that had been raised had not been settled. The question of whether Congress had the power to interfere with the interstate slave trade had received so much publicity that it was a certainty that neither the defenders nor the opponents of slavery would ever again lose sight of it. Certainly John Randolph did not. In 1824, when Congress was considering Henry Clay's proposal to provide federal funding for roads and canals, Randolph pointed out that if the power to regulate interstate commerce was broad enough to sanction such a program, then it was broad enough to threaten the interstate slave trade. "We are told," Randolph said, "that, along with the regulation of foreign commerce, the States have yielded to the General Government, in as broad terms, the regulation of domestic commerce—I mean, said Mr. R., the commerce among the several States, and that the same power is possessed by Congress over the one as over the other. It is rather unfortunate for this argument, that, if it applies to the extent to which the power to regulate foreign commerce has been carried by Congress, they may prohibit altogether this domestic commerce, as they have heretofore, under the other power, prohibited foreign commerce."[37]

While Randolph dreaded the prospect of congressional interference in the domestic slave trade, others welcomed it. In the aftermath of the Missouri crisis, voices from within the nascent antislavery movement began almost immediately to call upon Congress to use its alleged power to attack the interstate slave trade. Antislavery activists at the time were few and scattered, and their notions of what measures would be constitutionally permissible were often vague. For example, in 1822 James Jones, president of the Manumission Society of Tennessee, gave a speech in which he started out on firm ground by saying that Congress had the power to interfere with slavery in the District of Columbia and so could declare that the children born to slaves there should be free. But he next made the shaky assertion that, "Should Congress become unanimous in that, from the same righteous principle it will follow (as I conceive) that it has full power to put the declaration of American Independence fully into operation by declaring that there shall be no more slaves born in the United States of Republican America." He then claimed (without explanation) that Congress could fine or tax anyone who broke up slave marriages. Finally, he stepped back onto *terra firma* by declaring that Congress had full power to fine or tax "all those who are guilty of worse than the savage custom of driving human flesh, and souls of men to market in chains, from one state or territory to another."[38]

The Pennsylvania Abolition Society took a leading role in condemning the slave trade, both on its own and through collective action via the American Convention, a biennial meeting of delegates from state and local antislavery societies. In 1823 the Pennsylvania society submitted a memorial to the Pennsylvania legislature lamenting that in the western country the number of slaves was on the increase: "Raised like cattle for the market, they are driven from one state to another, and sold to the highest bidder." The Pennsylvania society also raised the slave trade issue at the American Convention that same year, declaring that the evil cried out for a remedy. Two years later, in their address to the 1825 American Convention, the Pennsylvanians asked how a nation that imposed the death penalty for engaging in the African slave trade could nevertheless still permit a trade in the descendants of Africans born on American soil, for, "when we pronounced the slave trade to be piracy, did we not forever extinguish our title to a slave? for is he not the product of that traffic?" In 1827 they used even stronger language, declaring that the domestic slave trade was "a cruelty, scarcely equalled by the enormities of the African slave trade, and for which our land cries aloud to Heaven for judgment. . . . That such a barbarous violation of Christianity, and even the common decencies of life, should have been practiced in this age, will be looked at by our posterity, with as much surprise, as we now feel that our ancestors could have tolerated the *African* trade."[39]

Other state abolition societies also raised the issue at the American Convention meetings, but, like the Pennsylvanians, were unsure what could be done about it. In 1826 the Anti-Slavery Society of Maryland lamented that in no other state than theirs were slaves more subjected to "the painful and distressing evils of family separation" as a result of slave trafficking. But although such trafficking was "odious and disgusting" it would be pointless to pass laws against it because there are "too many ways in which the most wholesome laws may be evaded" when they conflict with greed. "We consider, therefore, that the only effectual measure that can be devised for the abolition of this trade, is the emancipation of the slave population." In 1828 the Maryland society characterized the slave trade as "barbarous and inhuman" and said that it produced "wretchedness and misery . . . which beggars all description," as traders gathered slaves from various parts of Maryland and then despatched them "chained together in gangs, and driven off under the lash" to distant markets. But the Marylanders still said, "This appears to be one of the necessary evils of slavery, which cannot well be prevented, as long as the system itself is continued."[40]

Some antislavery groups, however, did believe that federal action to curb the interstate slave trade was possible. In 1826 the New York Manumission Society asked the American Convention to recommend to Congress that it "prohibit, by law, the rendering asunder of the family ties of slaves . . . by sales of parts of families into distant states or countries." In 1828 the Manumission Society of Tennessee proposed that antislavery activists should "load the tables of Congress" with memorials against the entire interstate trade. The Tennesseans had no doubt that Congress had the constitutional authority to ban it: "If Congress have power to regulate commerce between the several states, &c., let all the friends of man solicit the Congress to pass laws to prohibit that species of commerce, to wit: the Internal Slave Trade that's carried on to a very great (and shameful) extent between several of these states. . . . It's time for the people to be roused to their duty, and ask their rulers to abolish such things in plain explicit terms." On several occasions the American Convention appointed committees to consider proposals like those from New York and Tennessee, but the Convention never did take any concrete action to petition Congress or otherwise campaign effectively against the interstate slave trade.[41]

A frequent participant at the American Convention meetings was Benjamin Lundy. Born into a Quaker farm family in New Jersey in 1789, Lundy at the age of nineteen made his way west to Wheeling, Virginia. While working there as a saddler's apprentice, he was so horrified at the sight of the coffles of chained, ragged, and barefoot slaves that he saw trudging through the mud and snow on their way to the riverfront that he "made a solemn vow to Almighty God he would break at least one link of that ponderous chain of oppression." He began making good on that pledge in 1821 when he started publishing his pioneering antislavery journal the *Genius of Universal Emancipation.* In the January 1823 issue of his paper, Lundy published a "Plan for the Abolition of Slavery," a key point of which was to proscribe the transportation of slaves from one state to another "under the severest penalties, in all cases except the actual removal of their owners for the purpose of settlement." Lundy described slave trading as a "scandalous and outrageous business" that was "so aggravating in its nature, so demoralizing in its tendency, and so cruel and unjust in its operations, that it is doubtful whether any government can long exist that is weak or wicked enough to tolerate it." Lundy said that the domestic slave trade should be squelched not only because it was an evil in itself but also because it created an incentive both for the smuggling of slaves from abroad into the United States and for the kidnaping of free blacks in order to supply slaves to domestic traders. Lundy was at that time uncertain about the precise extent of federal authority over the slave trade. "If the government of the U.S. is not empowered to put a stop to this detestable traffic," he wrote, "the different state legislatures should pass laws for that purpose." But by the end of the year he seems to have decided that Congress did have the power to end the interstate slave trade just as it had the importation of slaves. "Does our Constitution, or anything else in nature, authorize us to extend our edicts to the ocean, when we are not permitted to enforce them within our own jurisdiction on the land?" he asked. "Legislators of North America . . . you are called to legislate! — you have it completely in your power to put a final stop to the accursed traffic in negroes carried on in the United States . . . and it were sincerely to be hoped that a consideration of these things might engage the early attention of the representatives in our national Legislature, & all other statesmen who value their individual fame; the weal of their constituents, or the perpetuity of our republican institutions." Lundy was an early and unabashed advocate of political action against slavery. He declared, "I wish it to be understood that I do not expect to *'persuade' the advocates of slavery* to do justice. Such persons cannot be honest; and I am not for making a covenant with dishonesty. WE MUST VOTE THEM DOWN."[42]

Lundy's hatred for the slave trade landed him in trouble when he condemned Austin Woolfolk, Maryland's leading slave merchant, as a "monster in human shape." When the two men met on the street, Woolfolk knocked Lundy down and beat him severely. Woolfolk was found guilty of assault but fined only a dollar, the judge in the case declaring that he had "never seen a case in which the provocation for battery was greater." The judge remarked also that the domestic slave trade was good for Maryland because it got rid of rogues and vagabonds. In September 1829 Lundy took on a young assistant named William Lloyd Garrison. They had met a year earlier when Lundy visited Boston and

GENIUS OF UNIVERSAL EMANCIPATION.

EDITED AND PUBLISHED BY BENJAMIN LUNDY, GREENEVILLE, TEN. AT $1 PER ANN. ADV.

"We hold these truths to be self-evident: that all men are created equal, and endowed by their Creator with certain unalienable rights; that among these are life, liberty, and the pursuit of happiness." —— *Declaration Independence U. S.*

No. 7. Vol. II. *FIRST MONTH,* 1823. Whole No. 19.

UNITED STATES' INTERNAL SLAVE TRADE.

"Hail Columbia, Happy Land!"

"SHALL THY FAIR BANNERS O'ER OPPRESSION WAVE?"*

TO THE AMERICAN PEOPLE.

The above is a faint picture of the *detestable traffic in human flesh,* carried on by citizens of this Republic in the open face of day, and in violation of the fun-

Figure 3. Benjamin Lundy attacks the slave trade. The January 1823 issue of the *Genius of Universal Emancipation* features a crude engraving of a trader brandishing a whip over a group of migrating slaves, one of whom carries a flag. Courtesy Oberlin College Library, Special Collections.

made a speech advocating petitions against slavery in the District of Columbia. Garrison heard the speech and then published a letter supporting Lundy and refuting the argument of a clergyman who had responded to Lundy by claiming that the slave trade was a blessing because it would lead to the demise of slavery in the District as well as in Maryland and Virginia. In Baltimore, Garrison joined in the feud with Woolfolk, denouncing him as the largest shipper of slaves to New Orleans. Garrison also attacked Francis Todd, a shipowner from Garrison's hometown of Newburyport, Massachusetts, for having allowed his vessel the *Francis* to transport slaves from Maryland to Louisiana, an act that Garrison denounced as "domestic piracy." A Baltimore grand jury indicted Garrison for criminal libel. He was tried and convicted, in spite of the fact that Todd's ship had indeed carried slaves from the upper to the lower South. Garrison spent forty-nine days behind bars before being freed when Arthur Tappan, a wealthy and sympathetic New York merchant, paid his fine. Meanwhile, Todd successfully sued Garrison for $1,000 in civil damages. Todd never collected the money, however, for as soon as Garrison was released from prison he fled to Boston. Garrison had assailed a collaborator in the interstate slave trade and had suffered for it. That bitter experience helped motivate him to view slavery and its defenders in a new light.[43]

Another important influence on Garrison was his interaction with the free black community. In the 1820s urban free blacks, especially those residing in Boston, New York, Philadelphia, and Baltimore, became increasingly outspoken in their opposition to slavery, racism, and discrimination. In part, they were reacting to the emergence of the American Colonization Society and its plan to remove African Americans to Liberia. Some free blacks embraced colonization, but the vast majority regarded it as a menace that threatened to snuff out their hope for equal rights and opportunities in America. In 1825 two former slaves published autobiographies, thus initiating what was to become a major genre of antislavery propaganda. "It grieved me to see my mother's tears at our separation," wrote William Grimes, who, at age ten, had been purchased in Virginia by a man who "came down from the mountains" in 1794 "to buy negroes." Grimes was later sold to another man, who took him to Savannah. He passed through the hands of ten different masters before escaping from bondage. The author of the other autobiography, Solomon Bayley, told how he had been taken illegally from Delaware (where slave exportation was forbidden) into Virginia (where slave importation was forbidden), leaving his family behind. He tried to sue for his freedom but was thrown into jail at Richmond and then put on a wagon heading west. He escaped and made his way back to Delaware. His master caught up with him there and, in exchange for Bayley's agreeing to drop his freedom suit, allowed him to work off his own purchase price and eventually to buy the freedom of his wife and children too.[44]

In 1827 John Russwurm and Samuel Cornish of New York City began publishing *Freedom's Journal,* the first black newspaper in the United States. Although Russwurm and Cornish disclaimed any desire "to harrow up the feelings of our readers by frequent attention to these scenes," they printed several articles, some of them copied from Lundy's paper, that described slave coffles on the move and coastal vessels clearing upper South ports for New Orleans. They also published a letter from an English abolitionist, who, noting that "Virginia is now the greatest seat of the internal slave trade," declared, "I feel at a loss to know what humanity has gained by, the abolition of one slave trade, and the substitution of another, perhaps, quite as extensive, and, in some of its features, even more horrible." Another letter focused on slave trading in the District of Columbia. The writer imagined a scene in which a slave family is separated. The master's daughter asks if the slaves have done anything to deserve being sent away. "No, my child," replies the master, "but they are *black,* and I want money to hord [*sic*] up for old age, or to spend in pleasure and dissipation." The letter ended by saying that Congress should be petitioned "to pass a law on this subject." Finally, in their issue of 17 October 1828, the editors of *Freedom's Journal* themselves called for the suppression of the domestic slave trade. They declared:

> It is high time that the citizens of the Union should arise as one man and put an end to a traffic which all civilized nations are endeavouring to abolish: we do not mean the foreign slave trade alone; we refer to our and their internal slave trade. In our humble opinion, the thousands which are annually appropriated for the suppression of the foreign slave trade, is to be considered but a seconds [*sic*] object, while our domestic trade is suffered to be carried on from one State to another. We may declaim as much as we please upon the horrors of the foreign slave trade, but we would ask, are the horrors of the internal trade less—are the relations of life less endearing in this country than in Africa—are the Wood-folks [i.e., Austin Woolfolk, the great trader of Baltimore] of the South less cruel than the slavers on the [African] coast [?]. Surely not.[45]

The black militancy of the 1820s reached its climax with the publication of David Walker's *Appeal to the Coloured Citizens of the World.* Although he was the Boston agent for *Freedom's Journal,* Walker's views ranged far beyond the reformist impulses of that newspaper. In his *Appeal,* Walker preached black racial pride, denounced the colonization movement, and called for violent black resistance to oppression. He reprinted a newspaper account of a rebellion by a slave coffle. A trader named Gordon had gathered about sixty slaves in Maryland and was marching them overland through Kentucky toward the Mississippi River. Unbeknownst to Gordon and his two assistants, the slaves somehow obtained a file, and sixteen of them surreptitiously cut through their handcuffs in such a way that they could free themselves in an instant. On the morning of 14 August 1829, two of the slaves staged a fight. As the distracted whites moved to break up the disturbance, they were surprised and overwhelmed by the other conspirators. Gordon's two helpers were killed, and he himself was beaten and left for dead, as the attackers fled into the woods. At that point the tables began to turn. Gordon, who in fact had not suffered a disabling injury, was helped onto his horse by one of the slave women. He raced to a nearby plantation and raised the alarm. The rebels were swiftly rounded up. Walker viewed the incident with consternation. He was scornful of "the *ignorant* and *deceitful actions*" of the "*servile woman*" who had helped Gordon get away, and he found it incomprehensible that he had survived. "The black men acted like *blockheads,*" Walker declared. "Why did they not make sure of the wretch? He would have made sure of them, if he could." To Walker it was obvious that all slave traders deserved to die for their sins of carrying off men and women in chains and handcuffs and "driving them around the country like *brutes.*" Walker asked, "Should the lives of such creatures be spared? . . . Are they not the Lord's enemies? Ought they not to be destroyed?" The lesson for black rebels was clear: "If you commence, make sure work—do not trifle, for they will not trifle with you."[46]

William Garrison did not embrace David Walker's celebration of violence, but he was won over by the arguments of Walker and other free blacks who opposed all compromise with slavery, demanded equal rights for all free African Americans, and denounced the colonizationists. Unlike Lundy, who remained ambivalent about colonization, Garrison now viewed it with repugnance. Garrison was through with half measures and temporizing. Now he would become the founder of a new and far more radical antislavery movement, one in which blacks and whites would join together to demand the immediate abolition of slavery and the slave trade.

4

Different Opinions at Different Times

The excitement engendered by the Missouri Debates had scarcely subsided before the South confronted a new menace to the slave trade, as the United States Supreme Court, in the case of *Gibbons v. Ogden,* contemplated for the first time the meaning of the interstate commerce clause of the Constitution. But neither then nor at any other time did the Supreme Court ever issue a definitive ruling on whether Congress could use its authority over commerce to suppress the domestic slave trade. Because no act of Congress ever attempted to ban the slave trade, there was no occasion to test the constitutionality of such an act before the judiciary. There were, however, a series of cases in which the court assessed the legitimacy of state actions that arguably conflicted with the federal commerce power. In its ruling on any one of those cases, the court might have made clear what the scope of the federal power actually was. The court never did so, at first because of a wise refusal by Chief Justice John Marshall and his colleagues to attempt a judicial resolution of this profoundly political issue, and later because of clashing views among the justices of the court headed by Marshall's successor, Roger B. Taney, that made it impossible for the judges to agree upon an answer to a question that could be as complex as it was incendiary. It was only in the midst of the great sectional crisis of the 1850s that the court implicitly veered toward the proslavery side in such an extreme way as to help plunge the nation into catastrophe.[1]

The Supreme Court first contemplated the meaning of the commerce power in the famous case of *Gibbons v. Ogden.* The case was first scheduled for consideration in 1821, when the surfacing of the slave trade issue in the Missouri Debates was still fresh in the public mind, but for procedural reasons was put off until 1824. The case concerned a New York state law that granted to Robert Fulton and his associates the exclusive right to operate steamboats in New York waters. The Fulton monopoly was challenged by rival boat owners, who claimed that the New York statute was an unconstitutional invasion of the federal government's power to regulate interstate commerce. Although the case had nothing directly to do with slavery, it was obvious that it could have important implications regarding state versus federal control over the passage of slaves from state to state. Moreover, the case also could have implications regarding the constitutionality—or lack of it—of the Negro Seamen's Act, a law that had been enacted by South Carolina in the aftermath of an attempted slave insurrection, the Denmark Vesey conspiracy of 1822. The Negro Seamen's Act was aimed at preventing free blacks from the North or from abroad from contaminating the state's slaves with ideas of resistance and freedom. The law provided that any black crewman debarking from a vessel at a port within South Carolina was to be jailed until his vessel was ready to depart. The cost of incarceration was to be paid by the ship's captain. Any sailor not redeemed by his captain could be sold into slavery. In the United States Circuit Court for South Carolina, in 1823, Justice William Johnson declared the Negro Seamen's Act unconstitutional, on the grounds that the power of the federal government over interstate commerce was paramount and exclusive. South Carolina ignored Johnson's decision, however, and continued to enforce its statute. The governor of the state urged upon its legislature "a firm determination to resist, at the threshold, every invasion of our domestic tranquillity and to preserve our sovereignty and independence," because, he said, "there would be more glory in forming a rampart with our bodies on the confines of our territory" than to become either the victims of a successful slave rebellion or "the slaves of a great consolidated government."[2]

Chief Justice Marshall of the Supreme Court regarded Johnson's action as rash. Marshall had himself confronted on circuit a Virginia law comparable to that of South Carolina but had avoided pronouncing it unconstitutional. In a private letter to Justice Joseph Story, Marshall said, "Our brother Johnson, I perceive, has hung himself on a democratic snag in a hedge composed entirely of thorny state rights in South Carolina. . . . The subject is one of much feeling in the South. Of this I was apprized, but did not think it would have shown itself in such strength as it has. . . . the sentiment has been avowed that if this be the constitution, it is better to break that instrument than submit to the principle." Marshall then explained how he himself had avoided becoming similarly snagged. Alluding to the South Carolina law that Johnson had denounced, Marshall said, "We have its twin brother in Virginia, and a case has been brought before me in which I might have considered its constitutionality had I chosen to do so; but it was not absolutely necessary, and, as I am not fond of butting against a wall in sport, I escaped on the construction of the act."[3]

In *Gibbons v. Ogden*, the attorneys who defended the New York law granting the steamboat monopoly argued that commerce encompassed only the exchange of goods and did not include either navigation or the transport of passengers. They also maintained that the federal power to regulate commerce, although admittedly supreme, was not exclusive. That is, it did not preclude states from exercising a concurrent power over commerce so long as their actions did not actually conflict with any federal legislation. After all, the lawyers said, both before and after the adoption of the Constitution, many states had prohibited the importation of slaves not only from foreign countries but from other states as well. Thus the states possessed and were actually exercising a concurrent power over commerce. Interestingly, the lawyers acknowledged that the power to regulate included the power to prohibit, because, "The difference between regulation or restraining and interdiction, is only a difference of degree in the exercise of the same right, and not a difference of right."[4] (While most of these lawyers' arguments would support the case for state authority over the slave trade, this last one—that a power to regulate included the power to prohibit—would have been music to the ears of advocates of a federal ban on the interstate slave trade.)

Daniel Webster, one of the attorneys for the other side, dismissed the notion of a concurrent commerce power. The authority of Congress, he said, was "complete and entire." If Congress had not regulated some aspect of interstate commerce, then its decision not to act was as valid an exercise of the federal authority as was a decision to do so. In either case, a state had no right to stray into an area of exclusive federal jurisdiction. Despite this fiercely nationalist stance, however, Webster hinted that there remained some opening for state action. Probably he left the door ever so slightly ajar because he surmised that the court would not dare to adopt an absolutist position on so volatile an issue. Webster said that the federal power over commerce was exclusive "so far, and so far only, as the nature of the power requires." (What that Delphic statement meant was anybody's guess.) More concretely, he said that state quarantine laws were an exercise of police power rather than of commercial regulation and so did not trespass upon the federal jurisdiction over commerce. He hedged on the touchy question of whether a state law prohibiting the importation of slaves could be constitutional, saying that it would depend upon the law's particular provisions. Here Webster perhaps intended to signal both that South Carolina's law on Negro seamen could be defended as a police regulation, and that all of the states might still be allowed to control the entry or non-entry of slaves, even though Congress had exclusive authority over what Webster termed "the higher branches of commercial regulation."[5]

The decision of the court, delivered by the chief justice, was a masterpiece of bold assertion coupled with discreet sidestepping. John Marshall defined commerce broadly so as to include both navigation in general and the transport of people in particular. On the latter point, he cited the 1808 clause of the Constitution, noting that "it has always been considered an exception to the power to regulate commerce, and certainly seems to class migration with importation. Migration applies as appropriately to voluntary, as importation does to involuntary, arrivals, and, so far as an exception from a power proves its existence, this section proves that the power to regulate commerce applies equally to the regulation of vessels employed in transporting men, who pass from place to place voluntarily, and to those who pass involuntarily." Marshall also declared that the federal power over commerce "is complete in itself, may be exercised to its utmost extent, and acknowledges no limitations." It is vested in Congress as absolutely as it would be in a unitary government in which there was no sharing of power with the states. Referring to Webster's contention that the states could not encroach upon the federal jurisdiction even in those areas where Congress had as yet done nothing, Marshall said, "There is great force in this argument, and the Court is not satisfied that it has been refuted." Marshall thus adopted initially a nationalist stance that was, if anything, even more uncompromising than Webster's. But Marshall then went on to declare that it was not necessary in this case for the court to decide whether the states possessed any concurrent power over interstate commerce. The competitors of Robert Fulton had obtained a license under the federal Coasting License Act of 1793, Marshall said, and the New York law that gave Fulton his monopoly was unconstitutional because it conflicted with that license. (That the New York law really clashed with the federal coasting license was doubtful, for the license merely gave to American vessels some privileges that were denied to foreign ones, but it suited Marshall's purpose to claim that there was a conflict.) Through this maneuver, Marshall was able to have his cake and eat it too. He made a strong argument for exclusive federal power over interstate commerce but did not make it a formal ruling of the court. That is, he made it quite clear that he agreed with Webster that the federal authority over interstate commerce was exclusive and precluded any trespassing by the states onto the federal turf. But he ruled definitively only that a state law was invalid when it conflicted with an actual federal regulation of interstate commerce. The latter was a relatively narrow ruling that was unlikely to provoke virulent opposition. Thus, with the adroitness that was his trademark, Marshall avoided bringing down upon his head the southern denunciations that surely would have followed a stronger decision that more clearly threatened the slaveholding interest.[6]

Only one member of the court refused to shuffle along with Marshall in his sidestepping of the question of whether a concurrent power to regulate interstate commerce remained with the states. William Johnson concurred with the court's unanimous decision to annul the Fulton steamboat monopoly, but he rejected Marshall's explanation that the law that had created it was invalid because it conflicted with a federal regulation. The New York statute would have been just as invalid, Johnson said, even if there were no such thing as a federal coasting license. The federal commerce power, he insisted, "must be exclusive," for "the grant of this power carries with it the whole subject, leaving nothing for the State to act upon." Thus Johnson held firmly to the nationalist position that he had adopted when he declared unconstitutional South Carolina's Negro Seamen's Act. But once again Johnson's was a lone voice crying in the wilderness, for not even so fervent a nationalist as John Marshall had dared to join with him in his unabashed insistence upon an exclusive federal power.[7]

Thirteen years later, in *New York v. Miln* (1837), the Supreme Court rehashed the question of federal versus state power over interstate commerce, but without clarifying it. By this time, Marshall had passed from the scene and the court was headed by Roger B. Taney. The new Chief Justice had served as Attorney General under Andrew Jackson between 1831 and 1833. In that capacity, he had defended the constitutionality of the South Carolina Negro Seamen's Act, saying, "South Carolina or any other slave holding state has a right to guard itself from the danger to be apprehended from the introduction of free people of color among their slaves—and have not by the Constitution of the United States surrendered the right to pass the laws necessary for that purpose."[8] Taney now led his mostly like-minded colleagues in edging away from the rigorous nationalism that had been so dear to his predecessor. But by this time too the radical abolitionist movement had arisen and was inundating Congress with petitions signed by thousands of people demanding that it outlaw the interstate slave trade.

Like *Gibbons v. Ogden*, the *Miln* case focused on a New York state law, but this time the statute in question was one that imposed regulations on ships bringing immigrants into the port of New York. The attorneys who defended the law before the Supreme Court repeated the now familiar claim that the states possessed a concurrent power over commerce. In evidence, they cited the 1808 clause of the Constitution, arguing that the clause's mention of "such Persons as any of the States now existing shall think proper to admit" was proof that states, and not just the federal government, had the power to allow or deny the entry of people. They warned that if the court declared the federal power to be exclusive and on that basis struck down the New York immigration law, then many other state laws also would have to be considered invalid, including "a class of laws peculiar to the southern states," among them those "prohibiting masters of vessels from bringing people of color in their vessels."[9]

The attorneys for the other side repeated the equally familiar claim that the states could not transgress upon what was an area of exclusive federal jurisdiction. As to the idea that the 1808 clause was proof of concurrent state power, the opposing lawyers said, "This is not considered a correct deduction. If a state law prohibiting migration or importation, shall be brought into question; the point will arise, as to the power of the state to legislate upon it." The 1808 clause did not negate any part of the federal power over commerce; it only temporarily suspended one aspect of it. "It is fully granted, and could have been executed instantly, but for the limitation; and when that expired, it came into active existence. It was, from that time, as full as if it had never been interfered with." (In other words, the right of states to regulate migration or importation expired in 1808 when the federal power came into full force and thereby extinguished all state authority over such matters.)[10]

In its ruling in *Miln,* the court again avoided saying whether the federal commerce power was exclusive, and again a single justice dissented. Speaking for the majority, Justice Philip Barbour upheld the New York law as constitutional on the grounds that it was "not a regulation of commerce, but of police," and each state possesses, in its police power, "the same undeniable and unlimited jurisdiction over all persons and things, within its territorial limits, as any foreign nation; where that jurisdiction is not surrendered or restrained by the constitution of the United States." Thus the official ruling of the court avoided making any new statement about the nature of the commerce power. In separate opinions, however, two justices chose to address the unresolved issue of concurrent commerce power, one in order to defend the concept, and the other to denounce it. In his concurring opinion, Justice Smith Thompson said that the New York law would be constitutionally acceptable even if it did regulate commerce, because Congress had made no regulation with which it conflicted. Thompson declared (rather clumsily) that he considered it "a very important principle to establish, that the states retain the exercise of powers; which, although they may in some measure partake of the character of commercial regulations, until congress asserts the exercise of the power under the grant of the power to regulate commerce." In stark contrast, Justice Joseph

Story, who was the lone dissenter in the case, said that the New York law should have been struck down as a violation of the exclusive authority of the federal government over commerce, a subject "cut off from the range of state sovereignty and state legislation." Echoing the earlier words of John Marshall, and through him Daniel Webster, Story said, "it has been remarked with great cogency and accuracy, that the regulation of a subject indicates and designates the entire result; applying to those parts which remain as they were, as well as to those parts which are altered. It produces a uniform whole, which is as much disturbed and deranged by changing what the regulating power designs to leave untouched, as that upon which it has operated." Thus, although back in 1824 he had gone along with Marshall's equivocation on the issue in *Gibbons v. Ogden* (and, in fact, there is even a possibility that he was the principal author of the ruling that Marshall delivered), Story now opted for the uncompromisingly nationalist position that only William Johnson had been willing to adopt in the earlier case.[11]

Miln did nothing to clear the muddied waters left by *Gibbons v. Ogden.* Slaveholders could draw comfort from the fact that the *Miln* decision ascribed to the states a police power that, although only vaguely defined, appeared plenty broad enough to encompass measures like the South Carolina Negro Seamen's Act, but they worried that the court still shrank from ruling definitively that the states possessed a concurrent power over commerce such as would unquestionably allow them to control the domestic slave trade. Radical abolitionists, on the other hand, could take heart from Justice Story's declaration that interstate commerce was totally within the realm of federal power and entirely beyond the reach of state sovereignty. Thus the abolitionists could continue to trumpet their claim that Congress had both the right and the duty to abolish the interstate slave trade. Consequently, both the friends and the enemies of slavery had good reason to hold their breath when, in the 1841 case of *Groves v. Slaughter,* the court for the first and only time in its history took on a case that focused directly upon the question of which level of government had authority over interstate slave trafficking.

In 1832 Mississippi adopted a state constitution that contained a clause prohibiting the bringing in of slaves as merchandise after 1 May 1833. The clause was not an antislavery measure. It did not stop new settlers from bringing slaves with them when they came to live in Mississippi, nor did it prevent residents of the state from traveling beyond its borders, doing their slave-buying there, and then bringing their acquisitions home with them. Rather, the measure reflected concerns that too much capital was being drained away from the state, that the price of the slaves already there was being undermined, and that the slaves brought in by commercial traders often were misrepresented and so were more likely to turn out to be unhealthy, unreliable, or rebellious. Even the attempted curbing of the commercial trade was easily evaded by those slave dealers who simply shifted their transactions to places just outside Mississippi's borders. Yet many of the traders did not bother to do even that, and the commercial slave trade continued to flourish within Mississippi itself despite what the state constitution said. The case that eventually reached the Supreme Court was brought by a trader, Robert Slaughter, who had sold some slaves on credit inside Mississippi in 1835 and 1836. The purchaser, whose personal notes for $7,000 had been accepted by Slaughter, refused to make good on the notes when they became due, on the grounds that the original sale contract was invalid because the aforementioned clause of the Mississippi constitution made the whole transaction illegal. The arguments in *Groves v. Slaughter* lasted a full week and attracted unusual attention. According to a newspaper account, the ladies of Washington occupied all of the vacant seats and crowded everyone but the judges and lawyers out of the bar. Many Senators played hooky from their own chamber and went to watch the court proceedings instead. Even John Quincy Adams abandoned the House of Representatives to go listen to the closing arguments.[12]

An attorney defending the validity of the notes, and thus of Slaughter's right to receive payment for the slaves that he had sold, evidently believed in covering all bases, for he presented the court with an initial position, a fall-back from that one, and then a fall-back from the fall-back. First, he said that the relevant clause in the Mississippi constitution was not a regulation of commerce but an exercise of police power, because it aimed to do such things as "guard against the admission of the vicious, through the deceptions of negro-traders," actions which were "evidently objects of proper municipal regulation." Next, he said that even if the clause was a regulation of commerce, "it is one excepted from this power of congress, and remains in the state." (He did not explain why.) Finally, the attorney said that even if authority over the interstate slave trade was vested in Congress, it nevertheless "may also be exercised by the state"—in other words, that the states possessed an authority over interstate commerce that was concurrent with the federal power.[13]

A more outspoken defense of his home state's right to regulate the slave trade was presented by Mississippi Senator Robert J. Walker. Walker acknowledged that the federal commerce power was "supreme and exclusive," but insisted that Congress nevertheless could not control the interstate slave trade because slavery was exclusively a state concern "over which it never was designed by the constitution, that congress should have the slightest control. . . . Such a power in all its effects and consequences, is a power, not to regulate commerce among the states, but *to regulate slavery,* both in and among the

SLAVES! SLAVES!! SLAVES!!!

FORKS OF THE ROAD, NATCHEZ.

THE SUBSCRIBERS have just arrived in Natchez, and are now stopping at Mr. Elam's house, Forks of the Foad, with a choice selection of slaves, consisting of

MECHANICS,

FIELD HANDS,

COOKS,

WASHERS AND IRONERS, and

GENERAL HOUSE SERVANTS.

They will be constantly receiving additions to their present supply during the season, and will be sold at as reasonable rates as can be afforded in this market.

☞ To those purchasers desiring it, the Louisiana guarantee will be given.

Planters and others desirous of purchasing, are requested to call and see the Slaves before purchasing elsewhere. nov27—d:wtf GRIFFIN & PULLUM.

Mules! Mules! Mules!

JUST ARRIVED, and in excellent order, a large lot of MULES, raised in Missouri, and recommended for their size and condition.

They can be seen at the mule yards of Mr. Joseph E Kirk, and will be sold on favorable terms. A finer lo of Mules is rarely offered to the public.

nov27—d;wtf W. H. RIGHTER.

Figure 4. Slaves for sale in Mississippi. In 1833 Natchez passed an ordinance requiring traders to move their pens outside the city limits. Thereafter, the "Forks of the Road" straddling the city's eastern boundary became Mississippi's greatest slave trading center. It remained so down to the Civil War. Advertisement from *Natchez Daily Courier*, 27 November 1858. Courtesy Mississippi Department of Archives and History.

states. It is abolition in its most dangerous form, under the mask of a power to regulate commerce." Turning the tables on the abolitionists, Walker declared that if Congress were held by the Supreme Court to have power over the interstate slave trade, then the *free* states would not be able to forbid the entry of slaves. "The slave trader might . . . encamp them in chains at Boston, Lexington, Concord, or Bunker Hill. . . . This the abolitionists would regard with horror and dismay; but to all this they subject their own states . . . in their efforts to force their doctrines upon the southern states." Walker appealed to the court to banish the specters of "anarchy and civil war . . . death and desolation" by declaring that "over the subject of slavery, congress possesses no jurisdiction." Walker was so proud of his argument that he later sent a copy to ex-president Martin Van Buren, saying that he had addressed "the great constitutional question of the power of congress to prohibit the importation of slaves from state to state" and claiming that "the opinion of the court on *that point* was in my favour." But Walker's oratory had not impressed John Quincy Adams, who wrote in his diary, "I left the House, and went into the Supreme Court, and heard the argument of Mr. Webster . . . and the closing argument of Mr. Walker, the Senator from Mississippi, in reply. The question is whether a State of this Union can constitutionally prohibit the importation within her borders of slaves as merchandise. Mr. Walker threatened tremendous consequences if this right should be denied to the State — all of which consequences sounded to me like argument for the constitutional authority [of Congress?] to prohibit it in all the States, and for the exercise of it."[14]

The lawyers for the other side included both Daniel Webster and Henry Clay, "the Ajax and the Achilles of the bar." Clay declared that Mississippi could not prohibit the introduction of slaves as merchandise, because only Congress has the power to regulate interstate commerce. That power, he said, is not "one in which the states may participate. It is exclusive. It is essentially so." It might appear that Clay's strong assertion of exclusive federal power would place him in the company of the radical abolitionists, who agreed that Congress possessed such power, and who wanted Congress to use it to outlaw slave trafficking. But Clay was quick to squelch any such inference. The interstate commerce clause of the U.S. Constitution, he said, gives to Congress the power only "to regulate commerce, to sustain it, not to annihilate it. It is conservative. Regulation implies continued existence — life, not death, preservation, not annihilation, the unobstructed flow of the stream, not to check or dry up its waters. But the object of the abolitionists is to prevent the exercise of this commerce. This is a violation of the right of congress under the constitution." Clay thus rendered the interstate slave trade invulnerable. States could not attack it because the federal government possessed exclusive power over it. But the federal government could not attack it either, because Congress had power only to promote rather than inhibit slave trading.[15]

Clay claimed that the lawyers for the other side, in defending the right of Mississippi to prohibit the entry of slaves for sale, were "on the abolition side of the question." Here Clay deliberately misrepresented abolitionist views. It was perhaps true that some abolitionists might have mistakenly taken Mississippi's ban on the entry of slaves for sale to be an antislavery measure, and therefore welcomed it, without thinking about the constitutional issues that the measure raised. But Clay knew perfectly well that abolitionists argued for the supremacy of federal rather than state authority over the interstate slave trade. Indeed, Clay himself had implied as much when he said that the object of the abolitionists was "to prevent the exercise" of that particular kind of commerce. Abolitionists agreed with Clay's argument that the federal commerce power was exclusive. But abolitionists vehemently rejected Clay's contention that the authority of Congress over the interstate slave trade could be used only to sustain that trade and not to annihilate it. For the annihilation of the interstate slave trade by act of Congress was precisely what the abolitionists were seeking.[16]

Daniel Webster seconded Clay's claim that the national government could not use the commerce clause to attack the domestic slave trade nor could states interfere with it. At the time the Constitution was adopted, Webster said, slavery existed in the majority of the states, and the Constitution recognized the validity of slave property by requiring the return of fugitives. Therefore, "the protection of this right of property in the intercourse between the states, became a duty under the constitution." Slaves are articles of commerce and do fall within the federal commerce power, but that power cannot be used to deprive slaveholders of their property rights. A state has the right to abolish slavery. But so long as a state continues to recognize slaves as property, the state cannot prohibit slave trading. "If the right in states recognising slavery exists, to prohibit trading in them, it will allow non-intercourse between the states of the Union by the legislative enactments of the states; and will authorize retaliation. This is negatived by the decision of this court in Gibbons v. Ogden; and the question is closed."[17]

Despite the fact that *Groves v. Slaughter* confronted the court squarely with the question of the status of the interstate slave trade under the commerce clause, the court once again avoided making any official determination upon the crucial issues of exactly what Congress could or could not do, and of what states could or could not do. That happened not because the justices did not have strong opinions on the subject, but because their views were so diverse as to make agreement impossible. The official opinion of the court focused entirely upon a technicality that had been disputed in the case: Was the clause of the Mississippi constitution self-executing or was it ineffectual until it was implemented by an act of the state legislature? Slaughter's lawyers had argued that legislation was required. In reply, the attorneys for the other side had made the seemingly cogent point that if legislation was required, then it could be refused, and if it could be refused, then "we have that actually done, which the words of the constitution forbid to be done." But the court accepted the view that the constitutional clause was not self-executing. It did so because, in the words of Justice Smith Thompson, who delivered the official opinion of the court, "this view of the case makes it unnecessary to inquire whether this article in the constitution of Mississippi is repugnant to the constitution of the United States; and indeed, such inquiry is not properly in the case, as the decision has been placed entirely upon the construction of the constitution of Mississippi." Four years earlier, in his concurring opinion in *Miln,* Thompson had declared that the states could exercise a concurrent power over commerce so long as they did not come into conflict with a federal law. Now he suppressed that personal view in order to enunciate the only thing that a majority of the court could agree upon, which was that the clause in the Mississippi constitution was not self-executing.[18]

No sooner had Thompson finished reading his terse ruling than his colleague John McLean kicked open a hornets' nest by addressing head-on the explosive issue that the court's majority had contrived to evade. To the evident surprise of the other justices, McLean read out a concurring opinion in which he declared that although it was "not necessary to a decision of the case" at hand, he nevertheless wished to make clear his own conviction that Congress had no power to regulate "the transfer and sale of slaves from one state to another." Congress could not interfere with slave trafficking, McLean said, because "the constitution acts upon slaves as persons, and not as property." Because it was only state and not federal law that made slaves property, only the states have power over slavery, "and the transfer or sale of slaves cannot be separated from this power. It is, indeed, an essential part of it." McLean defended state authority over the slave trade in terms that seemingly went beyond even the broad boundaries of state police power. "Each state," he said, "has a right to protect itself against the avarice and intrusion of the slave-dealer; to guard its citizens against the inconveniences and dangers of a slave population. The right to exercise this power, by a state, is higher and deeper than the constitution. The evil involves the prosperity, and may endanger the existence of a state. Its power to guard against, or to remedy the evil, rests upon the law of self-preservation; a law vital to every community, and especially to a sovereign state."[19]

Stung by McLean's boldness, his colleagues swatted about in various directions. Chief Justice Taney, while declining to present any argument to sustain his position, stated his belief that the slave trade was exclusively under the control of the states, "and the action of the several states upon this subject cannot be controlled by congress, either by virtue of its power to regulate commerce, or by virtue of any power conferred by the constitution of the United States." Justice Henry Baldwin disagreed with McLean's notion that the Constitution treats slaves only as persons. If states recognize slaves as property, Baldwin said, then "they become the subjects of commerce between the states which so recognize them, and the traffic in them may be regulated by congress, as the traffic in other articles; but no further." He went on to say, however, that because property rights are protected by the Fifth Amendment, Congress can only facilitate rather than inhibit the interstate slave trade. Thus Congress has the power to prevent states from infringing upon the right of citizens to transfer their slave property from one state to another for sale. "Such transit of property, whether of slaves or bales of goods, is lawful commerce among the several states, which none can prohibit or regulate, which the constitution protects, and congress may, and ought, to preserve from any violation."[20]

To add to the confusion, the official report of the case contains, in between the opinions of Taney and Baldwin, the statement that Justices Story, Thompson, James Wayne, and John McKinley "concurred with the majority of the court in opinion, that the provision of the constitution of the United States, which gives the regulation of commerce to congress, did not interfere with the provision of the constitution of the state of Mississippi, which relates to the introduction of slaves, as merchandize, or for sale." Presumably the four judges asked the official reporter to insert that peculiar statement. Thompson apparently wanted to be included, even though he had earlier ruled, speaking for the majority, that the issue was not to be addressed. McLean and Taney perhaps did not join in the statement because each of them had already stated independently his view of the matter. Thus all but one of the seven justices who participated in the case agreed that a state could enact a regulation of the sort Mississippi had attempted, although there was no consensus among them as to whether the constitutional justification for such state action was state police power, concurrent power over interstate commerce, or even (in the case of McLean) a supraconstitutional right of self-preservation. The only dissenter was Baldwin, who believed that although a state might legitimately use its police power to prohibit *all* importation of slaves, it could not, as Mississippi had tried to do, allow its own citizens to import slaves while forbidding the citizens of other states to come in and sell slaves. To discriminate against the slave traders of other states, Baldwin thought, was to infringe upon the federal commerce power.[21]

Whether the federal government could use its commerce power to inhibit the interstate slave trade had not been at issue in the case, yet three of the justices had seen fit, nevertheless, to say that in their view it could not. Taney made that assertion but did not attempt to justify it. McLean said it was because the Constitution bore upon slaves only as persons. Baldwin said that Congress could use the commerce power only to facilitate the slave trade because curbing it would interfere with property rights. The other four justices were silent on the issue. Having their objective attacked by three judges and supported by none obviously offered no encouragement to the abolitionists to pursue their campaign for federal suppression of the interstate slave trade. But they could console themselves with the fact that the question still had not been ruled upon officially. It remained in legal limbo.

Unlike *Groves v. Slaughter,* the next important commerce cases to come before the court did not directly involve slavery, but they did reopen the vexing questions that had been addressed in *Miln,* with all of their implications for control of the interstate slave trade. The *License Cases* (1847) focused on state attempts to control the sale of alcoholic beverages, while the *Passenger Cases* (1849) concerned a new round of state attempts to regulate immigration. By this time, abolitionist agitation had achieved a considerable impact upon northern public opinion. To be sure, only a tiny minority of northerners had actually embraced radical abolitionism, with its call (in principle, at least) for the immediate, uncompensated emancipation of all of the slaves. But more and more northerners were becoming restive over what they saw as southern determination to dominate the national government and to compel the free states to cooperate with the slave states in shoring up the latter's disagreeable labor system. Consequently, the sense of comity between the free and the slave states was coming unglued. Northern states were increasingly reluctant either to return runaway slaves or to assist the South in prosecuting anyone who had helped them to escape from bondage. In the late 1830s the governors of Maine and New York refused to extradite individuals who had been indicted for "kidnaping" slaves in Georgia and Virginia. In the early 1840s both South Carolina and Virginia passed laws restricting the departure from their port cities of slaves on ships, especially ships that had come from New York. If the Supreme Court should ever rule that the federal commerce power was exclusive, thus voiding all state actions encroaching upon it, what would become of such laws? "In the name of Heaven," exclaimed a Virginia newspaper, "what power would the States have of protecting the lives and property of their own citizens, if this sweeping power of Commerce were admitted? . . . What becomes of the power to keep the citizens of New York from stealing our property and refusing to give it up or those who stole it, if we cannot pass such a bill as may authorize us to search their vessels, or to demand bond and security for the indemnity of masters, whose slaves may be stolen, by every kidnapper?"[22]

Equally at peril was South Carolina's Negro Seamen's Act, still in force despite its denunciation in 1823 by Justice Johnson, and now paralleled by similar statutes in several other slave states. In 1844 Massachusetts sent the distinguished reformer Samuel Hoar to Charleston to launch a test case challenging the Negro Seamen's Act. He had no sooner arrived than the South Carolina legislature passed a resolution calling for his expulsion, and reports of a gathering mob forced him to flee for his life. Finally, as if all of that were not enough, the conclusion of the Mexican War in 1846 unleashed an acrimonious debate in Congress over whether slavery would be allowed to expand into the newly acquired territories in the West. In the highly charged atmosphere of the late 1840s, it was inevitable that both counsel and judges would be even more acutely conscious of the slavery entanglements that threatened to engulf them whenever they grappled with the commerce power.[23]

In the *License Cases*, the court dealt collectively with three separate cases. The states of Massachusetts, New Hampshire, and Rhode Island had all enacted laws regulating the sale of alcoholic beverages that had been produced outside their borders. The validity of all three laws was challenged by the liquor interests, on the grounds that they intruded upon the federal commerce power. The Court heard numerous arguments on all three cases, but none of them (insofar as they have been preserved) brought up the slave trade issue. Still, according to a newspaper account, in one argument Daniel Webster did allude to "such laws as those of South Carolina affecting the privileges of persons of another State visiting that State" and "thought it time—high time—that the Court should give an opinion on questions of so much interest." The court did not oblige. In its decision, the court upheld all three state liquor laws as constitutional, but there was no doctrinal agreement among the eight participating justices, who, in a bewildering array of separate and conflicting opinions, locked horns over the extent and nature of the police and commerce powers. Taney came out for concurrent state commerce power, McLean defended exclusive federal power, and Justice Levi Woodbury (who had been appointed to the court in 1846) said that in this instance the states were exercising only police power rather than commerce power. Woodbury also anticipated a future direction of the court by tossing out the idea that the commerce power might be exclusively federal when commerce was national in character but concurrent with the states when commerce was local.[24]

The two legal disputes that the Supreme Court considered jointly as the

Passenger Cases first appeared on the court's docket in 1843 and 1844, respectively. One of the cases arose from an attempt by the state of New York to support a marine hospital by levying a tax on incoming passengers, both those arriving from abroad and those landing from coastal vessels. The other case stemmed from a Massachusetts statute taxing all arriving passengers in order to provide a fund for the support of foreign-born paupers. Partly because of vacancies and absences on the court, and partly because the justices were, according to Daniel Webster, "divided and puzzled," each of the two cases was heard three times. Only a partial record survives of the many arguments that were presented. The attorneys defending the state laws claimed that they were legitimate exercises of state police power. If the laws should be struck down, one of them warned, then the numerous laws of both free and slave states relating to the entry of both slaves and free blacks would be unsustainable. Slaves, after all, "are held and treated as property, being bought and sold like merchandise," whereas immigrant paupers "in no respect belong to trade, traffic, or commerce." Therefore, "If the law of Massachusetts [relating to paupers] comes within the wide grasp of the commercial power of the United States . . . how are such laws [relating to slaves] to escape? How have they escaped hitherto?" Another of the lawyers—John Van Buren, son of Martin Van Buren, and a rising star in the Democratic Party—in his defense of the New York law, said that states had concurrent power over commerce, and claimed that the Supreme Court had admitted as much when it held in *Groves v. Slaughter* "that the right to admit slaves from other States into Mississippi, or to forbid them to enter, rested exclusively with that State, and was unaffected by the authority of Congress to regulate commerce among the States."[25]

The attorneys for the other side contended that the federal power over commerce was exclusive. Believing (correctly, as it turned out) that he was making his last great defense of federal power before the Supreme Court, an aging Daniel Webster donned a blue coat over a buff vest with brass buttons, the same garb that he had sported in the Senate in 1830 when he delivered the greatest speech of his life, upholding the federal union as one and inseparable. Now Webster called upon the court to uphold the federal commerce power by striking down the state laws that encroached upon it. Only too aware of the states'-rights tendencies of the Taney court, Webster was pessimistic about his prospects for success, saying, in a private letter, that he had presented his argument "under great discouragements and evil auspices." Still, he believed that the court's judgment in the case would be "more important to the country than any decision since that in the steamboat cause. That was one of my earliest arguments of a constitutional question. This will probably be and I am content it should be my last. . . . Whatever I may think of the ability of my argument, and I do not think highly of it, I yet feel pleasure in reflecting that I have held on and held out to the end."[26]

The counsel for the two sides wrangled also over the meaning of the 1808 clause of the Constitution. Webster's opponents contended that although the clause gave Congress the right to control the "migration" as well as the "importation" of "persons," it was nevertheless intended to refer only to slaves being brought in from abroad and not to white immigrants. (The lawyers ignored the possibility that if "migration" did not refer to white immigrants, then maybe it *did* refer to slaves being transported from one place to another within the United States — and thus suggested that Congress could prohibit the interstate slave trade. Such an interpretation was, of course, not congenial to these defenders of states' rights.) An attorney allied with Webster, in contrast, said that the words used in the 1808 clause indicate that it was "not restricted to any particular class of persons, bond or free, and show that the whole power over such importations is confided to Congress."[27]

The decision of the court, when at last it came, was lengthy and confusing. By a bare majority of five to four, the justices declared the laws of both New York and Massachusetts to be unconstitutional. But there was no consensus as to *why* the laws were unconstitutional. Eight of the nine justices delivered their own opinions, running in all to nearly two hundred printed pages. The opinions contained such a diversity of views that the official reporter was forced to throw up his hands and admit that, although a decision had been rendered, the legal basis for it could not be explicated, for there simply was "no opinion of the court, as a court."[28]

Justice McLean said that the laws of New York and Massachusetts were unconstitutional because "a concurrent power in the States to regulate commerce is an anomaly not found in the Constitution." In *Groves v. Slaughter*, McLean had declared that although the federal power over commerce was exclusive, it could not be used to ban the interstate slave trade or to prevent states from controlling the admission of slaves. Now he scoffed at the notion that the exclusive federal power might be used to force the free states to accept the entry of slaves onto their territory. "Does anyone suppose that Congress can ever revive the slave trade?" he asked rhetorically. "And if this were possible, slaves thus introduced would be free."[29]

Justice Wayne said that he and three other justices agreed that the laws in question were unconstitutional, but thought that they should be declared so because they conflicted with existing federal laws and treaties, not because the federal commerce power was exclusive. Wayne added that he himself actually agreed with McLean that the federal power *was* exclusive, but felt there was no need to say so in this case. Wayne went on to reassure southerners that the federal commerce power, whether exclusive or not, could not be used to interfere with slavery. The Constitution, Wayne said, was formed by a coalition of free states and slave states. That is its foundation, and the 1808 clause and other provisions within it recognize the fact. Consequently, "The Constitution is to be interpreted by what was the condition of the parties to it when it was formed, by their object and purpose in forming it, and the actual recognition in it of the dissimilar institutions of the States." Wayne said explicitly that there was no basis for southern fears that the federal government could force the slave states to allow the entry of free blacks. He might just as well have added that his rigorously proslavery conception of the Constitution also ruled out any possibility of federal tampering with the interstate slave trade.[30]

Justice McKinley, with the support of Justice Robert Grier, said that the word "migration" in the 1808 clause referred to free immigrants as opposed to slaves. Then Grier, with the support of Justice John Catron, reinforced Wayne's point that the slave states had nothing to fear from the federal commerce power. Any state "whose domestic security might be endangered by the admission of free negroes" could use its police power to exclude them, said Grier. "This right of the States has its foundation in the sacred law of self defence, which no power granted to Congress can restrain or annul." He remarked also that the question of whether the federal commerce power is exclusive "is one on which the majority of this court have intimated different opinions at different times; but it is one of little practical importance in the present case," since Congress has acted in this area, and thus the state laws being disallowed by the court are in actual conflict with federal policy.[31]

Chief Justice Taney, with the support of Justice Samuel Nelson, presented a lengthy and vigorous dissenting opinion, in which he said that the states possess a concurrent power over commerce and that they, not Congress, have the right to determine what persons are or are not to be allowed to enter their domains. To suggest the opposite he thought absurd. "I cannot," he said, "believe that it was ever intended to vest in Congress, by the general words in relation to the regulation of commerce, this overwhelming power over the States." The statesmen who created the Constitution were "too wise and too well read in the lessons of history and of their own time" to have done such a thing, and "I cannot imagine any power more unnecessary to the general government, and at the same time more dangerous and full of peril to the States." Taney said also that the 1808 clause, despite its use of the words "migration or importation," had referred only to slaves. Because the founders were unwilling to use the word "slaves" in the Constitution, Taney explained, they referred to slaves as "persons," and having done that, "they employed a word that would describe them as persons, and which had uniformly been used when persons were spoken of, and also the word which was always applied to matters of property. The whole context of the sentence, and its provisions and limitations, and the construction given to it by those who assisted in framing the clause in question, show that it was intended to embrace those persons only who were brought in as property."[32]

Another dissenter, Justice Peter Daniel, made similar points. He too said that the states have a concurrent commerce power. Daniel recalled that Justice Baldwin in his opinion in *Groves v. Slaughter* had defended the notion that the federal power was exclusive. But Daniel said that Baldwin's view counted for little because it was "a dissent by a single judge," and still less because it had "asserted the extraordinary doctrine that the States of this Union can have no power to prohibit the introduction of slaves within their territory when carried thither for sale or traffic, because the power to regulate commerce is there asserted to reside in Congress alone" — which Daniel regarded as an "eccentric and startling conclusion." Daniel also agreed with Taney about the 1808 clause, saying that it "was intended to apply to the African slave-trade, and to no other matter whatever."[33]

Finally, Justice Levi Woodbury added his voice to the dissenting minority. He thought that Taney was likely correct about the meaning of the 1808 clause, although Woodbury left the door open to a slightly wider interpretation. Woodbury said, "The word 'migration' was probably added to 'importation' to cover slaves when regarded as persons rather than property, as they are for some purposes. Or if to cover others, such as convicts or redemptioners, it was those only who came against their will, or in a quasi servitude." He added explicitly that under the 1808 clause, "no authority was conferred on Congress over the domestic slave-trade, either before or since 1808." Woodbury also declared forcefully that the states possessed both a concurrent commerce power and a broad police power, and therefore had an unquestionable right to exclude anyone they chose. Since all sovereign states can exclude any categories of persons, including "cargoes of shackled slaves," he said, the American states can, if they choose, exclude emigrants "only when slaves, or, what is still more common in America, in Free States as well as Slave States, exclude colored emigrants, though free." Woodbury concluded with a warning and a final rhetorical flourish: "A course of harshness towards the States by the general government," one that interferes with their "domestic policies in doubtful cases, and this by mere implied power," would "tend ultimately, no less than disastrously, to dissolve the bonds of that Union so useful and glorious to all concerned. 'Libertas ultima mundi, Quo steterit, ferienda loco' [The remaining liberty of the world was to be destroyed in the place where it stood]."[34]

The judges had expressed such disparate views that nobody then or since has been able to make any overall sense of them. Only one thing was clear: the court majority had struck down the immigration laws of New York and Massachusetts as unconstitutional. That fact alone was enough to inflame southern opinion. For if the two northern states could not control the entry of immigrants into their port cities, then how could any of the southern states be sure of their own power to control the entry of slaves or free blacks? "If we correctly understand the points decided," cried the *Charleston Mercury,* "they sweep away our inspection laws enacted to prevent the abduction of our slaves in Northern vessels. They sweep away also our laws enacted to prevent free colored persons—citizens of Massachusetts—or whatever abolition region, from entering our ports and cities. Thus it seems as if the Union is to be so administered as to strip the South of all power of self-protection and to make submission to its rule equivalent to ruin and degradation." Actually, the *Mercury* did not correctly understand the points decided, for there were none. And the notion that any southern laws had been swept away was ridiculously alarmist, as the judges had been at pains to signal that nothing of the sort was going to happen. Even McLean and Wayne, the only two justices who had declared that the federal commerce power was exclusive, had nonetheless also made it equally clear that states had a right to control the entry or nonentry of slaves and free blacks, and that the federal government could not use its commerce power to interfere.[35]

Given the doctrinal anarchy of the *Passenger Cases* decision, it seems astonishing that only three years later a court comprised, with just one exception, of the same men who had produced that dog's breakfast issued a decision in which a solid majority was able to agree not only upon the outcome of a commerce case but also upon the doctrinal basis for it. In *Cooley v. Board of Wardens of the Port of Philadelphia* (1852), the court upheld the constitutionality of a Pennsylvania law that required vessels entering the port of Philadelphia to either hire local pilots or make a compensatory payment. The newcomer to the court, Justice Benjamin R. Curtis, pulled off the near miracle of persuading five of his colleagues to join him in a majority decision that provided at last an official ruling on the perennial question of whether the interstate commerce power was exclusively federal or was concurrent with the states. Curtis's solution was to have it both ways. He said that some commerce matters called for exclusive federal power and others did not. "Whatever subjects of this power are in their nature national, or admit of only one uniform system, or plan of regulation, may justly be said to be of such a nature as to require exclusive legislation by Congress," he explained. Other commerce matters, such as the hiring of harbor pilots, are essentially local in character, and therefore in those areas the states can exercise a concurrent authority. Not surprisingly, Justices McLean and Wayne dissented from the majority and clung to their view of the federal power as exclusive, full stop.[36]

Although the *Cooley* decision appeared to be an improvement over the *Passenger Cases,* it was not. For it merely replaced one unanswered question with another one. Previously the question had been: Is the commerce power exclusive to the federal government, or do the states possess a concurrent power? The answer provided by *Cooley* was that federal power is exclusive over matters that are inherently national, but that states have a concurrent power over matters that are inherently local. But now a new question arose that was scarcely less troubling than the one that had been answered: How can we differentiate the matters that are inherently national from those that are local? *Cooley* provided no answer, aside from saying that pilotage belonged to the latter category. From the point of view of both defenders and opponents of the domestic slave trade, the court had settled nothing. For who could say for certain whether interstate slave trading was of a national or a local character? And even if there were some magical way to separate all national from all local concerns, neither side in the slavery debate would have been satisfied, for neither side was consistent in its demands. Both sides favored states' rights when it suited them, but both also had no hesitation in opting for national power when it was advantageous to their cause. Proslavery spokesmen always insisted that slave trading was a local matter that the federal government must not touch. Yet those same spokesmen were all in favor of a vigorous enforcement of the federal Fugitive Slave Act, so as to coerce the free states into yielding up the men and women who had managed to shed their chains and follow the drinking gourd northward to freedom. Abolitionists, on the other hand, did everything they could to defy and defeat the Fugitive Slave law, which they denounced as an unconstitutional abuse of states' rights as well as human rights. Yet those same abolitionists continued to insist that the federal government had both the right and the duty to abolish the interstate slave trade.

The struggle over slavery and the slave trade entered its climactic phase in the 1850s. The decade began auspiciously with a compromise agreement between North and South on what to do with the lands seized from Mexico. California was admitted as a Free state, and the territories of Utah and New Mexico were organized without any restriction on slavery. Yet while the Compromise of 1850 quieted for the moment the quarrel over the territories, it contained two other provisions that worsened rather than eased the sectional conflict. First, a new and draconian federal fugitive slave law delighted proslavery southerners but outraged antislavery northerners. Second, the prohibition of commercial slave trafficking in Washington, D.C., applied a cosmetic balm to northern sensibility over that ugly spectacle but provoked southern anxiety that it might be a first step toward the suppression of the entire interstate slave trade. In 1852 Harriet Beecher Stowe's best-selling novel *Uncle Tom's Cabin* brought home to hundreds of thousands of northern readers the cruel separation of slave families that was endemic to that trade. In 1854 the Kansas-Nebraska Act reopened the toxic conflict over whether slavery should be allowed in the territories.

When the Taney court, in *Dred Scott v. Sandford* (1857), declared that Congress did not have the constitutional power to ban slavery in the territories, even the most moderate opponents of slavery were horrified. There was, however, another aspect to the *Dred Scott* decision that also was important at the time but is less remembered today, and that is the fact that most of the majority justices grounded their ruling upon an extreme defense of the property rights of slaveholders. In the official opinion of the court, Chief Justice Taney said that for Congress to prohibit slavery in a territory was to violate the Fifth Amendment guarantee that a citizen could not be deprived of property without due process of law. "An act of Congress which deprives a citizen of the United States of his liberty or property, merely because he came himself or brought his property into a particular Territory of the United States, and who had committed no offence against the laws, could hardly be dignified with the name of due process of law," Taney declared. (The fallacy in Taney's reasoning here is obvious. If Congress has outlawed slavery in a territory, then the slaveholders he speaks of *have* committed an offense against the law. Therefore, the loss of their property *does* come about through due process of law. Of course Taney denies that because he holds that the law in question is unconstitutional. But why is it unconstitutional? Well, Taney says, it is unconstitutional because it takes property away from slaveholders who have committed no offense. Taney's reasoning is circular.) Taney added that the only power conferred by the Constitution upon the federal government with regard to slave property was "the power coupled with the duty of guarding and protecting the owner in his rights." Justices Wayne and Grier concurred fully with Taney. Justice Daniel stressed property rights even more strongly, saying that "the only private property which the Constitution has *specifically recognised*, and has imposed it as a direct obligation both on the States and the Federal Government to protect and *enforce*, is the property of the master in his slave; no other right of property is placed by the Constitution upon the same high ground, nor shielded by a similar guaranty." Justice John Campbell (the only newcomer to the court since the *Cooley* case) claimed that it was already a "settled doctrine" of the court that the federal government "can exercise no power over the subject of slavery within the States, nor control the intermigration of slaves, other than fugitives, among the States." Whatever state law makes property, Campbell said, must be recognized as property by the federal government in all areas within its jurisdiction. Therefore, "wherever a master is entitled to go within the United States, his slaves may accompany him, without any impediment from, or fear of, Congressional legislation or interference."[37] Thus five justices—a majority of the court's members—had explicitly affirmed that Congress could not ban slavery from a territory because to do so was to violate property rights.

The other four justices disagreed. Justice Catron concurred with the majority's decision but not with their reasoning. Catron held that the Louisiana Purchase treaty had guaranteed equal rights to all settlers, including slaveholders. He also said that because the Constitution (Article IV, section 2, clause 1) declares that the citizens of each state are entitled to the privileges and immunities of citizens in the several states, slaveholders may not be denied their equal enjoyment of the territories. Justices Curtis and McLean wrote vigorous dissents. Yet even as McLean upheld the right of Congress to ban slavery in the territories, he reiterated his denial that Congress could ban the interstate slave trade. McLean said (inaccurately) that in *Groves v. Slaughter*, "Messrs. Clay and Webster contended that, under the commercial power, Congress had a right to regulate the slave trade among the several States; but the court held that Congress had no power to interfere with slavery as it exists in the States, or to regulate what is called the slave trade among them. If this trade were subject to the commercial power, it would follow that Congress could abolish or establish slavery in every State of the Union." The ninth justice, Samuel Nelson, did not address the great issues that so preoccupied his colleagues. Instead, he simply upheld the earlier ruling by the U.S. District Court that Dred Scott was not free.[38]

The court majority's extreme solicitude for the property rights of slaveholders not only was bad news for the radical advocates of a ban on the interstate slave trade, whose cause obviously stood no chance before a court so doctrinaire about the sanctity of slave property; it also was disquieting to the far more numerous antislavery moderates, who now wondered how far the court majority might push its doctrine. Abraham Lincoln, for one, predicted that in some future case the court would rule that no state could exclude slavery. "We shall lie down pleasantly dreaming that the people of Missouri are on the verge of making their State free," Lincoln said, "and we shall awake to the reality instead, that the Supreme Court has made Illinois a slave State." After all, Lincoln explained, if, as the Taney court had avowed, "the right of property in a slave is distinctly and expressly affirmed in the Constitution," then it followed that "nothing in the Constitution or laws of any State can destroy the right of property in a slave."[39]

That Taney and his colleagues would have dared to try to transform the free states into full-fledged slave states is scarcely believable. But it is not far-fetched to surmise that the court's extreme commitment to property rights in slaves might have led it to make inroads in that direction. The court might, for example, have established a constitutional right of transit for slaveowners wishing to traverse a free state along with their human chattels. A case that could have provided the context for just such a ruling was, in fact, in the pipeline. In 1852 the courts of New York State had freed eight slaves belonging to Mr. and Mrs. Jonathan Lemmon, who had brought them from Virginia to New York City in order to board a steamer for New Orleans. The resulting case of *Lemmon v. The People,* 20 N.Y. 562 (1860) was headed for the Supreme Court on appeal. Charles Sumner, Salmon Chase, and Horace Greeley all predicted that if the Democrats won the presidency in 1860, then the Taney court would use this case to force the introduction of slavery into the free states. The Democrats did not win the presidency, however, and the *Lemmon* case was overtaken by events, as the nation spiraled into the maelstrom of secession and civil war.[40]

Throughout the antebellum decades the Supreme Court never made a definitive ruling as to whether Congress could interfere with the interstate slave trade. At first, under the wise leadership of John Marshall, it did not because Marshall realized that it would be foolhardy to ignite southern public opinion over so inflammatory an issue. Later, under the lesser genius of Roger B. Taney, it did not primarily because of doctrinal disagreements among the judges. If they had at any point issued a formal ruling on the question, it appears almost certain that the justices who served under Taney would have been unanimous in holding that Congress did not possess the constitutional authority to abolish the interstate slave trade. Not a single justice had ever stated it to be his belief that Congress did have such power, whereas eight of them had made evident their personal conviction that it did not. Five of the eight (McLean, Taney, Baldwin, Woodbury, and Campbell) had said explicitly that Congress could not interfere with the slave trade, and the other three (Wayne, McKinley, and Grier) had made remarks carrying such a strong implication to that effect as to make their stance unmistakable. The justices would not have been unanimous in their legal reasoning as to *why* the interstate commerce clause did not give Congress the power to halt the slave trade. But by the time of the *Dred Scott* decision, a majority of them had coalesced around a doctrine that held that the right to property in slaves was constitutionally sacrosanct and untouchable.

In its zeal to prevent the struggle over slavery from threatening the unity of the nation, the Taney court in *Dred Scott* had rashly sought to resolve by judicial fiat the ambiguous constitutional legacy of the founding fathers. To the founders, the long-term fate of slavery in the republic had been a question left open for political resolution by future generations. To Taney and his like-minded associates, the question was now closed. Slavery and the interstate slave trade were safe behind the bulwark of such a court as this. But even justices of the Supreme Court are not immortal. The character of the court changes as vacancies occur and new judges are appointed. By 1860 a great political party had arisen in the North that was openly hostile to slavery and the slave trade. A man who had denounced the *Dred Scott* decision and called for it to be reversed had been elected to the presidency. It was Abraham Lincoln who would be proposing any new justices to join the court. How safe was the interstate slave trade now? The South's answer to that question is part of the explanation for the nation's declension into bloodshed and horror.

5

The Door to the Slave Bastille

On New Year's Day 1831 William Lloyd Garrison published the first issue of his new paper *The Liberator.* It was the beginning of an organized, militant movement against slavery that was unlike anything America had ever seen before. "I am aware," Garrison wrote, "that many object to the severity of my language; but is there not cause for severity? I *will* be as harsh as truth, and as uncompromising as justice. On this subject, I do not wish to think, or speak, or write, with moderation. . . . I am in earnest — I will not equivocate — I will not excuse — I will not retreat a single inch — AND I WILL BE HEARD." In the following year, Garrison and a small band of followers founded the New England (later called the Massachusetts) Anti-Slavery Society, and the year after that they advanced from the state to the national arena by organizing the American Anti-Slavery Society (AA-SS). Gone was the elitism, deference, and moderation that had characterized the earlier antislavery organizations. Garrison and his comrades sought to create a mass movement that would for the first time involve anyone and everyone who agreed that slavery was an evil that should be abolished immediately. Not only were men of any social rank allowed to join, even women and African Americans were welcomed into the fold. Indeed, the vast majority of the original five hundred or so subscribers to Garrison's *Liberator* were free blacks, who were pleased that at last a white reformer had partially caught up with black opinion on slavery and colonization.[1]

Historians of radical abolitionism often say that the movement was apolitical until the 1840s. They assert that "in the early years of the AASS its members gave little thought to the political implications of their movement," and that it was only in the late 1830s that some members proposed "to transform the American Anti-Slavery Society into a political pressure group." Such assertions are misleading. That the movement was apolitical in its early years is true only in the extremely narrow sense that the abolitionists did not then organize a separate political party of their own. But from the beginning they articulated an explicit political program and vigorously pursued their political objectives. "Does the American Anti-Slavery Society intend *political* action?" asked an editorial in one of their newspapers. "The answer must depend on what is *meant* by political action. If it is meant that the society will enter the scramble for political offices, will set up its candidates and measure its success by theirs, it certainly does not intend any such action. . . . But if by political action be meant, inducing *men,* by moral considerations, to act politically for the single object of the abolition of slavery, it certainly does intend political action. . . . How is slavery ever to be abolished except by political action?"[2]

In calling for the establishment of a national organization, Garrison and his cohorts declared that they would "take up those branches of the subject which are acknowledged to be of a national character," including slavery in the territories, slavery in the District of Columbia, and "the criminal and disgraceful commerce between the States, in slaves." They believed that Congress could take action on each of those issues by virtue of the powers granted to it by the U.S. Constitution, and they aimed to pressure Congress to attack slavery by all constitutional means. The constitution adopted by the AA-SS at its founding convention declared explicitly that the Society intended, "in a constitutional way, to influence Congress to put an end to the domestic slave trade." Although the creators of the AA-SS conceded that Congress had no authority to interfere with slavery within the slave states, they issued a "Declaration of Sentiments" in which they proclaimed that the national legislature had both the right and the obligation "to suppress the domestic slave trade between the several States."[3]

Despite those clear statements of abolitionist intent, the abolitionist assault upon the interstate slave trade has received remarkably little notice from historians. That is so for two reasons. One is that Garrison and those abolitionists who remained loyal to him later gravitated toward a Christian anarchist perspective from which they denounced all forms of coercion and renounced all participation in politics. The other and more important reason is that the struggle over the expansion of slavery into the territories eclipsed all other issues during the climactic phase of the antislavery crusade. Yet the attack on the slave trade deserves to be rescued from obscurity, for it was a significant facet of immediate abolitionism in the early years of the movement. Banning the interstate slave trade was advocated by many prominent abolitionists, was endorsed by two New England legislatures, and was called for in a host of abolitionist petitions, pamphlets, and speeches, many of which afford insight into the abolitionist conception of the slave-based southern economy. Agitation of the slave trade issue helped to define the radicalism of the abolitionists, earning them denunciation not only from proslavery zealots but also from advocates of compromise and moderation. Finally, the slave trade issue figured in the internal disagreements that fragmented the abolitionist movement in the late 1830s. Before considering all of those matters, it is appropriate to first explore how and why the founders of the AA-SS came to launch their attack upon the domestic slave trade.

It has been claimed that William Jay, a New York judge and son of founding father John Jay, was the individual chiefly responsible for the inclusion of the proposed attack on the interstate slave trade in the AA-SS Constitution and Declaration of Sentiments. William Jay had engaged in antislavery activity as early as 1826, when he was involved in petitioning for an end to slavery in the District of Columbia. In thus speaking out against slavery, he obviously was following in the footsteps of his eminent father. In June 1833, Arthur Tappan, the wealthy New York merchant who three years earlier had rescued Garrison from a Baltimore prison cell by paying his fine, wrote William Jay to ask whether he thought it would be a good idea to try to establish a national antislavery society. Jay replied cautiously that if such a society were to be formed, it must give southerners no grounds for fearing an unconstitutional invasion of their rights. Jay suggested that all antislavery societies should incorporate into their constitutions a statement on the order of the following: "We concede that Congress, under the present National Compact, has no right to interfere with any of the slave States in relation to this momentous subject. But we maintain that Congress has a right and is solemnly bound to suppress the domestic slave-trade between the several States and to abolish slavery in those portions of our territory which the Constitution has placed under its exclusive jurisdiction." In October, Jay received a circular letter signed by a committee consisting of Arthur Tappan, Joshua Leavitt, and Elizur Wright, Jr., inviting him to attend what was to become the founding convention of the AA-SS. (Leavitt was a Congregational minister and editor of the *New York Evangelist.* Wright was a professor of mathematics at Western Reserve College in Hudson, Ohio, who had accepted Tappan's call to come to New York City and help organize the national abolitionist movement.) At the same time, Jay received another letter, that one a personal appeal from Samuel J. May, also urging him to come. (May was a Unitarian preacher and ardent reformer who had been an ally of Garrison since 1830.) In his reply to the committee, Jay declined to attend the convention, saying that he doubted the expediency of forming a national society, but he repeated his advice that any national organization must avow correct constitutional principles.[4]

At the founding convention of the AA-SS in December, Jay's letter was read in his absence. The convention subsequently adopted the society's constitution, which included the statement that the organization would seek to obtain a congressional ban on the domestic slave trade, and it appointed a committee to draw up a declaration of principles. After a long but inconclusive discussion, the latter committee delegated its task to a subcommittee consisting of William Lloyd Garrison, Samuel J. May, and John Greenleaf Whittier. (Whittier's career as a notable man of letters had begun in 1826 when Garrison published one of his poems in the Newburyport, Massachusetts, *Free Press*. Whittier had agreed to join the radical abolitionist movement both out of sincere antislavery conviction and because he owed Garrison a favor.) According to the later recollection of Whittier, the subcommittee met and, "after a brief consultation and comparison of each other's views," left the actual drafting of the document to Garrison. "We agreed to meet him at his lodgings in the house of a colored friend early the next morning. It was still dark when we climbed up to his room, and the lamp was still burning by the light of which he was writing the last sentence of the declaration. We read it carefully, made a few verbal changes, and submitted it to the large committee, who unanimously agreed to report it to the convention."[5]

Because Garrison was the principal author of the AA-SS Declaration of Sentiments, it seems likely that William Jay's urgings were only one factor in bringing about the AA-SS stand against the slave trade. As a former associate of Benjamin Lundy, Garrison may have known about Lundy's 1823 plan for abolishing slavery partly by ending the slave trade. Certainly he was still smarting from his own experience of being jailed in Baltimore for attacking a shipowner for engaging in the "domestic piracy" of carrying slaves coastwise. Also, Garrison was undoubtedly familiar with more recent interest in such action by other abolitionists. In a speech that he gave in January 1833, David Lee Child caustically condemned the domestic slave trade. (Child was a Massachusetts lawyer who was more interested in promoting social reform than in practicing his profession. Fortunately, his wife, Lydia Maria Child, was not only a fellow abolitionist but also a successful novelist whose royalties enabled the couple to live in modest comfort.) David Child had joined with Garrison and a dozen others to found the New England Anti-Slavery Society in 1832. Now, at the first annual meeting of that society, held in Boylston Hall in

Boston on 9 January 1833, Child pointed out that while Britain had ended the slave trade within its empire, the United States still permitted the "wicked traffic" to go on in the United States. In September an article in the New England society's magazine challenged the idea that slavery was solely a concern of the southern states by noting that the U.S. Constitution permitted prohibition of the slave trade after 1808. The author of the article had no doubt that the federal authority extended to the interstate as well as to the foreign slave trade. Finally, in the 5 October 1833 *Liberator,* Garrison himself published a long, unsigned article describing the evils of the slave trade and concluding with a plea for congressional action:

> I do from the bottom of my heart declare that in my opinion, the internal slave trade of this Republic, is very little inferior in horrors and atrocities to the foreign trade of Africa. I do believe that Virginia is become another Guinea, and the Eastern Shore an African Coast.
>
> Is there no remedy for this?
>
> I believe that Congress has the same power over the domestic slave trade between the different states, which it had over the foreign slave trade after the expiration of the disgraceful "twenty years." Let Congress exercise this power.[6]

It seems reasonable to conclude that in 1833 William Jay was only one of several, perhaps many, abolitionists who had in mind the idea of demanding congressional action against the interstate slave trade. It was an idea whose time had come. Influenced by the precedents of the 1820s, alarmed by the mushrooming slave trade resulting from the cotton boom of the 1830s, and inspired by the example of Great Britain's suppression of slave trading within its empire, American abolitionists were ready to take their stand against the domestic trade in the bodies of men, women, and children.

Perhaps the first abolitionist to agitate the slave trade issue in the aftermath of the December 1833 founding of the AA-SS was Henry B. Stanton, a recent recruit to the cause. As a young newspaper writer and county clerk in Rochester, New York, Stanton had been "saved" by the evangelist Charles G. Finney and had enrolled as a student at Lane Theological Seminary in Cincinnati. Because Cincinnati was a thriving river port, Stanton was in a good position to observe the slaves being carried aboard steamboats down the Ohio River and onward via the Mississippi to the markets of the lower South. In the fall of 1834 he was among the famous "Lane rebels" who organized an antislavery society and then left in protest when the trustees of the seminary forbade any further agitation of the slavery issue. Even before that, however, he had attacked the slave trade. In the spring of 1834, he published a searing description of the removal of slaves from Virginia and Kentucky to Louisiana by "*soul drivers,*" whom Stanton characterized as "usually brutal, ignorant, debauched men" who exercised "despotic control over thousands of down-trodden, and defenceless men and women." Stanton described the manner in which the slaves were transported downriver, often sharing deck space with horses and sheep. The slaves, he said, were "usually chained, subject to the jeers and taunts of the passengers and navigators, and often, by bribes, or threats, or the lash, made subject to abominations not to be named." Other slaves made the journey by land, walking up to a thousand miles and sometimes carrying heavy chains the entire distance.[7]

Another early propagandist was David Lee Child, who, along with four other committee members, submitted an extensive "Report on the Slave Trade" to the 1834 annual meeting of the New England Anti-Slavery Society. Printed in full in the *Liberator,* the report presented a wealth of anecdotal evidence about the burgeoning interregional trade and called for petitions to Congress to end it. "It is a fact worthy of observation," the report noted, "that just at the precise time that the foreign slave trade was *permitted,* by our Constitution to cease, the Domestic was ready to begin. The turn of the tide could not have been calculated with more accuracy!"[8]

Stanton and Child were for a time almost alone among abolitionists in campaigning against the interstate slave trade. Even William Jay in his early and influential *Inquiry into the Character and Tendency of the American Colonization and American Anti-Slavery Societies* (1835) only touched on "the suppression of the American slave trade" as one of the objectives of the AA-SS, choosing instead to dwell upon the power of Congress to abolish slavery in the District of Columbia. Yet Jay's mere mention of the AA-SS stand on the interstate trade drew fire from his critics. In a published reply to Jay's *Inquiry,* colonizationist David Reese challenged Jay's claim that the AA-SS intended no interference with slavery in the slave states. "Is it no 'interference with the slave states *in relation to slavery,*' to 'suppress the domestic slave-trade between the several states,' which the society declare congress not only to have a right to do, but to be 'solemnly bound' 'to exercise it'[?]," Reese asked, adding that Jay's opponents consequently "have some reason to say abolitionists are endeavouring to 'cause the national legislation to bear directly on the slaveholders,' and in 'a great degree *against and in defiance of the will of the South.*' "[9]

Even in 1836 it was still possible for Lydia Child in her famous *Appeal in Favor of that Class of Americans Called Africans* to ignore the interstate trade while imploring her readers to petition for a congressional ban on slavery in the District of Columbia "year after year, until a reformation is effected." Other abolitionists, however, were now looking beyond the District of Columbia question to the larger issue of the interstate trade. In February 1836, John Greenleaf Whittier, in response to an anti-abolitionist message from the governor of Massachusetts, asserted that the overthrow of slavery could be accomplished without any change to the U.S. Constitution. Whittier discussed the power of Congress over the federal district, but he then went on to single out also the potential for congressional action against the interstate trade. Noting that the "right of Congress to abolish the Domestic traffic is admitted in the Boston Memorial on the Missouri Question signed by DANIEL WEBSTER and others," Whittier concluded that such power "is evidently given" by the U.S. Constitution, "but of the expediency of its exercise the people must judge for themselves." A few months later, the clergyman, abolitionist, and Underground Railroad conductor John Rankin of Ripley, Ohio, made the slave trade the subject of a forceful speech to the Pittsburgh Anti-Slavery Society. Rankin told of a slave who lived within sight of his own house, just across the Ohio River in Kentucky. The slave's master had agreed to allow him to purchase his freedom for $550, but just as he was on the brink of raising that amount, the master suddenly sold him to a trader, who took him away by riverboat "to a returnless, hopeless distance from his wife and tender babes, without being allowed even the consolation of just bidding them farewell." Rankin stressed that slave trafficking was not an abuse of slavery but an essential part of it. Without the interstate slave trade, slavery could not exist in Kentucky or Virginia. But of course, "There is no possible source of a good title to a slave. Hence the criminality of the slave trade, and hence the criminality of slavery."[10]

Also in 1836, an anonymous abolitionist published *Remarks on the Constitution, by a Friend of Humanity, on the Subject of Slavery.* Compiled from a series of essays that had appeared originally in the Philadelphia *Evening Star* ("the only daily paper in this city which has shown a willingness to admit matter opposed to Slavery to be presented to the public"), this pamphlet presented the most elaborate analysis of congressional power over the interstate trade since Robert Walsh's similar effort of 1819. Indeed, it appears probable that Walsh was the author also of this new work. *Remarks on the Constitution* discussed the antislavery sentiments of the U.S. founding fathers and argued that they had intended that the domestic as well as the foreign slave trade should cease in 1808. The treatise ended with the statement that "the United States in Congress assembled ought not only to have declared the Foreign but the Domestic Slave Trade PIRACY—after the year 1808. And each and every state was bound in honor to abolish Slavery, from the same time."[11]

Alvan Stewart was a Utica, New York, lawyer who joined the AA-SS in 1834 and was a key figure in founding the New York Anti-Slavery Society the following year. In October 1836, Stewart made the internal slave trade the principal topic of his address on behalf of the first annual meeting of the New York organization. Stewart claimed that more than 120,000 slaves were being transferred annually from the upper South into the lower slave states. According to Stewart, that figure was double the number of slaves ever imported into the United States from Africa in any year prior to the abolition of the external trade, and it was an even greater offense to humanity, because the slaves born in America, being "better informed and cultivated in the knowledge of right and wrong," suffered even more from being "torn from their natal soil" than did native Africans. "The slave," Stewart said, "has no interest in property or things, or in the soil. His whole earthly interest is in the love and sympathy of his relations, and in the beings for whom he has formed strong attachments in his youthful days. Therefore he is by a removal from those places where he was raised, and in severing all the bonds that make life supportable, doubly robbed —always of himself, and lastly of his friends and relations."[12]

Stewart said that the abolition of the interstate trade not only would end the suffering of the transported slaves, it also would cripple the slave economy. If the "slave-growers" of the upper South could not sell off their surplus slaves, they would "sink under the weight of a population whom their old exhausted slave soil could never support," while the slaveholders of the lower South would be compelled "to abandon slave labor and employ free colored people, in a great degree, if they could no longer import slaves . . . to supply the havoc created by overworking, underfeeding, and an unhealthy climate." Stewart added that the abolition of slavery in the District of Columbia and in the territories would be ineffectual so long as slaves could readily be moved out of those areas. But, "were a rigorous law passed by Congress, forbidding the internal slave trade between the States, it would be equivalent to the manumission on the soil of two-thirds of the slaves in the United States in less than ten years." Stewart concluded with the earnest plea "that every anti-slavery society, or individual who may petition Congress on the subject, may make the annihilation of the domestic, or internal slave trade between the States, a point of the most prominent importance, and pray for its entire ABOLITION."[13]

Because Stewart's views were to be echoed in many other writings by himself and other abolitionists, it should be noted that in the light of modern scholarship his belief that an interruption of the interstate transfer of slaves would be all but fatal to the slave economy appears exaggerated yet not altogether off the mark. It is true that by the 1830s it was not uncommon for Virginia planters to own more slaves than they could productively employ, because their slaves had multiplied while their landholdings had not. (James Madison, for example, reluctantly parted with sixteen slaves in the fall of 1834, because he could no longer afford to maintain them. Madison did not sell his slaves to a trader, however, but to a relative in Louisiana. He claimed that the slaves consented to the move.) Soil exhaustion in the upper South was not so significant a stimulus to the interregional movement of slaves as Stewart supposed, but it is true that the soils of Maryland and Virginia could not compare in productivity with the rich alluvial lands of Louisiana and Mississippi. Consequently, the capital gains accruing from the reproduction of the slave population were an important component of the economic returns to slaveholding in the upper South. In the lower South, contrary to Stewart's implication that the slave population could not sustain itself, more slaves were needed primarily not to replace those that died but because of the enormous demand for labor arising from the rapid clearing of new lands and expansion of agriculture. It was only in the sugar-growing region of Louisiana that slave deaths exceeded births. Working conditions on the sugar plantations were brutal, particularly during harvest time, when slaves worked eighteen hours a day for weeks on end, as planters drove the slaves unmercifully in order to harvest and process the cane during the brief period of opportunity after it ripened and before it began to spoil. An unbalanced sex ratio (sugar planters preferred males), a low fertility rate, and high mortality among both adults and (especially) children all meant that the sugar parishes conformed to Stewart's stereotype of the lower South as a place where the slave population was overworked and unable to maintain itself through natural increase.[14]

The most inaccurate aspect of Stewart's description of the interstate slave trade was his claim that 120,000 slaves a year were caught up in it. Because there was no way for anyone to determine accurately how many slaves were involved, it is understandable that white southerners generally underestimated the extent of slave trading while abolitionists exaggerated it. Although 1836 probably was the peak year in the entire history of the interstate slave trade, it is improbable that slave migration of all kinds, much less the commercial slave trade alone, reached even in that exceptional year anything like the 120,000 figure that Stewart claimed was being attained annually. Michael Tadman estimates that net slave movements out of the exporting states totaled 284,750 over the entire decade of the 1830s.[15]

In sum, then, Stewart's view of the potential impact of a ban on the interstate slave trade upon the institution of slavery was somewhat overstated but not wrong. However, from the perspective of a present-day historian, Stewart's belief that such a ban could have been imposed successfully appears highly unrealistic. It would be quite ahistorical to imagine that Congress could have seriously contemplated taking such a radical step as to ban the interstate slave trade in a nation where slaveholders held so much sway. And it would be even more ahistorical to suppose that such a ban could have been enforced.

Slave traders routinely circumvented state laws aimed at interfering with their activities, and no doubt would have done the same in response to any federal legislation. Moreover, for a federal ban to be effective it would have had to apply not only to the commercial traders but also to those migrating slaveowners who crossed state lines with their own slave property in tow. Otherwise, how could bona fide settlers be distinguished from others who might arrive with a coffle of slaves, settle briefly if at all, and then sell off their chattels? There was no easy way to sort out traders from settlers. But that planter migration could have been considered, in a nineteenth-century context, an aspect of interstate commerce is exceedingly doubtful. Still, from a purely theoretical point of view, it is true that if Congress banned all movement of slaves across state lines, and if that ban was effectively enforced, then the slave economy would indeed be dealt a grievous blow. Slaveholders' profits in the upper South might decline so much that moderate antislavery sentiment there might revive, especially in Virginia, where plans for gradual abolition had been considered by the state legislature as late as 1832. Slavery would survive, even prosper, in the lower South, but economic growth there certainly would be curtailed by the labor constraint arising from the shutting off of slave imports.[16]

In the first years of their propaganda campaign, the abolitionists naively believed that they could convince white southerners to see the error of their ways and turn from the sin of slaveholding. Consequently, the abolitionists directed much of their effort at the South, mailing their antislavery tracts in large quantities to influential southerners such as officeholders, editors, and clergymen. The southerners reacted in fury. In Charleston on 29 July 1835, a mob broke into the post office, seized all of the abolitionist literature that could be found, and burned it along with effigies of William Garrison and Arthur Tappan. In December, President Andrew Jackson urged Congress to enact a federal law banning such incendiary literature from the mails. John C. Calhoun wrote the report of a Senate committee charged with responding to Jackson's call. Calhoun's report rejected Jackson's proposed federal law as a violation of the First Amendment guarantee of freedom of the press, but strongly upheld the right of states to take whatever measures they believed necessary to protect their "internal peace and security," including "the unquestionable right to pass all such laws as may be necessary to maintain the existing relation between master and slaves." The report declared, furthermore, that the federal government must fully cooperate with all such measures taken by the states. In making the latter point, the report said specifically that the federal government must so cooperate when exercising "the powers of Congress over the mail, and of regulating commerce with foreign nations and between the States." Calhoun's mention of the commerce power was gratuitous, as his preceding discussion focused entirely on freedom of the press and the responsibility of the government to deliver the mail. Calhoun evidently had been rattled by the abolitionist calls for a ban on the interstate slave trade. He was now trying, rather awkwardly, to put Congress on record as holding that the federal authority over interstate commerce could be used only to help states preserve their peace and security—or, in other words, only to protect the domestic slave trade and never to interfere with it. The Senate did not endorse Calhoun's report, but his idea that the federal government could only enhance and not harm the slave trade was rapidly becoming axiomatic to white southerners.[17]

Between 1837 and 1839, abolitionist political activity assumed massive proportions. Local antislavery societies began querying candidates for public office, often asking them to commit themselves to the position that Congress had both the right and the duty to interdict the interstate slave trade. Some politicians who responded favorably to such requests, perhaps without giving them a great deal of thought, would be much embarrassed later on in their careers when publicity was given to the fact that they had once gone on record as endorsing a ban on the slave trade. Millard Fillmore of New York fell into that trap. When Fillmore ran for the vice presidency in 1848, he denied the accusation of the *Richmond Enquirer* "that I hold it to be within the power of Congress to interfere with, or break off, the transportation, removal, or disposal of persons held as slaves, from one slaveholding State to another." Abolitionists then publicized the fact that ten years earlier Fillmore had replied in the affirmative to an abolitionist query, "Are you in favor of Congress exercising all the constitutional power it possesses to abolish the internal slave trade between the States?" Although saying yes, Fillmore had added that he was "much engaged" and so would "leave, for some future occasion, a more extended discussion of the subject."[18]

Undeterred by the gag rule of 1836, in which the House of Representatives resolved that antislavery petitions should be tabled unread, abolitionists inundated Congress with a blizzard of such petitions, and again the slave trade issue frequently was included. Female abolitionists were particularly active in circulating petitions, for, as one group of abolitionist women explained, "It is our only means of direct political action. It is not ours to fill the offices of government, or to assist in the election of those who shall fill them. We do not enact or enforce the laws of the land. The only direct influence which we can exert upon our Legislatures, is by protests and petitions. Shall we not, then, be greatly delinquent if we neglect *these?*"[19]

The most famous of the female abolitionists were Angelina and Sarah

Grimké. Because they were the daughters of a prominent South Carolina plantation owner and jurist, their conversion to the radical antislavery cause in the mid-1830s thrilled abolitionists. In a letter published in April 1837, the Grimkés urged northerners to petition for "the entire breaking up of the inter-state slave trade." A month later, at a national convention of abolitionist women, Angelina moved and the convention adopted a resolution declaring "that it is the duty of every woman in the United States, whether northerner or southerner, annually to petition Congress with the faith of an Esther, and the untiring perseverance of the importunate widow, for the immediate abolition of slavery in the District of Columbia and the Territory of Florida, and the extermination of the inter-state slave trade." On behalf of the convention, she and Mary S. Parker later sent out a circular imploring antislavery women to carry out their duty:

> Sisters, will you not use the power which God has intrusted to your hands for good? Will not each one of you throw a faggot on the flame destined to melt the chains of the slave.
>
> Many say they would gladly sign our petitions if their fathers, husbands, and brothers were willing. Our beloved friend Ann G. Chapman, while she was visibly with us used to say she believed this objection came most frequently from women, who could be very obstinate concerning a gay party, a projected journey, or a new service of china; but when great principles were at stake, they very promptly sacrificed them to earn the reputation of meek and submissive wives. . . .
>
> We would exhort you not to be easily discouraged in the task of obtaining signatures. . . .
>
> Do not take it for granted, that any woman will refuse to sign a petition because she has hitherto opposed us. Visit every house, ask every individual. Annually renew your appeals. Make them uncomfortable in their sinful negligence, by giving them repeated opportunities to decline their duty. . . .
>
> We cannot leave this subject without again urging that petitions to Congress constitute the one central point, to which we must bend our strongest efforts.

At about this same time, the national office of the AA-SS sent a circular containing petition forms to "every town in the free states where an Abolitionist can be found who will circulate them." The petitions asked Congress, along with other antislavery actions, "so to regulate commerce among the several States, as that the traffic in slaves may be immediately prohibited."[20]

James G. Birney, a former Alabama plantation owner who, like the Grimké sisters, had seen the light and become an abolitionist, reported that between January 1837 and March 1838, the U.S. House of Representatives received petitions signed by 23,405 men and women praying for a ban on the interstate slave trade. That figure exceeded the number of petitioners against admitting new slave states (22,161) and for abolishing slavery in the territories (21,212) but was dwarfed by the 130,248 signers of petitions for abolishing slavery in the District of Columbia. During the third session of the Twenty-fifth Congress, December 1838 through March 1839, the House received another great wave of petitions, and this time the number of signers against slavery in the District of Columbia fell to 80,755 while the number against the interstate slave trade rose to 54,547.[21]

The great petition campaign was accompanied by extensive agitation on the part of those abolitionists already on record as advocating a congressional ban on the interstate slave trade. In an article, William Jay rectified his original omission of that issue from his *Inquiry.* He now defended the constitutionality of a ban on the interstate trade by citing the opinions expressed by his own father as well as by Daniel Webster in 1819. Then, in a new book entitled *A View of the Action of the Federal Government, in Behalf of Slavery,* Jay elaborated upon his views, saying that since under the federal law of 1807 the coastwise transport of slaves in vessels of less than forty tons had been prohibited, "It would not be easy to show that the Constitution forbids its prohibition in vessels over forty tons burthen. We may therefore take it for granted that the . . . coasting trade will be legally abolished. Should the land traffic not be also destroyed, it would not be for want of disposition, or constitutional power in Congress, but on account of the extreme difficulty which would exist in preventing evasions of the law." In a speech to the sixth anniversary meeting of the AA-SS, Henry Stanton argued that the free states possessed the political power to extinguish slavery in America if only they would support antislavery measures, including a ban on the interstate trade. Stanton said that "through the influence of the internal slave trade, slavery is made profitable. . . . If there were no great sluice-way to let off the superabundance of slavery its turbid waters would overthrow, and slavery would be drowned in the northern slave states." Slavery would die in the lower South also, because "the ranks of humanity are thinned there, by working to death the slaves, to such an extent as would depopulate the globe in two centuries." Stanton concluded that "the internal slave trade is the great jugular vein of slavery; and if Congress will take the same weapon with which they cut off the foreign trade, and cut this vein, slavery would die of starvation in the southern, and of apoplexy in the northern slave states." In successfully urging Pennsylvania abolitionists to embrace the banning of the interstate trade as an objective, Alvan Stewart told them that if Congress were to exercise that power, then "slavery would die of its own superincumbent weight in 10 years." In

Figure 5. Abolitionist propaganda. This print was taken from a copper plate found amid the ruins of a hall that was set on fire by an anti-abolitionist mob at Philadelphia in 1838. Although dated 1830, the plate more likely was created closer to the year of the fire. It depicts two traders readying a group of slaves for shipment coastwise. At the left a rowboat ferries slaves to a sailing ship anchored beyond. On the right a woman and her children stand chained together. Behind them, a slave is being flogged while others toil in the fields. In the distance, the national flag flies over the U.S. Capitol. Courtesy Library of Congress, Prints and Photographs Division, LC-USZ62-89701.

persuading the Vermont legislature to call for congressional action, Stewart called the abolition of the interstate trade "the great door to the slave Bastile"; without the interstate market, "the slaves of Maryland and Virginia would eat up their masters, and the masters must emancipate in self-defence, to save themselves from destruction," while in Alabama, Louisiana, and Mississippi, "there is such havoc annually by death among the slaves of the great planters, by the unhealthiness of the climate and the cruelty of overseers, that in less than seven years, if no slave could be imported, into those southern regions, one half of the plantations would lie uncultivated for want of slaves."[22]

Meanwhile, new voices joined the chorus of calls for action against the movement of slaves across state lines. Samuel J. May asserted that in its commerce clause the Constitution had placed in the hands of Congress "a mighty power" to break up "effectually, entirely, in all its parts, the accursed system of merchandise in men"; so great was the power of abolitionists to combat slavery politically that the slaveowners "may vapor, and vaunt, and threaten and rave. But all this will be of no avail. . . . They may secede from the Union, but this will give them no relief. They will be just as near to God, just as near to truth, just as near to the abolitionists." Elizur Wright, Jr., described the export of slaves from Virginia and asked, "Is it not time for freemen to say through their representatives in Congress, we will no longer bear the responsibility of this crime? . . . If . . . the federal government cannot touch the principle of forced labor, let it lay its whole power upon the principle of raising laborers for sale." James G. Birney said that it was the failure of Congress to exercise its powers against slavery, including its power to prohibit the interstate trade, that had at length made slavery "so audacious, as openly to challenge the principles of 1776 . . . to menace the integrity of the union and the very existence of the government itself." Myron Holley, an upstate New Yorker, declared that the invention of the cotton gin and the acquisition of Louisiana accounted for the fact that Congress had not carried out its duty to destroy the interstate slave trade after 1 January 1808; the suppression of that trade, he added, "is not intrinsically of difficult accomplishment. It requires nothing but common sense, in Congress, to provide perspicuous prohibitory enactments, and common honesty, in our judiciary and executive authorities, to enforce them." Quaker meetings condemned the slave trade and called for congressional action. And yet another anonymous pamphleteer upheld at length the "high, yet simple, duty of Congress, *as the authorised regulator of commerce,* to extinguish, without delay, this nefarious traffic." The latter author described in colorful language the allure of the interstate market to:

> the slaveholder of Virginia, who, seated in his old and gentleman-like mansion, surveys the wide demèsnes, which . . . long since exhausted by slave labor, present to his eye a brown and dreary aspect, except where they have become overgrown by a miserable forest of pines. His black people have multiplied around him, and he scarcely knows how to feed them. . . . The slave jobber is prowling about the neighborhood, with his tempting offers of five hundred dollars for a lad or girl, or one thousand dollars for an adult person. The temptation soon becomes irresistible, and slave after slave supplies the southern market.[23]

The most spectacular abolitionist tract of the 1830s appeared in the final year of the decade. *American Slavery As It Is: Testimony of a Thousand Witnesses* was a substantial book crammed into the format of a mere pamphlet. Printed in minuscule type and priced at thirty-seven and a half cents, it presented a stupefying array of evidence on the horrors of slavery. Although published anonymously, it was the work of Theodore Dwight Weld, his wife the former Angelina Grimké, and her sister Sarah. Weld had led the Lane rebels of 1833 and then with his gift for impassioned oratory had spread the gospel of immediate abolitionism throughout northeastern Ohio. After damaging his vocal cords to the point that he could no longer carry on with his lectures, he turned from the spoken to the written word. By sending out a form letter asking for eyewitness accounts of slavery, he gathered hundreds of testimonies, each carefully ascribed to a respectable person. Meanwhile, Angelina and Sarah combed through twenty thousand issues of southern newspapers, extracting damning evidence from both the editorial content and the advertisements. Thus the Welds and Sarah Grimké compiled and eventually published their propaganda masterpiece, a stupendous catalogue of slavery atrocities.[24]

American Slavery As It Is was a haphazardly organized mountain of evidence peppered with Theodore Weld's strident polemics. Topics were introduced and abruptly dropped only to reappear later on. Yet those weaknesses in presentation somehow added to the emotional impact of the work, as readers became immersed in a surreal nightmare, turning each page with trepidation over what might come next. Above all, the Welds emphasized the sheer physical brutality of the slavery regime, with evidence ranging from recurring descriptions of slaves suspended by their hands and flogged until their flesh was in ribbons and the ground below soaked with blood, to strange and unique barbarities, such as a slavemistress using a hammer and chisel to strike off a servant's toe. The Welds gave no special emphasis to the evils of the interstate slave trade—it would take the passing of another decade and the genius of Harriet Beecher Stowe before the potential of making the slave trade the central theme of a brilliant antislavery propaganda piece would be realized—but scattered through *American Slavery As It Is* was abundant evidence of the nature and extent of the trade, the casual brutality that permeated it, and the ocean of sorrows that it left in its wake.

In their introduction, the Welds appealed to readers to imagine how they would feel if they saw the wrists of their own spouses and children bound to coffle chains. Later on, a witness described how gangs of slaves were marched westward over the mountains from Maryland and Virginia to the Ohio River, then shipped to the deep South on flatboats, guarded by keepers armed with dirks and pistols. Another witness explained exactly how a coffle was formed:

> The "*coffle chain*" is a chain fastened at one end to the centre of the bar of a pair of hand cuffs, which are fastened to the right wrist of one, and the left wrist of another slave, they standing abreast, and the chain between them. These are the head of the coffle. The other end [of the chain] is passed through a ring in the bolt of the next handcuffs, and the slaves being manacled thus, two and two together, walk up, and the coffle chain is passed, and they go up towards the head of the coffle. Of course they are closer or wider apart in the

> coffle, according to the number to be coffled, and to the length of the chain. *I have seen* HUNDREDS *of droves and chain-coffles of this description,* and every coffle was a scene of misery and wo[e], of tears and brokenness of heart.

This witness had once seen a "drove" numbering 350 slaves, divided into five coffles of seventy slaves each. Obviously only the largest of traders operated on such a massive scale. Other witnesses described the far more numerous small-time speculators who moved lesser numbers. In Louisiana, a certain Methodist preacher was said to dabble in the business, buying a handful of Negroes at Natchez when he went there to preach, then bringing them to New Orleans for sale. Another small trader could not afford chains, so he simply tied his slaves' hands behind their backs as he drove them three or four hundred miles along the rutted roads from Virginia to Georgia. He said that he often bought a husband or a wife, leaving the spouse and children behind, "but then I made them amends by marrying them again as soon as I had a chance, that is to say, I made them call each other man and wife, and sleep together, which is quite enough for negroes."[25]

The Welds used newspaper clippings to show how the slave trade sundered family ties. An advertisement in a Charleston paper announced the sale of "one hundred and twenty *likely young negroes*" just arrived from Petersburg, Virginia, including "*small girls* suitable for nurses, and several SMALL BOYS WITHOUT THEIR MOTHERS." Dozens of advertisements described runaways as trying to return to the families from which they had been parted. A jailer in Madison County, Tennessee, announced that he had in custody "a negro woman, who calls her name Fanny, and says she belongs to William Miller, of Mobile. She formerly belonged to John Givens, of this county, who now owns *several of her children*." Theodore Weld appealed to the reader to imagine what it must have been like for Fanny to make her way from Alabama to Tennessee, "through the wilderness, hundreds of miles, to clasp once more her children to her heart," only to be seized when within a few miles of them, thrown into jail, and her capture advertised so that her owner could arrange for her to return, alone, to her bondage in the deep South.[26]

Witnesses told of mothers separated even from their babies. A preacher who had resided in Kentucky knew a young woman who had been present when two traders were about to leave Louisville with a group of slaves bound for the deep South. "Just before the steamboat put off for the lower country, two negro women were offered for sale, each of them having a young child at the breast. The traders bought them, took their babes from their arms, and offered them to the highest bidder; and they were sold for one dollar apiece, whilst the stricken parents were driven on board the boat, and in an hour were on their way to the New Orleans market." Even those women who were allowed to keep their infants could not be sure the babes would survive the arduous journey. The coffles were driven many miles every day and often slept without shelter at night. A young man from Virginia had once stayed at a tavern where, because of extremely muddy conditions, a drove of slaves was given the rare privilege of sleeping indoors, crammed together on the floor of a room. But first they were fed their dinner. A servant entered the room bearing on her head a tray containing a mix of potatoes and cornmeal, "*the dirtiest, blackest-looking mess I ever saw* . . . not as clean, in appearance, as that which was given to a *drove of hogs,* at the same place the night previous." Before the woman had time to remove the tray from her head, the famished slaves began seizing the food in handfuls and devouring it. At another tavern, this one on the national road in Maryland, another traveler had heard the screams of a woman being punished by a trader for crying over the loss of her child. The child had died along the road three days earlier. Its body had been "thrown into a hole or crevice in the mountain, and a few stones thrown over it."[27]

Unable to accept permanent separation from their loved ones, some victims of the slave trade took their own lives. A speculator was overheard telling how he had deceived a young mulatto woman into thinking he was taking her to her mother. When the young woman realized that he had in fact bought her and was taking her out of the state to be sold, she escaped in the night and drowned herself in a river. The speculator lamented that he had "lost a good five hundred dollars by this foolish trick." Another trader, who had repented and given up the business, told of a male slave in handcuffs who drowned after leaping from the deck of a riverboat. Other victims of the trade survived physically but were maimed psychologically by the ordeal of separation. A former southern clergyman recalled that his neighbor once sold a fourteen-year-old boy to a speculator. The boy's mother was so devastated by the loss of her son that she became hopelessly insane. "With tears rolling down her cheeks, and her frame shaking with agony, she would cry out, 'don't you hear him—they are whipping him now, and he is calling for me!'" With myriad examples like these, the Welds drove home their message that slavery and the slave trade bred unspeakable evil and suffering. *American Slavery As It Is* was by far the most successful and influential abolitionist publication of the 1830s. In its first year it sold 100,000 copies. Its vast store of evidence and anecdote would be drawn upon countless times by abolitionist speakers and writers during all of the remaining years of the antislavery crusade.[28]

By agitating antislavery issues, querying candidates, and circulating petitions, New England abolitionists achieved some political successes at the state level in the late 1830s. But because the abolitionist call for a ban on the interstate slave trade was the most radical of their political proposals, it met with more resistance than the other demands. The Vermont legislature in 1836 adopted a resolution calling upon Congress to ban slavery in the District of Columbia, and in 1837 passed a whole raft of antislavery resolutions, turning down only the one declaring that Congress has the power to ban the interstate slave trade. At last, in October 1838, the legislature adopted joint resolutions instructing the state's senators and representatives in Congress to use their utmost efforts to secure, among other things, the abolition of the slave trade between the several states and territories. In the meantime, the Massachusetts legislature adopted a similar set of resolves, including statements that "Congress has, by the Constitution, power to abolish the traffic in slaves, between different States of the Union," and that "the exercise of this power is demanded by the principles of humanity and justice." A joint special committee of the General Court had examined the question and had concluded that the power to ban the interstate slave trade:

> is, perhaps, the most important power which is attributed to Congress, over the subject of slavery, and yet it has not often been discussed. Some of your committee had doubts upon this subject, at the commencement of their investigations, but the result of their individual study, and interchange of opinions, has been to remove those doubts, and they are unitedly of opinion, that Congress does possess the power to regulate or entirely prohibit, at its discretion, the trade in slaves, as in any other article which is made the subject of commerce, between the different states.

At about the same time, the successful candidate for the governorship of Rhode Island responded to an abolitionist query by agreeing that Congress could and should abolish the slave trade between the states.[29]

In the United States Congress, however, abolitionist proposals got nowhere. On the floor of the House of Representatives, only John Quincy Adams was willing to say that he would vote for a ban on the interstate slave trade. In the Senate, Daniel Webster would make no such commitment. He did say that as to "the power to regulate the transfer of slaves from one State to another, there was no doubt in his mind but that Congress also possessed this power," but he added that "he would refrain from expressing any opinion as to the expediency of the exercise of the above powers; he only wished to be understood as claiming that Congress possessed them." In a line of argument that could not have pleased abolitionists, Webster then "referred to the act of Congress on the subject of slaves escaping from one State to another" to show that Congress had already exercised its power to control the interstate movement of slaves. Only one maverick Senator was willing to go further than Webster.

Thomas Morris, a Democrat from Ohio, introduced a series of antislavery resolutions. The Senate refused to print them, but they apparently included one calling for the abolition of the interstate slave trade, for John Calhoun declared that they "displayed the absolute *creed* of the Abolitionists fully developed." For his pains, Morris was denied renomination by his party when his term drew to a close.[30]

Beginning in 1836, antislavery petitions to the House of Representatives were tabled unread under the gag rule, and in 1838 the Atherton resolutions (introduced by Charles Gordon Atherton, a doughface Democrat from New Hampshire) not only continued the gag but also declared explicitly that "Congress has no jurisdiction whatever over the institution of slavery in the several States," that "Congress has no right to do that indirectly which it cannot do directly," and that therefore "all attempts on the part of Congress to abolish slavery in the District of Columbia, or the Territories or to prohibit the removal of slaves from State to State . . . are in violation of the Constitution, destructive of the fundamental principle on which the Union of these states rests, and beyond the jurisdiction of Congress."[31]

In a major Senate speech in 1839, Henry Clay declared that Congress could not prohibit the interstate slave trade, on the grounds that the power to regulate commerce does not include the power to annihilate any particular branch of that commerce. Although hailed by a racist pamphleteer as the funeral sermon for abolitionism, Clay's argument was neither novel nor troubling to his opponents. Gerrit Smith and other antislavery writers soon pointed out that inasmuch as Congress had abolished the external slave trade in 1808 under its authority to regulate foreign commerce, an analogous power to abolish the internal slave trade must be implicit in the congressional authority to regulate interstate commerce. Clay himself seems to have lacked confidence in his own argument, for he had earlier confided in a private letter his fear that the abolitionists might gain sufficient political clout to carry out their plans:

> The danger is that the contagion [of abolitionism] may spread until it reaches all the free States; and it it ever comes to be acted on as a rule among them, to proscribe slaveholders [from elective office], they have the numbers to enforce it. Union and concert with them will throw the whole Government into their hands, and when they have once possession, the principle by which they have acquired it will urge them on to other and further encroachments. They will begin by prohibiting the slave trade, as it is called, among the slave States, and by abolishing it in the District of Columbia and the end will be ——[32]

Congressional intransigence in the face of abolitionist demands contributed to the breakup of the unified abolitionist movement in the late 1830s. To

William Lloyd Garrison and his following, the hostile response of the national government reinforced a growing disenchantment with participation in the political process, while to some of Garrison's opponents the same experience taught a different lesson: not that abolitionists should abandon politics but rather that they should cease trying to work through the existing political parties and instead should launch an abolitionist third party in a renewed struggle to achieve their political aims. Alvan Stewart typified the latter reaction when he declared to Myron Holley that to induce the slaveholders to free their slaves "is a task beyond the highest conquest of moral suasion." The liberation of the slaves therefore must be brought about by political action, Stewart believed, but "to petition congress to abolish slavery in the Dis. Col. or the internal slave trade, in its [i.e., Congress's] present shape, is a waste of labor." Some abolitionists spurned both the Garrisonian drift toward anarchism and the anti-Garrisonian focus on partisan politics. William Jay, for example, condemned the "no-government" stand of the Garrisonians but also opposed the launching of a political party. Jay regarded the latter as an ill-advised attempt "to change the antislavery enterprise from a religious into a political one," adding sardonically that "a scramble for the loaves & fishes has already commenced."[33]

Soon Alvan Stewart went public with his advocacy of a new approach to politics. "An independent abolition political party is the only hope, for the redemption of the slave!!" he proclaimed, justifying that assertion with a review of past abolitionist efforts:

> What have we done?
>
> In the first place, we have spent more money and time, delivered more addresses; printed, published, sold and distributed more publications, in this country, and held more state, district, city, town, county, and village meetings . . . than on any other topic of public interest ever put forth in this country.
>
> Secondly, we have presented more petitions to Congress, asking that body to exercise its admitted power, for the abolition of slavery in the District of Columbia and for the suppression of the slave trade between the States, than have ever been presented on all other subjects, since the foundation of the Government. So far from Congress regarding our prayers for the emancipation of the slave, we have been eminently in jeopardy of losing our own liberty; and the great right of petition has been solemnly put *to death,* by an American Congress. . . .
>
> . . . We have heretofore acted with those abolition brethren who say we ought to . . . rely on the old parties, to give us men to extirpate it wherever slavery remains in the free States, and members of Congress to abolish slavery where the power of Congress extends.
>
> Is not this hope a wretched failure?[34]

In 1839 and 1840 Stewart worked with James G. Birney, William Goodell (a New York journalist, editor of the *Friend of Man*), Myron Holley, Joshua Leavitt, Gerrit Smith, Henry B. Stanton, and Elizur Wright, Jr., to organize the Liberty Party. Each one of these founders of the Liberty Party already was or soon would be on record as an advocate of congressional abolition of the interstate slave trade.[35]

As early as November 1837, Elizur Wright, Jr., had objected to Garrison's "no-government" theory largely because it seemed to Wright inconsistent with the AA-SS call for political action against the interstate slave trade. "It does appear to me," wrote Wright to Garrison,

> that *your* "truth" that human government has no rightful authority, does conflict with *our truths,* as expressed in our Declaration of Sentiments as well as with the most important measures by which we seek to accomplish our object. In the Declaration we maintain that "the slaves ought instantly to be set free and brought under the *protection of law,*" and that "Congress has the *right* and is solemnly bound to suppress the domestic slave trade" &c. What miserable falsehood if human government has no *right* to exist![36]

Between December 1838 and January 1839, Massachusetts abolitionists split into two hostile camps, and the anti-Garrisonian group established a new abolitionist newspaper edited by Wright. The lead editorial of the first issue of that paper made it clear that the anti-Garrisonians were dedicated to political action because of their conviction that "Slavery in the District and Territories, and the slave trade between the States, must be abolished." The editorial went on to assert:

> that the people of this Pilgrim Commonwealth have it in their power to make the soil of the Federal republic as free as their own. If they cannot do it *directly,* they can do it *indirectly;* for, they have not yet imbibed the absurd doctrine of the Atherton school, that what cannot be done *directly* may not be done at all. Let them employ "moral and political action," without stint or measure, "as prescribed in the Constitution of the United States," and the glorious consummation is at hand.[37]

Abolitionist advocates of a ban on the interstate slave trade believed, and were fundamentally correct in believing, that such a ban would wreak havoc on the southern economic system. Deprived of the capital gains arising from their sale of surplus slaves, the slaveowners of the upper South would see their profits plummet. Deprived of the influx of slaves from the older slave states, the slaveowners of the lower South would be hard-pressed to meet the labor demands of an expanding staple-crop economy. While the idea of using the federal commerce power to prohibit the interstate slave trade originated prior to the emergence of immediate abolitionism, the demand for such action came into full flower after its incorporation into the AA-SS Constitution and Declaration of Sentiments in 1833. Publicized and promoted by Henry B. Stanton, David Lee Child, Alvan Stewart, William Jay, the Grimké sisters, Theodore Weld, and many other abolitionists, congressional interdiction of the slave trade became a major objective of abolitionist petitioning, querying of candidates, and general agitation. Although those efforts resulted in resolves by the legislatures of Vermont and Massachusetts for congressional action, those calls were spurned by the federal government. Stung by their failure to influence federal politics, some abolitionists rejected further political involvement, while others redoubled their efforts and launched an independent political party dedicated to attacking slavery by all constitutional means, including the destruction of the slave trade. Although their views were to diverge later on, the founders of the Liberty Party agreed at the outset that Congress could and should abolish the interstate traffic in slaves. In agitating for a ban on the interstate slave trade, the abolitionists of the 1830s raised a specter that was to haunt southern slaveowners down to the outbreak of the Civil War. As long as the southern states remained within the Union, the threat to the domestic slave trade would not go away. It remained the potential avenue for a devastating attack upon slavery within the confines of the American constitutional framework. It was the door to the slave Bastille.

6

Little Will Remain to Be Done Except to Sing Te Deum

By 1840 the stage was set for a vigorous political assault upon the interstate slave trade. For a time such an assault occurred. But then everything changed. Instead of increasing in importance, the slave trade issue received less and less attention from antislavery politicians, as the Liberty men of 1840 and 1844 gave way to the Free-Soilers of 1848 and 1852, and then to the Republicans of 1856 and 1860. What is the explanation for this curious waning of an issue that had seemed to offer the avenue for a devastating blow against slavery within the confines of the American constitutional framework? To answer that question, this chapter first describes the relatively prominent role that the slave trade question did play in antislavery politics between 1840 and 1848. Then it probes for reasons why that role diminished rather than expanded later on. Finally, it argues that the threat to the interstate slave trade, feeble as it was by the late 1850s, was nevertheless an important influence in making white southerners deeply fearful of the emergent political party that would soon sweep to victory under the leadership of Abraham Lincoln.

The founding convention of the Liberty Party met at Albany, New York, in April 1840, and nominated James G. Birney, the former slaveowner turned abolitionist, as its candidate for the presidency. The new party did not prepare a formal platform, but the delegates to the convention were agreed that the termination of the interstate slave trade should be one of their objectives. Eight weeks later a convention of the Liberty men of Massachusetts authorized an address that castigated the established parties for neglecting "the great duties, which devolve on the national government," including that of abolishing "the slave trade between the states." Meanwhile, delegates from the American Anti-Slavery Society attended a transatlantic gathering of abolitionists in London, England, where they submitted an elaborate compendium of information on American slave trading that had been compiled by Theodore Weld at the request of the British and Foreign Anti-Slavery Society. The London convention adopted a resolution viewing "with deep regret and sorrow" the existence of the American internal slave trade and declaring that "effectual means ought to be forthwith taken in the United States of America, to remove this stain from the character of that nation." As the 1840 presidential campaign went forward, Harriet Martineau wrote hopefully, if inaccurately, that "the usual federal and democratic questions are in many cases laid aside at the present elections for the all-important one of the abolition of slavery in the District of Columbia, and the prohibition of the inter-state slave-trade."[1]

In subsequent years the banning of the interstate trade was called for in resolutions or addresses issuing from various Liberty groups, including the national convention at New York in May 1841, the Pennsylvania state convention at Philadelphia in February 1844, the southern and western convention at Cincinnati in June 1845, the northwestern convention at Chicago in June 1846, and the Massachusetts state committee in August 1846. Meanwhile, the *Liberty Almanac,* an annual propaganda piece, often included material publicizing the party's intention of using the federal commerce power to end the slave trade. The 1846 *Almanac,* for example, declared that "Slavery in the District of Columbia, and the slave trade between the States, exist by the authority of Congress, and for their continuation the Nation is responsible. . . . With a Liberty Congress and Executive, we would abolish slavery in the District, and the inter-state slave trade. . . . Slave-breeding would cease, for slaves would no longer find a market; slavery itself would become unprofitable, and would speedily die of apoplexy in one portion of the South, and of consumption in the other."[2]

One Liberty man, Samuel Webb, probably expressed the hopes of many when he said that if the party could elect twenty-five of its members to Congress, it would hold the balance of power and thus could compel the major parties to "make concessions in favor of liberty—such as, regulating the trade between the States, so as to put a stop to the internal, or as it may be properly be [*sic*] called, the infernal slave trade—abolishing slavery in the District of Columbia or in some one or more of the territories of the United States, &c." Leading figures in the party readily acknowledged their intent to destroy the slave trade. Joshua Leavitt, Alvan Stewart, and James G. Birney all said as much in public statements. Writing to Henry B. Stanton and Elizur Wright, Jr., in 1845, Salmon P. Chase said that there were differences of opinion among Liberty men as to what national legislation against slavery was possible under the U.S. Constitution. "All, however, agree, that the inter-state slave trade can be prohibited," Chase observed, "and so long as we agree upon this, differences of opinion as to other points are harmless; for, let us once reach this point, and we shall find our work so nearly accomplished, that little will remain to be done, except to sing *Te Deum*." Despite what Chase said, it would be wrong to assert that the abolition of the interstate slave trade was the preeminent political objective of the Liberty men. When they spoke of ending the domestic slave trade, they usually spoke also of banishing slavery from the District of Columbia, the territories, and all federal property. Sometimes they added other measures, such as excluding slaveholders from public office, repealing the federal Fugitive Slave Law of 1793, or even amending the Constitution so as to end the partial counting of slaves in determining state representation in Congress. But the prospect of crushing the interstate slave trade was arguably the most potent weapon in the Liberty men's political arsenal, and friend and foe alike can have had little doubt that they intended to use it if they could.[3]

In the 1840s interest in attacking the slave trade was not confined to the Liberty Party. In 1846 a faction within the Whig Party of Massachusetts also adopted that aim. The antislavery Whigs included Charles Francis Adams, John Gorham Palfrey, Stephen C. Phillips, Charles Sumner, and Henry Wilson. Palfrey advocated abolition of the interstate slave traffic in a newspaper essay that was soon republished in his collection entitled *Papers on the Slave Power*. That work went through three editions and, according to Samuel May, "attracted much attention." May added that in a dinner conversation, Palfrey "expressed very strongly his conviction that they who lived 20 years longer would see the complete overthrow of Slavery in this land." At the September 1846 Massachusetts Whig state convention, Sumner asserted that the constitutional power of Congress to "abolish the slave-trade between the States" could no longer be questioned by "any competent authority," and Phillips submitted a series of resolutions, one of which asserted Whig support for "prohibiting the Slave Trade between the States." When the convention rejected Phillips's resolutions but adopted a platform that pledged to promote all constitutional measures for overthrowing slavery, the reformers were not mollified. Adams explained that the adopted platform was but a "hard dish of Tariff, garnished with as much anti-slavery as may give a popular relish to the dry and tasteless meat," whereas Phillips's defeated proposals had constituted "a strong and juicy joint." There were also some Democrats here and there who supported the banning of the interstate traffic in slaves. In 1846 a coalition of antislavery Democrats, Whigs, and Liberty men forced through the New Hampshire legislature a resolution calling upon the state's congressmen to press for antislavery measures that included suppression of the domestic slave trade. A similar coalition probably accounts for the passage by the Vermont legislature in both 1842 and 1849 of resolutions upholding the right of Congress to abolish the trade.[4]

While the slave trade issue was a prominent facet of antislavery politics throughout most of the 1840s, a change took place as politicians began girding themselves for the election of 1848. In October 1847 the Liberty party reached outside its own narrow ranks to nominate for the presidency John P. Hale, a Senator from New Hampshire who possessed good antislavery credentials but who did not believe that Congress had the constitutional power to suppress the interstate slave trade. Moreover, the Liberty Party and Hale soon yielded the limelight to the newly founded Free-Soil Party and its presidential candidate Martin Van Buren, a suspiciously late and opportunistic recruit to the antislavery cause who had absolutely no intention of interfering with slave trafficking. Van Buren and his "Bucktail" faction of the Democratic Party of New York State had been closely allied with the South until 1844, when they decided to change course because their constituents were becoming increasingly hostile to such doughface behavior. The gag rule in the U.S. House of Representatives came to an end in December 1844 when the Bucktails withdrew their support for it. Meanwhile, the southern Democrats, led by Robert Walker of Mississippi, had blocked Van Buren's nomination for the presidency. When Van Buren and his followers were further rebuffed at the 1848 national Democratic convention, they walked out and began organizing the Free-Soil movement.[5]

Only a radical minority within the Free-Soil Party was interested in combatting the slave trade. It is true that some Liberty men, including Henry Stanton and Lewis Tappan, refused to support the new party because it failed to endorse the full Liberty program, including the banning of the slave trade. It is also true that the Free-Soil platform called upon the federal government to relieve itself of any responsibility for slavery, which made it possible for both friends and enemies of the new party to claim, if they wanted to, that it was pursuing the old Liberty party goals.

A few weeks prior to the founding convention of the Free-Soil Party, Illinois abolitionist Owen Lovejoy declared that "an interdict should be placed forthwith on the inter-state and coastwise traffic in human beings." He asked rhetorically, "Does, for instance, Virginia law operate upon the broad Atlantic?

Clearly not. Why should it any more than that of New York? By what law, then, human or Divine, are those human beings held as chattels, while the bark in which they find themselves goes bounding onward upon the billows of God's mighty ocean?" After the convention, Lovejoy claimed that the speeches there "were essentially such as we have long been accustomed to hear in Liberty gatherings," and that the new party "is to all intents a movement against slavery, and must inevitably be a progressive one, and will not stop until slavery becomes extinct." In Massachusetts a few weeks later, Henry Wilson advocated as Free-Soil objectives virtually all of the old Liberty aims, including forbidding the interstate slave trade. Wilson declared that those measures would "discourage, localize, and destroy slavery." Meanwhile, a Pennsylvania politician wrote a series of public letters attacking the Free-Soilers and urged his readers to instruct their congressmen to vote for a resolution declaring that "to prohibit the sale of negro slaves by the citizens of one State to the citizens of another State" would be "against the *spirit* of the Federal compact." But such statements were largely the result of either wishful thinking or excessive apprehension. Clearly most people who gathered behind the Free-Soil banner were content to let the slave trade issue slide.[6]

Seeking the abolition of the interstate slave trade faded as an antislavery objective in part because abolitionists ceased to agree unanimously that it was a good idea. After 1840 only some abolitionists, and probably not the majority, continued to cling to the view that the federal commerce power could and should be used as an avenue for attacking slavery. Once William Lloyd Garrison repudiated all coercion and all participation in corrupt government, he and his coterie—including Wendell Phillips, Henry C. Wright, Edmund Quincy, and Samuel May—began to deny that any political action against slavery was possible within the American constitutional framework. The Constitution, the Garrisonians now insisted, was the result of a "guilty compromise" between the free and the slaveholding states. Consequently, "*It means precisely what those who framed and adopted it meant*—NOTHING MORE, NOTHING LESS, *as a matter of bargain and compromise.* Even if it can be construed to mean something else, without violence to its language, such construction is not to be tolerated *against the wishes of either party.*" Because construing the commerce clause so as to permit the banning of the interstate slave trade most certainly was contrary to the wishes of the South, it was not constitutionally permissible. Henry Wright even asserted that the clause in the Constitution that had allowed Congress to prohibit the further importation of slaves into the United States from abroad beginning in 1808 had been intended not to undermine slavery but to increase the value of the slaves already present in the South. Because of that increase in value, according to Wright, the 1808 clause "gave tenfold vigour to the horrible business of breeding slaves" in the upper South in order to supply the markets of "the more southern and western Slave States." Wright added that in his opinion, "If traffic in Slaves between Virginia and Africa be piracy, so is it between Washington and New Orleans," but he gave no hint that anything could be done to halt the domestic slave trade without repudiating the Constitution. Wright's overall argument clearly implied that the Constitution had been intended to foster the interstate slave trade rather than to threaten it.[7]

To the charge that the Garrisonian withdrawal from politics gave aid and comfort to the proslavery forces, Wendell Phillips replied that "honesty & truth are more important than even freeing slaves." To the charge that the Garrisonians were deviating from the course that the abolitionists had embarked upon in 1833, Edmund Quincy replied that the Garrisonians "still hold that it is the duty of the Free States to remove slavery by moral and political action. Only, they have attained, after long and bitter experience, to the conviction that it is a moral and political impossibility to remove it by political action. . . . Their present position they hold to be a perfect satisfaction of the intention, expressed or implied in 1833, of the duty of using 'political action' for the removal of slavery, as read in the light of the present day." Quincy thus tried to wriggle around the hard fact that the Garrisonians had indeed deviated from the 1833 AA-SS Declaration of Sentiments, of which Garrison himself had been the principal author. Echoing Phillips, Quincy added, "We do not refuse to hold office, or vote, under the United States Constitution, as abolitionists, but as honest men. It is not the emancipation of the slaves, primarily, that we contemplate in this course, but the preservation of our personal honor, of our individual integrity. We acknowledge that our *second* duty is to the slave; our *first* is to our own souls." Back in 1837 Samuel May had declared that the commerce clause provided Congress with "a mighty power" to break up "effectually, entirely, in all its parts, the accursed system of merchandise in men." But by 1845 May sang a different tune. Now he declared that Congress could impose no law interfering with slavery, because "the opposition of the people . . . continuing what it now is — how easily might they, in various ways, evade the Act." Only moral suasion could be effective against slavery, he now said. "Abolitionists, all of them, used to believe this, and act as if they so believed," insisted May, "and our early conquests were effected by the power of truth and not by partisan votes."[8]

To the dwindling band of political abolitionists still pressing for a ban on the slave trade, a problem even more vexing than the opposition of the Garrisonians was the defection of some of their own compatriots. As time went on, a minority of political abolitionists gravitated toward the extreme position exemplified by Lysander Spooner, who interpreted the Constitution as a totally antislavery document. (It was, however, only the basic idea of regarding the Constitution as an antislavery document and not the details of Spooner's interpretation that gained a wide following. Many of his arguments were bizarre. He claimed that because the commerce power belonged to the federal government, the states could not forbid slaves to engage in commerce. He denied that the 1808 clause had anything whatever to do with slaves.) Those abolitionists who came to believe that the federal government had the power to abolish slavery outright were usually no longer much interested in anything so paltry as the mere annihilation of the interstate slave trade. In 1844 William Goodell challenged the Garrisonian interpretation of the Constitution as a proslavery document by vigorously upholding the power of Congress to abolish the interstate trade, but by 1847 Goodell had embraced the extremist position and was of the opinion that any "Liberty party, or other political association against slavery" that hesitated to "raise the full broad flag of an anti-slavery constitution" would "find itself vastly behind the times." Goodell's close associate Gerrit Smith followed a similar course. In 1845 Smith had said, "There is no need whatever, that we claim more than the Constitution clearly yields us," but in 1848 he declared that he was not among those "who believe that the Federal Government has no higher power over slavery than to abolish it in the District of Columbia, and to abolish the inter-State traffic in human beings. On the contrary, I claim that this Government has power, under the Constitution to abolish every part of American Slavery."[9]

The Liberty Party tried to accommodate both moderates and extremists by keeping its 1844 national platform vague—hence the absence in the platform of an explicit call for the abolition of the interstate slave trade—but the incompatibility of the two constitutional views made an eventual schism almost inevitable. As early as 1845 a convention at Boston attended by more than a thousand political abolitionists resolved that the U.S. Constitution did not sanction slavery, and in 1848 those radicals who could not stomach the nomination of John P. Hale as the Liberty candidate for the presidency held their own rump convention, nominated Gerrit Smith, and resolved that the federal government had the constitutional power "to abolish every part of American slavery; and is supremely guilty for refusing to exercise it." For good measure, the radicals added that even if slavery were lawful and protected by the Constitution, then the government should override the Constitution and abolish it anyway. The extremists continued on their separate path in the 1850s and, in their zeal to discover constitutional justification for the outright abolition of slavery, largely ignored the possibility of using the commerce power to end the slave trade. Thus from opposite ends of the abolitionist spectrum, the Garrisonians and the constitutional extremists both undermined the efforts of those abolitionists who continued to labor for a congressional ban on the slave traffic.[10]

Another and even more important reason for the decline of the slave trade issue in antislavery circles was the urgency of the territorial question that arose at the end of the Mexican War. In the Treaty of Guadalupe Hidalgo, concluded on 2 February 1848, Mexico ceded to the United States a vast new region to the west. Opponents and defenders of slavery now joined battle over whether slavery should be allowed to expand into the new lands. Each side saw the other as conspiring to dominate the national government by creating new states that would tip the balance of power in its favor. Paradoxically, even though the antislavery forces concentrated their attention on the great struggle for the territories and therefore agitated the slave trade issue less and less, the proslavery forces grew to fear it more and more. Many southerners were convinced that if the North won the battle for the new territories, it would be only a matter of time until it would use its increased clout within the national government to begin implementing antislavery measures, including the abolition of the slave trade.

In November 1849 the Vermont legislature adopted resolutions condemning slavery as "a crime against humanity" and declaring that Congress might rightfully use its constitutional authority over the federal territories and over interstate commerce in order both to halt the expansion of slavery and to "abolish slavery and the slave trade wherever either exists under the jurisdiction of Congress." The resolutions directed Vermont's congressional delegation to resist slavery expansion and to support all prudent measures for both the exclusion of slavery from the District of Columbia and "the entire suppression of slavery on the high seas, and wherever else Congress has jurisdiction" so as to "relieve the Federal Government from all responsibility for the existence, maintenance, or tolerance of slavery, or the traffic in slaves." The Vermont resolutions were a last gasp of the vigorous agitation of the slave trade issue that had prevailed in antislavery circles before it was eclipsed by the territorial question. The resolutions were also rather cautious, touching the slave trade issue gingerly. Although the resolutions did implicitly call upon Congress to suppress the interstate slave trade *if* Congress possessed the constitutional power to do so, they left open the question of whether the national legislature actually had that power.[11]

Despite their relatively tepid approach to the slave trade question, the Vermont resolutions drew a fiery response from Jeremiah Clemens, a recently elected Senator from Alabama who had come to Washington firmly pledged to defend southern rights. In a major speech delivered on 10 January 1850,

Clemens declared that the Vermont resolves were proof that northerners, despite their frequent protestations to the contrary, did intend to interfere with slavery in the slave states. Northerners deluded themselves, however, in thinking that slavery could be ended by peaceful means. The South's slaves, Clemens said, were worth nine hundred million dollars, and "no people ever existed, or ever will exist, who would consent to the destruction of this vast wealth without a long and desperate struggle." Northerners must understand that southerners "do not intend to stand still and have our throats cut." The hostile intentions of the North were evident, according to Clemens: "We know well what we have to expect. Northern demands have assumed a form which it is impossible for us to misunderstand. First comes our exclusion from the territories. Next abolition in the District of Columbia—in the forts, arsenals, dockyards, &c. Then the prohibition of the slave trade between the States; and, finally, total abolition." Other southerners echoed Clemens's fears. In the Georgia state senate, a young westerner named Joseph E. Brown said that although the nation's new territories had been purchased "by the best blood of the South," he would be willing to give them up for the sake of preserving the Union, were it not for the fact that doing so would only lead to further northern aggression. Yield the territories, he said, "and you will be called upon to yield the District of Columbia. You will then be told that this is a small matter. That forced upon you, you must surrender the arsenals and dock yards. Those yielded, the internal slave trade will be abolished. By the time these are accomplished, states will be organized in the new territories, and by the force of numbers, the great object of all these movements will be consummated—an alteration of the Constitution and abolition in the States."[12]

Henry Clay tried to allay such fears. He presented to the U.S. Senate a series of resolutions that would, he hoped, not only end the squabble over the territories but also bring to a close the entire national controversy over slavery. Included in his list of eight specific proposals was a resolution declaring that "Congress has no power to prohibit or obstruct the trade in slaves between the slaveholding States; but that the admission or exclusion of slaves brought from one into another of them depends exclusively upon their own particular laws." Clay said that he did not regard that statement as a renunciation of any real constitutional power, because the Supreme Court had already decided that Congress could not regulate the slave trade. He added that he believed the court's decision was correct and trusted it would "forever put an end to the question whether Congress has or has not the power to regulate the intercourse and trade in slaves between the different States."[13] Clay must have had his fingers crossed behind his back when he said that, because as a former attorney in the case of *Groves v. Slaughter,* he of all people knew perfectly well that the court had in fact not ruled explicitly on the issue of congressional power over interstate slave trafficking.

Salmon Chase, who had recently been elected to the Senate by an alliance of Democrats and Free-Soilers in Ohio, attacked Clay's proposals in a magnificent speech that lasted more than two hours. In response to Clay's call for a resolution renouncing congressional authority over the slave trade, Chase repeated the hoary abolitionist argument that the federal Act of 1807 regulating the coastwise trade was a conclusive demonstration that Congress *did* have authority over interstate slave trafficking. The 1807 law prohibited the transport of slaves in vessels of less than forty tons burden. If Congress could enact that law, Chase said, then it could enact others. "If they can prohibit the trade in vessels of less than forty tons, then they can prohibit it in vessels of one hundred, five hundred—altogether." Chase continued:

> And why should not Congress prohibit this traffic? We hear much of the cruelty of the African slave trade. Our laws denounce against those engaged in it the punishment of death. Is it less cruel, less deserving of punishment, to tear fathers, mothers, children, from their homes and each other, in Maryland and Virginia, and transport them to the markets of Louisiana or Mississippi? If there is a difference in cruelty and wrong, is it not in favor of the African and against the American slave trade? Why, then, should we be guilty of the inconsistency of abolishing *that* by the sternest prohibition, and continuing *this* under the sanction of national law?[14]

Chase's senatorial colleague John P. Hale could not bring himself to agree. Conservative by nature and lethargic in temperament, Hale had become a Democrat early in his political career partly because he was attracted to the Jacksonian stress upon strict interpretation of the Constitution. Hale now said that he did not "clearly perceive" that Congress had the power to abolish the slave trade. "But I will tell gentlemen what I do believe," he added. "I believe that Congress has exercised powers which do not belong to them half so plausibly as does this power. They have exercised powers which do not vest in them any more than does this power to abolish the trade between the States." Hale acknowledged that slaves were articles of commerce and that Congress could regulate commerce. Yet he still insisted that Congress could not abolish the slave trade because, he said, "The right to regulate does not carry with it the right to destroy." Hale thus ended up agreeing with what had always been Henry Clay's position on the issue, although Hale claimed that the inspiration for his own stance came not from Clay but from a speech given by Daniel Webster in opposition to Thomas Jefferson's 1807 embargo policy.[15]

Unlike Chase and Hale, most members of Congress ignored Clay's call for a resolution renouncing federal power over the interstate slave trade. Probably they considered it unimportant compared to the other elements in Clay's scheme for sectional compromise. After all, a mere abstract statement would have little effect. The constitutional point at issue obviously would not be settled by a congressional resolution, for anybody who did not like it would pay no heed to it. Indeed, everyone appears to have forgotten that in 1838 the U.S. House of Representatives had actually adopted a comparable resolution, declaring that Congress had no jurisdiction over slavery in the states, that it had no right "to do that indirectly which it cannot do directly," and that therefore any attempt to "prohibit the removal of slaves from State to State" was "in violation of the Constitution" and "beyond the jurisdiction of Congress." All of Clay's other proposals, in contrast, would have tangible results. Clay's plans for dealing with the territories were the main focus of discussion, but there was also much debate over his calls for both the enactment of a draconian new federal fugitive slave law—a huge gain for the South—and for the abolition of the commercial slave trade in the District of Columbia—a supposedly balancing concession to the North. The latter proposal was purely cosmetic, however, because it would not end slavery in the nation's capital or even stop the slaveowners who resided there from continuing to buy and sell slaves. All it decreed was that commercial traders could no longer bring slaves into the district for the purpose of selling them, which merely meant that the traders would have to take their revolting coffles and pens somewhere else. But southerners were all too aware that the presence of slavery in the federal district had long been a prominent focus of abolitionist agitation. Consequently, they feared that even the minor sop to antislavery sentiment that Clay proposed would set a fearsome precedent. In the Senate, Robert M. T. Hunter of Virginia denounced the proposal as a first step toward the abolition of slavery in the District of Columbia. Still worse, he said, "It connects itself with one of the most delicate, dangerous, and to my State vital questions, of all that have grown out of this anti-slavery agitation. I mean what is called the abolition of the domestic slave trade." Hunter then launched into an elaborate defense of the interstate slave traffic, insisting that, despite occasional cases of individual hardship, it generally was a great blessing to the slaves because it permitted them to migrate to areas where agriculture was more profitable and where they could therefore receive a greater share of the product of their labor. Hunter concluded his argument by pointing out that if it was wrong to bring a slave into the District of Columbia to sell him, then surely it also was wrong to sell a slave from one state to another, or even from one slaveholder to another.

And if all of those things were wrong, then the whole institution of slavery could not be right.[16] Interestingly, that was a point with which even the most ardent of Hunter's abolitionist enemies could fully concur.

Clay replied that his proposal would merely prevent a trader from holding slaves in a pen in Washington after gathering them in Maryland and Virginia and before shipping them off to New Orleans or Mobile. Clay claimed that far from being an encouragement to abolitionism, the adoption of the proposal would provide "greater security against the agitation of the question of the abolition of slavery itself within the District." Unfortunately for Clay, Salmon Chase soon chimed in, cheerfully admitting that the abolition of slave trading was indeed a first step toward the abolition of slavery itself and that "gentlemen deceive themselves if they suppose it is the last step." Henry Foote of Mississippi then declared that any proposal to abolish slavery in the District of Columbia would mean the dissolution of the Union because it would be both a "hideous violation of the political compact of our fathers" and "the entering wedge to other and more aggressive measures, which are afterwards to follow."[17]

For months Clay's proposals for a sectional compromise were furiously assaulted by both proslavery and antislavery forces, not only inside but also outside the halls of Congress. In an open letter addressed to the House of Representatives and published in both the popular and the abolitionist press, William Jay condemned every one of Clay's ideas but poured especial scorn upon the proposed renunciation of congressional authority over the interstate slave trade. "The last item of this grand compromise," Jay said, "is virtually a guaranty that the American slave trade, vile and loathsome as it is, shall be held sacred from prohibition or obstruction by the federal government for all time to come. The stars and stripes shall forever protect each coasting vessel that shall be freighted with human misery and despair, and manacled coffles shall, without molestation, be driven across the continent from the Atlantic to the Pacific." Rather than accept Clay's compromise, Jay said, it would be better to dissolve the Union and allow white southerners to commit "the sin and folly of founding a new Republic upon the denial of human rights and of rendering themselves a bye-word, a proverb and a reproach among all the nations of the earth."[18]

Jay's denunciation of Clay's scheme was matched by some southerners, who were as vehement as Jay in their opposition to the proposed compromise, and every bit as willing to contemplate a dissolution of the Union, but for opposite reasons. They viewed Clay's resolutions as endangering rather than entrenching the South's peculiar institution. In June 1850 a southern convention at Nashville, summoned in response to a call from an earlier meeting in Mississippi that had been instigated behind the scenes by John C. Calhoun of South

Carolina, called for an unbending opposition to all antislavery demands, including the idea that white southerners should ever "submit to be legislated pirates for conveying slaves from one State to another," and warned that unless the South defended its rights, within fifty years twenty free states might be added to the Union and slavery abolished by a constitutional amendment.[19]

Soon after the Nashville meeting, Clay's omnibus bill embodying all of his compromise proposals was defeated in Congress. Stephen A. Douglas of Illinois then took over the leadership of the compromise effort from the aged and ailing Clay. By breaking the omnibus bill into pieces, and then wheeling and dealing so as to cobble together the different combinations of votes that he needed to get most of the pieces passed one by one, Douglas at last succeeded where Clay had failed. By September Douglas had secured the adoption of the series of measures that we now remember, collectively, as the Compromise of 1850. The Compromise as finally enacted did not include Clay's proposed resolution denying congressional power over the slave trade. The Compromise did, however, abolish the commercial slave trade in the District of Columbia, a step that many southerners continued to view with alarm and foreboding.[20]

Concern for the future security of the interstate slave trade was voiced by the legislature of North Carolina, at a second assemblage of southern delegates at Nashville, at state conventions in Georgia and South Carolina, and at a meeting of the Democratic Party caucus in Congress. In North Carolina, a joint committee of the state legislature recommended acquiescence in the Compromise of 1850 but called for retaliation should Congress take any further measures against slavery, including restricting the slave trade. At Nashville, elder statesman Langdon Cheves of South Carolina declared that in the wake of the Compromise of 1850 more northern aggression was to be expected, with attacks on slavery in the territories and in the federal district serving merely as "an entering wedge" for further assault: "We shall no doubt very soon hear of a proposition in Congress for regulating the slave trade between the States; and the surplus slaves of Virginia and North-Carolina, will not be allowed to pass to the new and unsettled country of the South and Southwest; . . . It is vain to say that such measures will be unconstitutional. Neither fanaticism nor power can be restrained by the privileges of a Constitution in parchment." The Georgia convention declared its reluctant acceptance of the Compromise of 1850 as a permanent settlement of the sectional conflict but vowed to resist any further antislavery measures, including "any act suppressing the slave trade between slaveholding States" even to the point of secession from the Union. The convention's resolutions became known as the "Georgia Platform" and served as a rallying point for southerners both inside and outside of Georgia. The South Carolina meeting, although it was in the long run much less influential than the Georgia one, explicitly upheld the right to secede in response to any further federal encroachments on slavery. A minority report spelled out those encroachments in a list that included "any attempt on the part of Congress to interfere with . . . the slave trade between the States." At a meeting of the Democratic caucus in Congress, an attempt was made to have the caucus take a stand similar to the Georgia platform, but the matter was tabled.[21]

Pamphlets published by the Southern Rights Association added to the hue and cry. In one of them, an anonymous Virginian predicted that once northerners had succeeded in routing slavery from the national capital and from all federal facilities, "the prohibition of what they call the slave trade on the high seas, and then on the Mississippi, whose waters, they pretend, are common property, and then between the States, will quickly follow each other. What would be left the South in such a condition?" In another, Edward Bryan of South Carolina insisted that the rights of the states must take precedence over the powers of the federal government, for otherwise the latter could "abolish the slave trade between the several States" as well as prohibit slavery in the territories. A third pamphlet reprinted an article by Jeremiah Clemens in the *Southern Quarterly Review* in which the senator from Alabama, after noting (correctly) that the Supreme Court had never ruled on the question of whether Congress could "interfere with the transport of slaves from State to State," warned that "the opinions declared by some of the judges, in the 'passenger cases,' raise very painful apprehensions on this subject. . . . Petitions to Congress, to prevent the transmission of slaves from State to State, for sale, and denunciations of the internal slave trade, will now become a staple of antislavery agitation."[22]

A few abolitionists tried their best to make southern nightmares come true by continuing to agitate for a ban on the interstate slave trade. The most prominent was Frederick Douglass, a former Maryland slave who had escaped to the North in 1838. Following the publication of his autobiography in 1845, he rapidly gained fame as an impassioned orator who could deliver a riveting firsthand account of life under slavery. In 1850 he broke with the Garrisonians and embraced political action, including the call for a ban on the interstate slave trade. During his years in bondage Douglass had not personally fallen into the clutches of the speculators, but as a mere infant he had been cruelly separated from his mother, and his kinship network had been devastated as his sister, two aunts, and many other relatives were carried off to the deep South by traders, while another aunt and uncle had escaped the same fate only by running away. In 1852 Douglass delivered his greatest speech, "The Meaning of July Fourth for the Negro." In it, he told how slave trafficking tore families apart. "I was born amid such sights and scenes," he said. "To me the American slave-trade is a terrible reality. When a child, my soul was often pierced with a sense of its horrors." Recalling "the piteous cries of the chained gangs that passed our door," he exclaimed, "My soul sickens at the sight."[23]

Douglass's was not the only voice raised against the slave trade in the 1850s. In an *Address to the Anti-slavery Christians of the United States,* William Jay appealed on behalf of the American and Foreign Anti-Slavery Society, a small organization that remained dedicated to the 1833 abolitionist political program, including action by Congress "to suppress the commerce in slaves between the States." Joel Tiffany, in *A Treatise on the Unconstitutionality of American Slavery,* argued that those same measures, including the authority of Congress "to annihilate the domestic slave trade," were "amply sufficient to put an end to slavery, and at once, if the people would exercise them," although he also supported the extremist idea that the federal government could abolish slavery itself. John Gorham Palfrey returned to the fray by writing *The Inter-state Slave Trade,* which described the horrors of the domestic slave traffic, made a crude attempt at drawing upon census data to estimate the movement of slaves from the upper to the lower South, and concluded that "whatever may be other political relations of slavery, the remedy for the unutterable wickedness of this traffic is in the hands of that Congress of the United States to which the free States send a majority of members." But those scattered publications were but a faint echo of the massive agitation against the slave trade that had been mounted by the unified abolitionist movement of the 1830s.[24]

Although the conventional abolitionist anti-slave-trade propaganda of the 1850s was relatively sporadic and ineffectual, that same decade saw the appearance of a work of fiction that may have had a greater impact upon northern public sentiment than the combined effect of all of the abolitionist tracts that were ever published. Harriet Beecher Stowe's *Uncle Tom's Cabin,* after being serialized to growing acclaim in Gamaliel Bailey's *National Era,* burst on the scene in book form in March 1852. It was an instant and phenomenal success. The first printing of 5,000 copies sold out in a few days. Domestic sales topped 20,000 within a few weeks and 300,000 within a year. By the end of the decade, they had passed the million mark. Abolitionists had long sought to turn public opinion against the slave trade by marshalling logical arguments and factual evidence. Stowe appealed less to her readers' intellects than to their emotions, and her fictional portrayal of the horrors of the slave trade pulled at the heartstrings. Drawing upon her own emotional devastation at the death of her infant son, her beloved Charley, from cholera in 1851, she portrayed vividly the agony of African Americans whose closest personal ties were sundered by a system that, Stowe said, "whirls families and scatters their members, as the wind whirls and scatters the leaves of autumn."[25]

Stowe made little attempt to challenge her readers' racist assumptions about African Americans, for she herself shared some of those assumptions. To her, there were profound differences between whites and blacks, although she did attribute the difference partly to historical experience rather than heredity. She contrasted "the Saxon, born of ages of cultivation, command, education, physical and moral eminence," with "the Afric, born of ages of oppression, submission, ignorance, toil, and vice!" Some of the black characters in *Uncle Tom's Cabin* are grotesque stereotypes straight out of a minstrel show. The only ones who display intelligence and initiative are mulattoes, whereas the full-blooded blacks belong to a "kindly race, ever yearning toward the simple and childlike." No matter how repellent some of Stowe's racial constructs may be to modern readers, however, they made her book more palatable to her white contemporaries. They enabled her to get across her central message that although African Americans may be inferior to whites in many respects, they are nonetheless human beings and deserve to be treated as people rather than things. Indeed, they are fully equal to white people in what matters most, the capacity to embrace the Christian faith and to live by its precepts.[26]

The pervasive theme of *Uncle Tom's Cabin* is the destruction of families by the interstate slave trade. The novel opens with a conversation between Arthur Shelby, a genteel Kentucky planter who has run into debt, and Mr. Haley, a trader, whom Stowe describes as "a short, thick-set man, with coarse, commonplace features, and that swaggering air of pretension which marks a low man who is trying to elbow his way upward in the world." Shelby reluctantly agrees to sell to Haley both the faithful servant Tom and the four-year-old son of a housemaid named Eliza. Tom bids a tearful goodbye to his wife and children and obediently departs with Haley, but Eliza runs away with her little boy rather than give him up. The novel's two alternating plots then unfold. The first describes Tom's experiences as he is taken southward and sold first to a kind if enervated master in New Orleans and then to the fiendish Simon Legree. The second plot tells the story of Eliza, who flees northward, pursued by slave catchers, and makes a heroic crossing of the Ohio River by leaping from one ice floe to another. Tom, because he will not forswear his Christian principles, perishes at the hands of Legree. Eliza, helped by Quakers who spirit her along the Underground Railroad, is reunited with her husband and achieves safety and freedom in Canada by crossing Lake Erie to "the blessed English shores."[27]

Although Stowe's only firsthand acquaintance with the South was a single brief excursion to Kentucky, she had become intimately acquainted with the

Figure 6. Scene from *Uncle Tom's Cabin.* Kentucky planter Arthur Shelby converses with the vulgarly attired slave trader Haley while the latter sizes up the beautiful Eliza and her little boy. *Uncle Tom's Cabin,* illustrated edition (Boston: John P. Jewett and Company, 1853). Courtesy University of Virginia Library, Special Collections.

realities of slavery and the slave trade while living in Cincinnati from 1832 to 1850. For example, in March 1833 she probably read an article in the *Cincinnati Journal* entitled "Unrighteous Traffic," in which the editor expressed his revulsion at having encountered at the city wharf a steamboat loaded with 150 slaves who had been bought up by speculators in Virginia and Kentucky and were on their way to be sold at Vicksburg, Mississippi. The editor expressed sympathy for those southern slaveholders who were merely making the best of "an evil which they have inherited from other generations and which they have a disposition, but not the power, to remedy." But he declared that "no character on earth is more intrinsically hateful or more universally despised" than the slave trader, who acquires wealth "by adding mountain weights to the already grievous load of human misery." Harriet had come to Cincinnati because her father, Lyman Beecher, had accepted the presidency of Lane Theological Seminary. Soon her father became immersed in turmoil as he tried, unsuccessfully, to mediate between the seminary's trustees and its rebellious student body led by Theodore Dwight Weld, who had converted his classmates to militant abolitionism. One of Weld's fellow rebels, Henry B. Stanton, published what appears to be the first abolitionist propaganda effort against the interstate slave trade following the founding of the American Anti-Slavery Society in December 1833. Nor did the eventual departure of Weld and his fellow rabble-rousers bring an end to antislavery agitation at Cincinnati. James G. Birney started publishing his antislavery *Philanthropist* there in 1836. When Birney was threatened by a proslavery mob, a local lawyer named Salmon P. Chase came to his defense. Soon Chase committed himself to radical abolitionism and became the attorney of choice for runaway slaves. Birney's assistant editor, Gamaliel Bailey, later took over the *Philanthropist* and continued to produce it until 1847, when he left to publish the *National Era* at the nation's capital.[28]

It was not only her acquaintance with the Lane rebels and her reading of antislavery literature that brought home to Harriet the evils of the southern labor system. When a servant girl in Harriet's own household was discovered to be in imminent danger of being seized by slave catchers, the Beechers delivered her to an agent of the Underground Railroad, who hid her away until the threat had passed. On another occasion, a dispirited woman from Kentucky knocked on Harriet's door. The woman had been freed by her master's will, but her two-year-old daughter had been sold to a trader. The woman showed Harriet a letter from the trader demanding two hundred dollars for the girl and stating that she would be sold at auction unless the mother came up with that sum by the end of the week. The Lane community quickly raised the money to reunite mother and child. When Harriet's brother Charles rejoined the family in Cincinnati after working for several years as a brokerage clerk in New Orleans, he told her what he had seen in that stronghold of deep South bondage and slave trading.[29]

Drawing upon everything that she had experienced, read, and heard during her seventeen years in Cincinnati, Stowe was remarkably successful in presenting within her novel a sweeping, plausible, and mostly accurate portrait of the routine workings and dreadful consequences of the interstate slave trade. In her vivid depiction of a trader's pen and slave auction in New Orleans, for example, she explains that the traders encourage "noisy mirth" among the slaves, "as a means of drowning reflection, and rendering them insensible to their condition." She tells also of one slave mother's pathetic and unsuccessful attempt to disguise the beauty of her innocent daughter in order to prevent her being sold, at age fifteen, into "a life of shame." Stowe augmented her personal knowledge and experience by borrowing incidents and details from abolitionist literature, notably Theodore Weld's *American Slavery As It Is.* She also appears to have lifted some of her characters and settings from an earlier antislavery novel, Richard Hildreth's *The Slave: or the Memoirs of Archy Moore* (1836). But it was her own imaginative genius that wove all of those disparate raw materials into her two compelling narratives. Moreover, just in case there were any readers too thick to draw the appropriate inferences, she often interrupted her stories in order to hector her audience with short sermons. When she describes Tom sobbing as he gazes for the last time at his sleeping children, she says that his are "just such tears, sir, as you dropped into the coffin where lay your first-born son; such tears, woman, as you shed when you heard the cries of your dying babe. For, sir, he was a man,—and you are but another man. And, woman, though dressed in silk and jewels, you are but a woman, and in life's great straits and mighty griefs, ye feel but one sorrow!" When she describes Eliza fleeing into the frosty night with her little boy in her arms, Stowe asks the reader, "how fast could *you* walk? How many miles could you make in those few brief hours, with the darling at your bosom,—the little sleepy head on your shoulder,—the small, soft arms trustingly holding on to your neck?" In her concluding remarks at the end of the book, she says that the domestic slave trade "is an inevitable attendant and result of American slavery" and that she has "given only a faint shadow, a dim picture, of the anguish and despair that are, at this very moment, riving thousands of hearts, shattering thousands of families, and driving a helpless and sensitive race to frenzy and despair."[30]

The conventions of her time made it impossible for Stowe to include any explicit discussion of sexuality, but she alluded frequently and unmistakably to the sale of slave women for carnal purposes. In the opening scene, Haley points out that Eliza, a beautiful mulatto, would bring a great price in New Orleans. Later, when Haley conspires with two slave catchers who plan to seize Eliza and falsely claim her as their own property while handing over her little boy to Haley, the schemers agree that she should not be pursued with dogs, lest they damage her good looks. Still later it is made clear both that Eliza's husband had a sister who was sold for sexual purposes, and that the same was true of Eliza's mother. Stowe necessarily left a great deal to the reader's imagination, but she pulled no punches in revealing the commodification of slave women's sexuality.[31]

Stowe clearly was familiar with southern defenses of the slave trade. Anticipating the objections that southerners would raise to her portrayal of it, she cleverly worked into her stories refutations of some of the principal southern myths and rationalizations. In the opening scene, Haley assures Shelby that blacks do not mind family separations because they are not like "white folks, that's brought up in the way of 'spectin' to keep their children and wives, and all that. Niggers, you know, that's fetched up properly, ha'n't no kind of 'spectations of no kind; so all these things comes easier." The events that immediately follow make it abundantly clear that family breakup does not come easily either to Tom or to Eliza. Stowe does not challenge the southern myth that the slave traders are a degraded class of men who are outcasts from polite society, but she does emphasize that the traders could not exist if respectable southerners did not do business with them. "But who, sir, makes the trader?" she asks the reader, in one of her little sermons. "Who is most to blame? The enlightened, cultivated, intelligent man, who supports the system of which the trader is the inevitable result, or the poor trader himself? You make the public sentiment that calls for his trade, that debauches and depraves him, till he feels no shame in it; and in what are you better than he?" Earlier Haley makes the same point more succinctly: "So long as your grand folks want to buy men and women, I'm as good as they is," he says. "'Tant any meaner sellin' on 'em, than 'tis buyin'!"[32]

Stowe does strike a false note when she portrays Shelby as compelled to sell his slaves to Haley. Stowe explains that Shelby had "speculated largely and quite loosely; had involved himself deeply, and his notes to a large amount had come into the hands of Haley." Here Stowe has bought into the southern myth that masters do not sell slaves for profit but only out of necessity. Some southern critics of the novel pointed out that Shelby could have chosen to sell his slaves locally and in that way raised the money to pay off his obligations to Haley. It is curious that southerners would bring up that point, but it is a valid one. No slaveholder ever had to sell to an interstate slave trader *if* the slaveholder was prepared to sacrifice his own financial self-interest by accepting what was likely to be a considerably lower sale price in the local market. Another valid criticism that can be made in this connection is that Stowe's notion that a trader would bully a slaveholder by buying up his notes is highly improbable. Traders found plenty of willing sellers without resorting to coercion, and it was in their interest to cultivate a good reputation among slaveholders. Southern critics did not raise this latter point, however, probably because the idea that traders were evil was part of southern mythology, and so the southern critics did not object to Stowe's portrayal of Haley as a blackmailer, implausible though it was.[33]

That Stowe's didactic masterpiece had a profound impact upon northern public opinion seems obvious, but there is no way of measuring the extent of that impact. We shall never know how many readers of *Uncle Tom's Cabin* subsequently switched their political allegiance to the Republican Party nor how important a factor their reading of the novel was in influencing their decision. The picture is still more clouded by the fact that besides the hundreds of thousands of readers of the book, there were additional hundreds of thousands of people who did not read it but instead saw one of the innumerable theatrical productions of *Uncle Tom's Cabin* that mushroomed everywhere because the copyright law of that time permitted anybody to adapt a novel to the stage without having to pay royalties. Stowe's central message about the evils of the interstate slave trade was muted in the play versions, because the producers knew that the paying public did not come to their theaters in order to be harangued. Audiences preferred to weep over the lugubrious death of little Eva (the sickly, saintly daughter of Tom's indulgent master in New Orleans) or to thrill to the spectacle of Eliza crossing the ice, usually with a pack of vicious dogs (live on stage) in hot pursuit. The theatrical adaptations had no time for such subtleties as the slave catchers' not using dogs in order to preserve Eliza's beauty so that they can sell her as a "fancy." Still, Stowe's message that the slave trade fractured families was never entirely lost. Tom nearly always died in Christlike agony far away from his Kentucky cabin and its occupants (albeit one early version of the play took the liberty of returning him there so as to provide a happy ending), and Eliza always clung for dear life to her little boy. Amid the myriad dolls and toys that were put on the market by entrepreneurs eager to cash in on the Uncle Tom craze, there was even a board game in which the players competed to reunite slaves with their spouses and children.[34]

However much *Uncle Tom's Cabin* may have raised northern awareness of the interstate slave trade, it did not result in any renewed effort by antislavery politicians to press for congressional action against it. Instead, the politicians focused on another antislavery issue that had received some attention in the novel. Although it was the devastating impact of the interstate slave trade that provided her central theme, Stowe said that her immediate inspiration for writing *Uncle Tom's Cabin* had come from the enactment of the Fugitive Slave Law of 1850. She had learned, she said, "with perfect surprise and consternation," that northern citizens were now duty-bound to help return escaped slaves to bondage. In her view, if the good citizens of the free states were properly informed, then they could not possibly do such a thing. "These men and Christians cannot know what slavery is," she declared, for "if they did, such a question could never be open for discussion." Antislavery politicians shared Stowe's abhorrence of the Fugitive Slave Law. But, ironically, their doing battle against that law led them to pull back from their struggle against the interstate slave trade, thus reversing Stowe's own implicit priorities.[35]

Because both Salmon Chase and Charles Sumner were determined to secure the repeal of the Fugitive Slave Law (or Fugitive Slave *Bill,* as Chase always called it, because he considered it unconstitutional), they found it expedient to retreat from their earlier endorsement of a wholesale ban on the entire interstate slave trade. They now gravitated toward the more moderate constitutional stance regarding the slave trade that had been adopted much earlier by Joshua Giddings, an antislavery Whig congressman from Ohio. In the 1840s Giddings had crusaded for repeal of the Act of 1807 by which Congress regulated the coastal slave trade. Giddings maintained that whenever a slave residing in an upper South state was taken to a port, placed on board a vessel, and shipped off to the lower South, "every slave thus taken from the jurisdiction of the slave State, is free the moment he leaves the bounds of such State and enters upon the high seas." But while Giddings insisted that it was unconstitutional for Congress to sanction the coastal slave trade, he did not believe that Congress had the authority to interfere in the inland traffic. In 1844 he expressed his agreement with "the doctrine of Mr. Clay, as set forth in his speech of 1839," and declared, "My political efforts are controlled by our constitutional compact. As the federal government possesses no power over it [slavery], we can exert no political power against it. Our political efforts therefore in regard to Slavery may extend to the repeal of all acts of Congress in favor of that institution, and to a total separation of the federal Government and the people of the free states from its support. To this point we are limited."[36]

In his March 1850 speech Chase had strongly upheld the right and duty of Congress to abolish the interstate slave trade. Sumner appears to have agreed, for in July 1850 he wrote the English reformer Richard Cobden that it was his earnest aim "to see slavery abolished everywhere within the sphere of the national government,—which is in the District of Columbia, on the high seas, and in the domestic slave trade." After 1850, however, both Chase and Sumner concentrated on attacking the allegedly unconstitutional coastal trade while ignoring the possibility of outlawing the entire interstate slave traffic. Indeed, in an 1852 speech Sumner even spoke approvingly of a Supreme Court opinion in which Justice John McLean had pondered whether or not Congress had the power to interfere with the interstate slave trade and decided that it did not. What accounts for this change? There is no possibility that the McLean opinion had caused Sumner to change his mind. For one thing, the opinion had been *obiter dictum* because the question of whether Congress had power over the slave trade was not before the court. For another, the case in question, *Groves v. Slaughter* (1841), had been decided a decade before Sumner altered his position. The explanation for Sumner's behavior emerges when it is noticed that his 1852 speech was made in support of a motion by him to repeal the 1850 Fugitive Slave Law. Sumner and Chase both insisted that the

Fugitive Slave Law was an unconstitutional infringement upon the right of the free states to prohibit slavery within their borders. But in adopting what amounted to a states'-rights stance vis-à-vis the Fugitive Slave Law, Sumner and Chase found it expedient to drop the idea of federal interference in the interstate slave trade, because that too could be condemned as an unconstitutional invasion of the right of states to do as they wished regarding slavery. It could be argued, after all, that if the federal government had unlimited power over the interstate slave trade, then perhaps an individual state had no right to prohibit the transport of slaves into its territory. Senator Robert J. Walker of Mississippi had raised precisely that point in his argument before the Supreme Court in *Groves v. Slaughter,* when he declared that if Congress had plenary power over the interstate slave trade, then the free states had no right to exclude slave traders, who could, if they chose, encamp their chained coffles at Boston, Lexington, Concord, or Bunker Hill before driving them on to some southern market.[37]

If their battle against the Fugitive Slave Law caused antislavery politicians like Chase and Sumner to stop talking about a congressional ban on the interstate slave trade, later developments conspired to keep that issue off their political agenda. In 1852 a New York court freed some slaves belonging to a Virginia couple who had stopped over in New York City while on their way to Texas. A prolonged appeal of that decision, supported by the state of Virginia, lasted the rest of the decade and prompted both Chase and Sumner to express fear that the Supreme Court might use the commerce power to protect slave transit through the free states just as had been predicted by Robert Walker. It had become all too clear that the power over interstate commerce given to Congress by the Constitution was a two-edged sword. It was possible that it could provide an avenue for Congress to cripple slavery by outlawing slave trafficking among the slave states. But it also was possible that it could provide an avenue for Congress to promote slavery by giving slaveholders the explicit legal right to take their slaves along with them whenever they passed through the free states without fear that their chattels might be liberated.[38]

The uneasy sectional truce that had followed the Compromise of 1850 was shattered in 1854. Stephen A. Douglas, the man who had created the truce, was also the man who destroyed it. Douglas was eager to open the region west of Iowa and Missouri to white settlement in order to facilitate the selection of a northerly transcontinental railroad route that would benefit his home state of Illinois. Despite the fact that slavery had been prohibited within the area in question by the Missouri Compromise, Douglas, in order to win southern backing for his plans, proposed that two new territories, Nebraska and Kansas, should be organized and that the status of slavery within each of them should be decided by its territorial legislature. In order to allow the territorial legislatures to thus exercise what Douglas called "popular sovereignty" on the slavery question, the Missouri Compromise was repealed. Douglas succeeded in shepherding his Kansas-Nebraska Bill through Congress, but he had drastically miscalculated the consequences that would follow. Antislavery spokesmen condemned the repeal of the Missouri Compromise as a betrayal and as proof positive that the federal government was under the control of the "Slave Power." In Kansas, guerilla warfare broke out between proslavery and antislavery settlers. In national politics, both the old Whig Party and the nativist American Party disintegrated because their adherents became hopelessly divided over Kansas and the issue of slavery expansion. A new political movement emerged that became known as the Republican Party. It was a coalition of former Whigs, former American Party adherents, and former Democrats, all of whom were united in their opposition to the Kansas-Nebraska Act and to any further expansion of slavery in the territories.

The Republican Party presented itself as a defensive movement opposing the efforts of the Slave Power to expand and to nationalize slavery. Opponents of the party, however, were not convinced that it harbored no other ambitions. In 1855 Richard W. Thompson, a former Whig Senator from Indiana who viewed the emerging Republican coalition with alarm, declared that what he called the "abolition party" had nine aims, one of which was "the abolition of the slave-trade between the States." Aware that no Republican platform had actually embraced that measure, Thompson added, "I do not say that in all the Northern States this party has put *all* these planks into its platform. That would not be expedient just now. But what I mean is, that what is now called the principle of political 'fusion' embraces all of them: — that is it brings into the same party those who advocate *all* of them . . . some one notion and some another." When the Republicans ran John C. Frémont for the presidency in 1856, John Perkins, Jr., a wealthy cotton planter and prominent Democrat in Louisiana, declared that "if Mr. Fremont be elected, the Union cannot and ought not to continue," because the Republican victory would lead to the banning of the interstate slave trade and other measures that would culminate in complete abolition. After the election, in which Frémont attracted a third of the popular vote, Edmund Ruffin of Virginia warned that "under the complete supremacy of a Northern administration," the "removal of slaves by sales from States where they were in excessive numbers, to other States or new territories where they were deficient" would be prohibited. In that event, Ruffin said, it would become impossible to create any new slave states, the bottled-up slaves of the old states would become "an unprofitable burden and a dangerous nuisance to the whites," and "the institution of slavery would be hastened toward its doomed extinction."[39]

The idea that the Republicans harbored a secret radical agenda evidently was sufficiently widespread for Stephen Douglas to try to exploit it during his famed series of debates with Abraham Lincoln in 1858. In their first encounter, Douglas asked Lincoln whether or not he was committed to a list of seven specific antislavery measures, including both the abolition of slavery in the District of Columbia and "the prohibition of the interstate slave trade between the different states." Taken by surprise, Lincoln made no immediate reply, but in their second joint debate he did answer Douglas's queries. Lincoln began by denying that he was pledged to anything on Douglas's list except the prohibition of slavery in the territories. He then elaborated on his views on all of the other issues that Douglas had raised. Lincoln said that he would be glad to see an end to slavery in the District of Columbia and that he believed that Congress had the constitutional right to abolish it there. He added, however, that he would support such abolition only on three conditions: that it be approved by the voters of the district, that it be done gradually, and that slaveholders be compensated for the loss of their property. Lincoln then turned to the issue of the interstate slave trade. He said:

> I must say here, that as to the question of the abolition of the slave-trade between the different States, I can truly answer, as I have, that I am *pledged* to nothing about it. It is a subject to which I have not given that mature consideration that would make me feel authorized to state a position so as to hold myself entirely bound by it. In other words, that question has never been prominently enough before me to investigate whether we really have the constitutional power to do it. I could investigate it if I had sufficient time, to bring myself to a conclusion upon the subject; but I have not done so, and I say so frankly to you here, and to Judge Douglas. I must say, however, that if I should be of opinion that Congress does possess the constitutional power to abolish the slave-trade among the different States, I should still not be in favor of the exercise of that power unless upon some conservative principle as I conceive it, akin to what I have said in relation to the abolition of slavery in the District of Columbia.[40]

Lincoln's waffling here is notable. His excuse that he had not thought about the slave trade issue will not bear scrutiny. As both a regular reader of the abolitionist press and a keen follower of all political controversies, Lincoln had almost certainly been well aware of the question for more than twenty years. Indeed, in their next debate Lincoln would confront Douglas with the example of an Illinois Democrat ("a political friend of Judge Douglas and opponent of mine," Lincoln pointed out) who as a candidate for Congress in the Galena District in 1850 had strongly endorsed the banning of the interstate slave trade, on the grounds that "so long as the slave States continue to treat slaves as articles of commerce, the Constitution confers power on Congress to pass laws regulating that peculiar COMMERCE, and that the protection of Human Rights imperatively demands the interposition of every constitutional means to prevent this most inhuman and iniquitous traffic." Furthermore, Douglas had posed his query a week before Lincoln answered it, so there had been time enough for Lincoln to adopt a clear position on the question, had he wanted to, even if it had been as new to him as he pretended it was. Finally, it is evident that Lincoln both as a prominent railroad lawyer and as a politician had already given plenty of thought to the commerce power. As a staunch Whig and an admirer of Henry Clay, he had taken a broad view of the Constitution. He had defended the constitutional legitimacy of both a national bank and of federal funding for improvements to transportation. On the latter issue, he had based his argument squarely upon a broad construction of the interstate commerce clause.[41]

It is easy to understand why Lincoln in his debates with Douglas would not commit himself to the view that Congress had the constitutional power to ban the interstate slave trade. Douglas was straining to portray himself as an unabashed champion of white supremacy and to convince Illinois voters that Lincoln was an abolitionist and an advocate of racial equality. Lincoln was doing everything he could to refute the radical image that Douglas was trying to foist upon him. But why, then, did Lincoln not state unequivocally that in his opinion Congress did *not* have the power to ban the interstate slave trade? Surely that would have been a much more effective response than was Lincoln's mealy-mouthed answer that he had not thought about the question. The explanation must be that Lincoln did not want to make his position clear, even though it would have been much to his immediate advantage to do so. Two years earlier, during the Frémont campaign, the radical political abolitionist Frederick Douglass had lamented that the first national Republican platform said nothing about the slave trade between the states and promised nothing beyond freedom for Kansas. Two years later, during the 1860 campaign, the Garrisonian abolitionist Wendell Phillips would sneer at Abraham Lincoln because he was not even in favor of stopping the interstate slave trade. But Lincoln would say no more. He was keeping his options open.[42]

Because of the defection both of the Garrisonians, who maintained that the Constitution protected the slave trade, and of the constitutional extremists, who maintained that Congress could abolish slavery itself, those abolitionists who continued to agitate in the 1840s and 1850s for a congressional interdiction of the interstate slave trade were but an echo of the powerful voices that had cried out for such action in the 1830s. The Liberty Party championed the idea of aggression against the slave trade, but its successors, the Free-Soilers and the Republicans, concentrated on the territorial question and shrank from more radical aims. Some antislavery politicians never subscribed to the notion that the federal commerce power could be used against the slave trade, and others found it expedient to cease advocating such action so as not to undermine their campaign against the Fugitive Slave Law of 1850. Yet, even as the interest of antislavery forces in attacking the slave trade waned, the fear of such an attack among proslavery spokesmen waxed strong as the turbulent decade of the 1850s drew to a close. Like their nemesis Abraham Lincoln, many slaveowners were coming to believe that the nation could not endure permanently half slave and half free.

7

Great and Terrible Realities

While historians once described the Civil War as arising from a clash over states' rights and the failure of politicians to compromise their differences in the national interest, such a view is no longer tenable. Implicit in the now discarded interpretation was the assumption that African Americans were marginal to American history and their fate of little consequence. Given that assumption, it followed that antebellum politicians should have made whatever deal was necessary in order to achieve sectional reconciliation. The fact that any such deal necessarily would have included a guarantee that southern slavery might continue indefinitely was glossed over with the pleasant fantasy that slavery was becoming less profitable and would soon fade away on its own. Nowadays most historians have faced up to the fact that the South's preoccupation with states' rights was but a thin veneer over the real issue. The only states' right that was under threat was the right to hold black people in slavery. And the only compromise that would have satisfied the South was a sectional agreement that not only would have recognized unequivocally the right of white southerners to hold black people as chattels in 1860 but also would have guaranteed that they could keep them and their progeny in bondage for ever. Abraham Lincoln and his party would agree to the former but not the latter. And the war came.

The South demanded guarantees for the perpetuation of slavery for two reasons. First, the present value of slave property was dependent upon the assumption that generations yet unborn would also be property. The buyer of a slave woman purchased not only her but also her future children and her children's children, descending along the maternal line in perpetuity. Thus even a remote threat to the permanence of slavery as a southern institution—just the smallest cloud on the far horizon—was an immediate menace to the material interest of the slaveholders. The second reason for southern determination was that the slaveholders were convinced that there was indeed a cloud gathering on the horizon, a dark one at that, and not far off. Consequently, the constitutional protections for slavery that had satisfied the southern delegates to the Great Convention of 1787 no longer satisfied the fire-eaters of 1860.

The chief focus of sectional strife was the territorial question. Stephen Douglas strove mightily to persuade both northerners and southerners to accept his idea of "popular sovereignty"—that is, to allow the settlers inhabiting any territory to decide whether they wanted slavery or not—and thus defuse the explosive national debate by rendering the question a purely local one. His effort was doomed, however, because too much was at stake. Both North and South realized that the issue of slavery expansion would define the American future. For the South, it was essential that slavery should expand. That was so not because the South was short of room to plant cotton, for there were millions of acres yet uncleared in the frontier areas of the states clustered around the Gulf of Mexico, but rather because the winning of new slave territories and thus eventually new states was necessary in order to preserve the sectional balance of power that provided political security for slavery. The legacy of the 1808 clause had caught up with the South. Year after year, the population of the North was swelled by the arrival of newcomers from Europe. Meanwhile, the South, forbidden to import black slaves and unattractive to white immigrants reluctant to enter a labor market dominated by servitude, saw its relative strength in the national political arena ebbing, as the population balance between the sections shifted inexorably in favor of the North. The loss of political clout mattered, because the Constitution did not provide absolute security for slavery. As abolitionists had long pointed out, there were federal powers that might be used to undermine it. Potentially the most damaging such power was the federal authority over interstate commerce, an authority which might be used to destroy the interstate slave trade.[1]

It is impossible to state exactly how important the threat to the slave trade was in shaping the course of events that ended in the catastrophe of civil war. The study of history is not a science like chemistry, in which an investigator can repeat an experiment over and over, adding or subtracting one or another ingredient and observing the effect. Because historical events happen only once, historians can only guess at rather than determine with finality the relative importance of the many factors that bring them about. But the more evidence historians search out and the more carefully they sift it, the more educated their guesses become. As to the case at hand, there is certainly some evidence that appears, at least at first glance, to suggest that the slave trade issue was not of critical importance in bringing on the secession crisis and the Civil War. Despite the primacy of the interstate commerce power in terms of its potential impact, southern spokesmen did not consistently stress it, either explicitly or implicitly, compared to the other constitutional provisions dangerous to slavery. Indeed, there was even one campaign pamphlet published during the run-up to the 1860 election that attacked Abraham Lincoln by discussing fugitive slaves, the admission of new slave states, slavery in the District of Columbia, slavery in the territories, and virtually every other conceivable issue *except* the interstate slave trade.[2] It is important to take into account, however, that part of the southern defense against abolitionism had always been to minimize the importance of the slave trade. If southerners now made too much of the devastation that a ban on the interstate slave trade would wreak on the southern economy, they would undermine their own defensive myth that the trade was small and economically insignificant. Thus it is understandable that southerners were reluctant either to single out the slave trade issue over other concerns or to be explicit about the enormous threat that it posed to the slave-based southern economy. Yet despite that restraint, the bulk of the surviving evidence amply demonstrates that white southerners were concerned about the threat to the slave trade should the Republican Party capture the presidency. While southern expectations varied as to exactly when or how the Republicans would attack the interstate slave trade, many influential southerners predicted that such an attack would occur, and they saw it as a key component in a series of measures whereby the South's peculiar institution might be swept away and its distinctive civilization destroyed.

As the election of 1860 approached, southern spokesmen voiced their anxiety. In December 1859, John C. Breckinridge, who was then Vice President under the James Buchanan administration and had just been chosen by the Kentucky legislature to serve a term in the U.S. Senate beginning in March 1861, listed what he said were "the present and *ulterior purposes*" of the Republican Party:

> To introduce the doctrine of *negro equality* into American politics . . . ;
> To *exclude the slave property* of the South from all Territory . . . ;
> To *prevent the admission* . . . of another slaveholding State;
> To *repeal the Fugitive Slave Law* . . . ;

> To refuse to prevent or punish, by State action, the *spoliation of slave property;* . . .
> To *abolish slavery* in the *District of Columbia;*
> To *abolish it* in the *forts, arsenals, dock yards,* and *other places in the South,* where Congress has exclusive jurisdiction.
> To *abolish* the *internal* and *coastwise trade.*
> To limit, *harass,* and *frown upon* the *institution* in *every mode of political action,* and by every form of public opinion.
> And, finally, by the Executive, by Congress, by the postal service, the press, and all other accessible modes, to *agitate without ceasing,* until the Southern States, without sympathy or brotherhood in the Union, worn down by the unequal struggle, *shall be compelled to surrender ignominiously,* and *emancipate their slaves.*

Breckinridge did not say how soon the Republicans would inflict all of these horrors upon the South, but he had no doubt that they would do so if they had the chance. "We stand," he said, "not in the presence of spectres and shadows, but of *great and terrible realities.* I see on one side, an *unrelenting purpose of aggression,* and on the other a *dauntless determination to resist.*"[3]

In North Carolina, the editor of the state's most important Democratic newspaper warned that the "forms" of the Constitution could be used to destroy the South and argued that the election of a Republican president would in itself be an overt act justifying secession. On the floor of Congress, Lucius J. Gartrell of Georgia demanded to know how far a northern colleague would go to advance the aggressive designs of the Republicans:

> If the Republican party succeed in electing a sectional candidate, and securing the control of both branches of the national Legislature, abolish slavery in the District of Columbia, the slave-trade between the States, prohibit the introduction of slavery into any of the Territories, and refuse the admission of a State because of slavery in its constitution—if, sir, the Republican party does any one or all of these things, and the South secedes from the Union, would the gentleman from Pennsylvania be ready to head a regiment and coerce her back?

In South Carolina, James Farrow claimed that it was unconstitutional to ban slavery from federal property, to interfere with the interstate slave trade, to block the recapture of fugitive slaves, to deny admission to new slave states, or to allow territorial legislatures to discourage slavery. Farrow hoped that the upcoming presidential election would focus on those matters and so provide once and for all "a verdict on the single issue of the *rights of the South under the Constitution on the subject of slavery.* We have cried 'peace' long enough—our only chance now is *agitation*—war to the knife against the disorganizing principles of the Republicans." Another South Carolinian, John Townsend, said that if the Republicans succeeded in their plans for "the *suppression of the inter-State slave trade*" and other aggressions, then "it would not be a difficult matter, under an *abolition interpretation* of the *constitution,* so to *cripple this vital Southern institution* of slavery as soon to render even a faithful Virginia field hand, now worth over a thousand dollars, *utterly worthless* to his master." In Maryland, former U.S. Senator Reverdy Johnson agreed that the Republicans, if victorious, would press for "the prevention of what is called the domestic slave trade" and predicted that "As sure as Heaven's clouds of fire and tempest carry desolation in their train, so sure is it that this now peaceful and happy land will be shaken to its very foundations, and the Union, the glorious Union of our noble ancestors, an inheritance to us more precious than was ever conferred on a people, will be tumbled into ruins, and the fondest hopes of the human race blasted forever."[4]

Unable to agree on a national platform and presidential candidate for the 1860 election, the Democratic Party broke in two. The majority faction nominated Stephen Douglas on a platform of popular sovereignty. The militant southern minority nominated John C. Breckinridge on a platform demanding federal protection for slavery in the territories. Meanwhile, the Republicans passed over their shining star William H. Seward and nominated instead dark-horse candidate Abraham Lincoln on a platform opposing slavery in the territories. Finally, a remnant of conservative former Whigs and nativists who could stomach none of the other three candidates established the Constitutional Union Party and nominated John Bell of Tennessee on a platform decrying sectionalism and avoiding a clear stand on the territorial question.

During the election campaign, both the Douglas Democrats and the Republicans generally avoided the slave trade issue. The Douglas camp naturally shied away from a question that offered more grist to its rivals' mills than to its own, and Douglas himself devoted the climactic speech of his campaign entirely to popular sovereignty and the territories. Meanwhile, the Republicans tried to broaden their appeal by portraying themselves as moderates on all slavery issues except that of expansion into the territories. Still, just weeks after Lincoln's nomination, Charles Sumner delivered a fiery Senate speech in which he said that advocates of popular sovereignty in the territories "most strangely forget the power of Congress 'to regulate commerce with foreign nations and among the several States.' . . . The migration or importation of slaves into any State existing at the adoption of the Constitution was tolerated until 1808, but from that date the power of Congress became plenary to prohibit their 'importation' from abroad or 'migration' among existing States, while from the beginning this power was plenary to prevent their 'migration' into the Territories." Sumner's focus here was on the territorial question, but his remarks cannot have been reassuring to southerners fearful of Republican interference in the interstate slave trade. Toward the close of the campaign, William M. Evarts, who had headed the New York State delegation to the Republican national convention, gave what appears to be the only Republican campaign speech that dealt directly with the slave trade, although he did not make clear whether he was talking about the domestic coastwise trade, the illicit external trade, or both. Evarts gave no hint that his party would interfere with slave trafficking, but he did vigorously deny that any Republicans participated in or encouraged it. Democrats claimed, according to Evarts,

> that we are a hypocritical race; that we are fond of money above every other thing, and trample, for gain-sake, our principles under our feet; that we fit out slave-traders; that our merchants furnish the means, the credit, and the insurance; and they say: "Look now at the North, which professes to be opposed to Slavery, and yet furnishes the means for this abominable traffic." Well, there is no fusion. It is not the North that is opposed to Slavery; it is the people, who have the sentiments of Freedom, who are opposed to Slavery; and those who have not those sentiments are engaged in anything, if you please, that the law will tolerate, or that the law will wink at, in advancement of Slavery. But let me ask that Democratic orator how many of those people that he thus classifies and stigmatizes, does he suppose vote the Republican ticket? [Laughter.] Whenever Republicans are caught in the service of Slavery we shall hang our heads! But when the orator who denounces our wickedness, counts among the voters of his party, captain and crew, the owner and merchant, the banker and district attorney, the officers and marshal, and the whole concern engaged in prosecuting, promoting, defending, protecting, or winking at the abomination, it is for them to cease their accusations. [Applause.][5]

The 1860 Republican national platform lambasted the Buchanan administration for its "attempted enforcement, everywhere, on land and sea, through the intervention of Congress and of the Federal courts, of the extreme pretensions of a purely local interest," but even the most vociferous anti-Republicans did not read into that vague bombast the implication that a Republican administration would interfere with either the landward or the coastwise slave trade. Only occasionally did a Republican spokesman hint at the possibility of radical action against slavery. In Chicago, newspaper editor and former mayor John Wentworth wrote a series of incendiary editorials and said that the election of Lincoln would mean "the emancipation of four millions of human beings." Because Wentworth earlier had become estranged from Lincoln and had backed Seward for the Republican nomination, some Illinois Republicans suspected him of deliberately sabotaging the campaign that he ostensibly was supporting. At St. Louis, perhaps the only southern city where a Republican could speak openly before a large and enthusiastic audience, German-American leader Carl Schurz predicted slavery's inevitable doom in the face of progress, pointing out that constitutional interpretation necessarily changes over time. "The predominance of interests determines the construction of the Constitution," Schurz said. "So it was and so it ever will be. . . . It is not an article of my creed—not a matter of principle—but a matter of experience; not a doctrine, but a fact." Finally, New York Republican and abolitionist John Jay waited until the evening before the election to proclaim that the new administration would first abolish slavery in the District of Columbia and then move to suppress the interstate trade. Like his eminent grandfather and father before him, Jay had no doubt that Congress possessed the authority to act. "The abolition of the internal slave-trade of the United States is a question upon which it will perhaps take a longer time to procure unanimity of opinion," he admitted, "but it is not possible for me to doubt that that time is not far distant. . . . The power of Congress to abolish it rests upon precisely the same clause in the Constitution under which they abolished the African trade, and it is as clear in the one case as in the other. It is a power in regard to which our most conservative statesmen have agreed in opinion."[6]

If most Republicans avoided the topic of possible federal action to undermine the South's peculiar institution, the Breckinridge Democrats and the Constitutional Unionists did not. In a debate that segued into the emerging contest between advocates and opponents of immediate southern secession should Lincoln be elected, the supporters of Breckinridge and Bell quarreled over whether or not a Republican administration would interfere with slavery. Following the lead of their presidential candidate, the Breckinridge camp proclaimed that such interference certainly would occur, and probably sooner rather than later. William Yancey, the Alabama elder statesman whose incontinent oratory led even fellow secessionists to regard him as a loose cannon, assured a Breckinridge campaign meeting in New York City that the Republicans intended to do more than just ban slavery from the territories:

> They say there shall be no more slave trade; that this is in accordance with the spirit of the Constitution and the teaching of the fathers. . . . Now, that slave trade between the states is incident to its life and prosperity. Confine a man to one spot and say that you must make a show right there and nowhere else, and would that man prosper and thrive and be a benefit to the community and to himself? You know it is not so. Trade must be allowed to seek its own mart and level. Otherwise you are interfering unconstitutionally and improperly and pursuing a bad policy as to trade. The great idea of the world at this time is for free trade. Now, take away the right to sell our slaves and you destroy

> the value of our property to that extent. It is so in regard to any property. Again, they endeavor to nullify the Fugitive Slave Law, and twelve states have passed laws to that end. They mean to abolish slavery in the District of Columbia, and in the arsenals and dockyards.
>
> *A voice.* Who says so?
>
> *Yancey.* The abolitionists and Black Republicans say so. (*Loud applause.*) I know no distinction. Seward says so. Lincoln says so. Lincoln first enunciated the irrepressible conflict. (*Applause.*) Put him in power and he will build up an abolitionist party in every Southern state; there is no doubt about it.[7]

A resident of Washington, D.C., writing in *De Bow's Review* predicted a similar series of events. He said, "The ultimate designs of the Republican party, although its present policy is to affect conservatism, are as 'plain as if written upon the arch of the sky.' Its immediate purpose . . . is to seize upon all the territories of the United States, and in due time, to bring them into the Union as free States." Once the Republicans had created enough new states to ensure their domination of the federal government, they would abolish slavery in the District of Columbia and at all federal naval yards, arsenals, and forts. "This will be followed," the writer said:

> by a prohibition to transport slaves by sea under the federal flag, from one port in a slave-holding State to another. This will result as a corollary from the doctrine which has already been proclaimed, that slave-property can only be protected by State authority, under positive law, and is not entitled to recognition outside of the limits of the State in which the domicil[e] of the owner of this property may be. After this has been done, the next step will be, under the provision of the Constitution which gives Congress the power to regulate commerce, to abolish the inter-State slave-trade, either directly in terms, or to do the same thing indirectly by taxation, or by burdensome restrictions.

After that the federal Fugitive Slave Law would be repealed, and then the Constitution would be amended in order to eliminate the partial counting of slaves in determining state representation in Congress. "It may not be a preconcerted plan of the Republican party to carry into effect each of these measures," the author admitted, but all of them would come about nevertheless, because "One will naturally beget another."[8]

Bell supporters denied the more extravagant claims of the Breckinridge camp about Republican intentions. In Tennessee, William G. Brownlow, editor of the *Knoxville Whig*, declared before an audience assembled to hear both him and Yancey that the latter and his fellow secessionists must "PASS OVER OUR DEAD BODIES ON THEIR MARCH TO WASHINGTON TO BREAK UP THIS GOVERNMENT." Brownlow insisted that only an overt Republican act damaging to slavery, certainly not the mere election of Lincoln, could justify secession. "Should Lincoln be elected," Brownlow said, "and should he, for instance, recommend the abolition of the slave-trade between the States, I shall advocate waiting to see if Congress will sustain him. If Congress will sustain him in the outrage and violation of the Constitution, I shall advocate an appeal to the Supreme Court; and if that tribunal sustain Lincoln, I would take the ground that *the time for Revolution has come*—that all the Southern States should go into it; AND I WOULD GO WITH THEM!"[9]

In Maryland, Congressman Henry Winter Davis gave a speech which, although ostensibly on behalf of Bell, was so defensive of Lincoln and the Republicans that some observers wondered where Davis's own real loyalties lay. Davis assured his listeners that conservative Republicans accepted the Fugitive Slave Law, the interstate slave trade, and slavery in the federal capital. "You are safe, then, at home," he averred. "You are safe in carrying, if you choose to carry, your slaves to Mississippi to sell them. You are safe from the example of freedom in the District of Columbia. There is nothing of that kind open at all." Also, as part of his defense of Lincoln's past record on slavery matters, Davis introduced the rather embarrassing point that the Constitutional Union Party's vice presidential candidate, Edward Everett of Massachusetts, had once responded to an abolitionist query by declaring himself opposed to the admission of new slave states and in favor of abolishing both the interstate slave trade and slavery in the federal district.[10]

In Virginia, both Bell and Douglas newspapers warned their readers that secessionism was a danger to the upper South because if the lower South states left the Union they would no longer be restrained by the 1808 clause of the U.S. Constitution and so could reopen the external slave trade. Residents of the seceded states who wished to buy slaves would then pay a few hundred dollars for an African rather than a thousand or more for a slave from Virginia. One newspaper even reported that slave prices were already down 25 to 50 percent because of the uncertain future of the interstate market. The most prominent Bell supporter in Virginia, former Whig leader John M. Botts, warned that even pressing the territorial question could backfire on the South. "It is a delicate subject," he said,

> and the man who proposes to take the institution [slavery] from the position which it now occupies as a *peculiar* institution, differing from all other property, and put it on an equality with merchandise generally, and say because you have the right to carry your merchandise into the Territories, you have the right to carry slaves as merchandise, he takes a very hazardous position . . . because the moment you propose to put it upon a footing with ordinary merchandise, then *may* come in another proposition, that Congress may regulate Slavery and the slave-trade between the States as it does merchandise. . . . I

do not know the lawyer who could successfully dispute the fact that Congress would have the power to regulate Slavery between the States, as it does in reference to every other article of commerce.

Botts also argued vehemently that the election of Lincoln would not justify secession. As proof that Lincoln had no radical intentions, Botts claimed that Lincoln, while a member of the Illinois state assembly in 1837, had voted against a resolution in which the legislature called upon the federal government to ban the interstate slave trade. Botts was mistaken. Lincoln in 1837 had in fact protested against the passage of a resolution in which the Illinois legislature declared that Congress did *not* have the constitutional power to abolish slavery in the District of Columbia. The surviving record gives no indication that the interstate slave trade issue was involved.[11]

That Botts could be so confused about Lincoln's past actions points up the fact that throughout the campaign the Republican presidential candidate himself made almost no attempt to clarify or even to reiterate the positions that he had taken in earlier years on the issues that so exercised his opponents. Unlike Breckinridge, who made a few speeches, and especially Douglas, who made many, Lincoln stayed home in Springfield and kept quiet. Nor would he gratify the many individuals, North and South, who wrote asking him to be specific about what he would or would not do if elected president. He had his secretary prepare a form letter announcing that Lincoln would say nothing, on the ground that his positions were already well known when he was nominated. In private correspondence, Lincoln explained that this policy of silence had been recommended by "all discreet friends." He said he would be willing to make a public statement disclaiming any intention to interfere with slaves or slavery in the states "if there were no danger of encouraging bold bad men to believe they are dealing with one who can be scared into anything." But for him to do so now would be represented by such men as an "*awful coming down,*" and anyone who did not already believe what he had said in the past would not believe a new repetition "though one rose from the dead." On at least one occasion, Lincoln evidently was sorely tempted to speak out, if only by proxy: In response to an opposition pamphlet making an unfavorable comparison between himself and Henry Clay, he began to draft what appears to be a letter to be sent under someone else's name in which Lincoln's actions in the 1837 Illinois legislature are explained. The letter was never completed or sent, however, so in the end Lincoln kept to his vow of silence.[12]

Lincoln held his tongue because he knew that the Republican Party was a fragile alliance of disparate elements. It included radical abolitionists who were eager to attack slavery in every way possible, even at the price of civil war if it came to that. It included also outright racists who cared nothing for the suffering of African Americans but simply wanted slavery excluded from the western territories so that white settlers there would neither have to compete with wealthy planters nor coexist with blacks. Most Republicans fell somewhere along a spectrum between those extremes, and Lincoln and his political confidants knew that anything he could say that might increase his appeal to some potential Republican voters would as likely alienate others. Therefore he and his "discreet friends" agreed that the safest course was for him to be mute and allow his past record to speak for itself. The strategy obviously was successful in that in the balloting on 6 November 1860 Abraham Lincoln was elected president of the United States. While he received less than 40 percent of the popular vote, his margin of victory in the electoral college was so substantial that he still would have won even if all of the votes garnered by Douglas, Breckinridge, and Bell had been polled by a single anti-Lincoln candidate rather than split up among three. It was the sectional polarization of the country, the fact that Lincoln received negligible votes in the South but swamped his combined opposition in the North, that gave him the prize.

That Lincoln's silence during the campaign was so successful as an election strategy has tended to divert the attention of historians from another important consequence of that silence, which was its impact upon the South. There, Breckinridge supporters spread their propaganda about the alleged radical antislavery intentions of a Republican administration without receiving any public rebuke from Lincoln. While the Bell campaigners did make some attempt to refute the most extreme Breckinridge charges by pointing out Lincoln's past moderate record, their efforts were far less effectual than an aggressive campaign by Lincoln himself might have been. Lincoln could have responded publicly to the Breckinridge charges, repeating what he had said in the past and giving reassurances about the future conduct of a Republican administration headed by himself. It is no doubt true, as Lincoln feared, that the Breckinridge camp—those "bold bad men" Lincoln referred to in his private correspondence—would have tried to turn everything Lincoln said against him, either by portraying him as a weakling or by distorting his meaning. But there is no certainty that they would have succeeded. Surely a vigorous effort by Lincoln to answer his opponents might have blunted the impact of the Breckinridge offensive. Not that any Breckinridge voters could have been won over to Lincoln, but some of them might have been motivated to switch to Bell or Douglas. This is an important point, especially bearing in mind that the eventual success of the radical secessionists owed more to their initiative and élan than it did to support from the mass of white southerners, many of whom remained unconvinced that withdrawal from the Union was either wise or desirable. Lincoln's silence allowed the Breckinridge camp to seize the initiative and achieve maximum impact upon southern opinion. In the North, Lincoln's silence helped win him the presidency, but in the South it strengthened the hand of the secessionists with whom the new president-elect would now have to contend.[13]

As soon as Lincoln's election was announced, the lower South states moved rapidly toward secession. A short-lived but lively debate ensued between the more ardent "immediatists," who wanted their home states to secede at once and unilaterally, and the relatively cautious "conditionalists," many of whom hoped that secession might yet be avoided, and all of whom wished to delay a decision until a coordinated plan of action could be agreed upon by several states. In a continuation of the dispute that had occurred during the presidential canvass, the immediatists insisted that Lincoln's election necessitated immediate action because the Republicans were certain to undermine and eventually destroy slavery by measures such as interference with the interstate slave trade. In Georgia, Thomas R. R. Cobb spoke out against those who believed that Republican intentions were too "indefinite and shadowy" to call for immediate resistance. "Let us inquire," Cobb said. "The inter-State Slave Trade is within the letter of the Constitution. Should Congress abolish it will my objector submit?" Georgia governor Joseph E. Brown took a similar stance, arguing that the election of Lincoln was the first step in a program that would lead to total abolition within twenty-five years. Brown said that after several preliminary moves, the Republicans "would then abolish the internal slave trade between the States, and prohibit a slave owner in Georgia from carrying his slaves into Alabama or South Carolina, and there selling them. These steps would be taken one at a time, cautiously, and our people would submit. Finally, when we were sufficiently humiliated, and sufficiently in their power, they would abolish slavery in the States."[14]

In a speech delivered in his home state on 26 November, Alabama congressman Jabez L. M. Curry described Republican intentions:

> Coming into power on the flood-tide of popular fanaticism, grown insolent by repeated submissions on the part of the South, . . . Denying to the South equality in the enjoyment of the common Territories, they seek to circumscribe the South, to prevent her growth and expansion, and localize slavery in the present States of its existence. Proceeding one step further, the inter-State and coast-wise slave trade is to be prohibited; slaves are not to be transported for sale beyond the limits of any State, nor shipped from Baltimore to Charleston, from Norfolk to Savannah, from New Orleans to Galveston. The saleable or transferable value is to be diminished, and the institution localized and made less profitable in the particular States which allow it. Advancing still

> further in the work of destruction, slavery is to be abolished in the District of Columbia, and other places subject to federal jurisdiction, and those points made the citadels of constant attack upon our peace and property.

Curry warned that the Republicans would eventually find a way to abolish slavery in the states in spite of its constitutional protections because, under "Black Republican torture," many clauses in the Constitution could "be perverted by hate or interest to authorize direct interference in the States." In Curry's opinion, "if any one in this audience now doubts that the Republicans, with Lincoln at their head, intend to abolish slavery in the states, he would not believe though one rose from the dead."[15] (It is interesting that Lincoln had earlier used the identical metaphor to describe those who refused to believe him when he said that he would *not* interfere with slavery.)

Even as Curry spoke, the governor of Florida, Madison S. Perry, was delivering a similar message to the legislature of that state. Perry said that he would not insult the intelligence or try the patience of his audience by detailing just how the "Northern fanatics" would carry out their "mad schemes," but he had no doubt that immediate secession was required. He noted that some southerners "object to secession until some overt act of unconstitutional power shall have been committed" and say "that we ought not to secede until the President and Congress unite in passing an act unequivocally hostile to our institutions and fraught with immediate danger to our rights of property and to our domestic safety." But that, said Perry, would be a fatal error. "My countrymen!" he cried, "if we wait for such an overt act, our fate will be that of the white inhabitants of St. Domingo!"[16]

Conditionalists tried to counter these arguments. In a remarkably outspoken speech opposing secession, Charles Anderson, a slaveowner who had recently moved from Kentucky to Texas, pointed out that both the Republican platform and the past record of Lincoln gave every indication "that he will faithfully execute the fugitive slave law, and that he would not attempt to interfere with slavery in the District of Columbia, nor with the inter-States slave trade." Anderson scoffed at those southerners who were spooked by "all the squads and cliques of old women in pantaloons and petticoats" who sent antislavery petitions to Congress. He even refused to be outraged by the Republican stance against slavery in the territories, maintaining that it was foolish to stake the security of all southern slave property on "the right of some brother Kentuckian of mine to take his black mammy (nobody was ever foolish enough to go thither with any more valuable slave) to the bleak snow-plains of Kansas." Such unequivocal opposition to secession was a rarity in the deep South, however. Most conditionalists readily acknowledged that secession might become necessary, but argued that it would be an appropriate response only to overt acts by the Lincoln administration, and perhaps might be avoided altogether if the Republicans would only provide ironclad guarantees that they would not interfere with slavery. In Georgia, Herschel V. Johnson, who had been Douglas's running mate in the election, now led the conditionalists in calling for a southern convention, which, he suggested, might demand amendments to the Constitution, including both a provision that "Congress shall have no power to prohibit or interfere with the slave-trade between the States" and another prohibiting states from depriving the citizens of other states of their slave property when they traveled or sojourned anywhere in the United States. Alabama conditionalists made similar proposals.[17]

Conservative northerners tried to reassure southerners that they had nothing to fear from the Lincoln presidency. Joel Parker, a Harvard law professor and self-described "old Bourbon of Massachusetts," declared that "Congress cannot prohibit the transportation of slaves from one State to another State, and so there is no occasion for constitutional amendments in relation to that subject." Furthermore, he said,

> If it may be supposed that regulations affecting a traffic in slaves, between the slave States, may be made under the constitutional power of Congress to regulate commerce between the States, it is not readily seen how that power can lawfully be exercised so as to do any essential mischief to the interests of the slave States, so long as they remain in the Union. The power must be exercised in relation to this subject, upon similar principles to those which will govern its exercise respecting other matters which form the subjects of commerce between the States. There is little or no legislation under this power at present, nor is there likely to be.

The anonymous author of a pamphlet published at Philadelphia considered it obvious, given his understanding of "the opinions of our President elect, and if I can judge of his character and sentiments from his public speeches," that "there would be no difficulty in giving every guarantee about the slave trade between the States." It is doubtful that propaganda of this sort received much attention in the South, however. Henry J. Raymond of the *New York Times* protested to William L. Yancey that wild charges against Lincoln and the Republicans were being circulated in Mississippi and elsewhere, while contrary information was being suppressed.[18]

All appeals for delay and moderation from both within and without were swept aside in state after state of the lower South, as the immediate secessionists prevailed. South Carolina formally seceded on 20 December 1860 and was followed over the next six weeks by Mississippi, Florida, Alabama, Georgia,

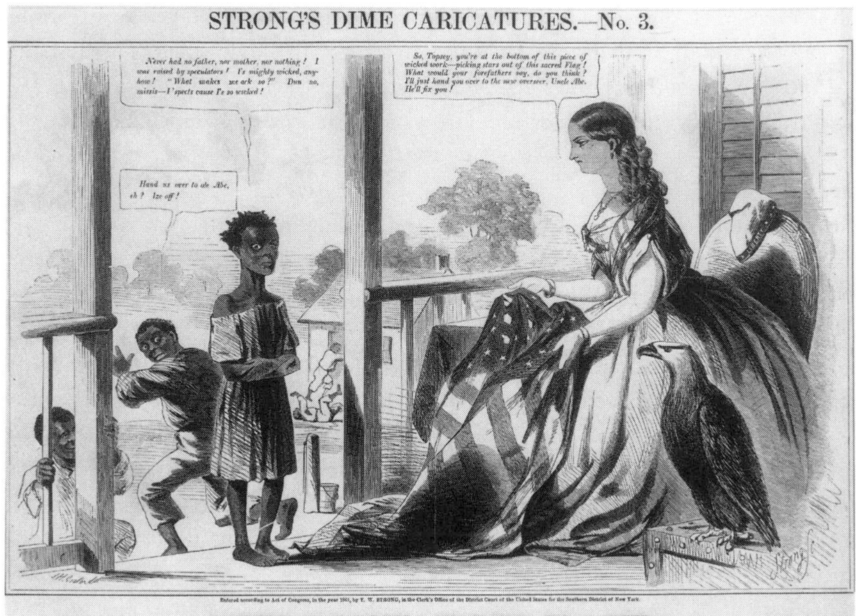

Figure 7. South Carolina as Topsy. The continued influence of *Uncle Tom's Cabin* is evident in this anti-secession cartoon. One of the more memorable subplots of Stowe's novel concerned the efforts of Miss Ophelia, a transplanted New Englander, to civilize Topsy, a wild and wily slave girl. Here the seated figure of Columbia plays the role of Miss Ophelia while Topsy personifies South Carolina. Columbia chastises Topsy for picking stars out of the sacred flag and threatens to hand her over to the new overseer, Uncle Abe. Topsy replies, "Never had no father, nor mother, nor nothing! I was raised by speculators! It's mighty wicked, anyhow! What makes me ack so? Dun no, missis—I 'spects cause I's so wicked!" (New York: T. W. Strong, 1861). Courtesy Library of Congress, Prints and Photographs Division, LC-USZ62-13954.

Louisiana, and Texas. The departing states left no doubt that it was the threatened future of slavery that had prompted them to take so drastic a step. "Our position is thoroughly identified with the institution of slavery—the greatest material interest in the world," declared the Mississippi convention; northern hostility to slavery "has grown until it denies the right of property in slaves, and refuses protection to that right on the high seas, in the Territories, and wherever the government of the United States had jurisdiction. . . . It knows no relenting or hesitation in its purposes; it stops not in its march of aggression. . . . We must either submit to degradation and to the loss of property worth four billions of money, or we must secede from the Union formed by our fathers, to secure this as well as every other species of property." Georgia's convention produced a list of grievances, including the fact that in several northern states "a citizen cannot travel the highway with his servant who may voluntarily accompany him, without being declared by law a felon and being subjected to infamous punishments. It is difficult to perceive how we could suffer more by the hostility than by the fraternity of such brethren." In Texas, the last of the Gulf states to secede, the convention stated simply that "recent developments in Federal affairs make it evident that the power of the Federal Government is sought to be made a weapon with which to strike down the interest and prosperity of the people of Texas and her sister slaveholding States, instead of permitting it to be, as was intended, our shield against outrage and aggression."[19] With secession a fait accompli in the arc of states stretching from South Carolina to Texas, the buoyant secessionists now looked hopefully to the more northerly slave states. There, however, the immediatists faced a larger and more determined opposition.

In the upper South, "commissioners"—informal ambassadors sent by the governments of the seceded lower states—repeated the arguments that they and their fellow immediatists had used to win the debates back home. Jabez Curry of Alabama, in an unsuccessful attempt to persuade the governor of Maryland to call that state's legislature into session, insisted that the Republicans did not recognize slaves as property that they had a constitutional obligation to protect. Rather, said Curry:

> the opinion of nearly every Republican is, that the slave of a citizen of Maryland, in possession of and in company with his master, on a vessel sailing from Baltimore to Mobile, is as free as his master, entitled to the same rights, privileges, and immunities, as soon as a vessel has reached a marine league beyond the shores of a State and is outside the jurisdiction of State laws. The same is held if a slave be carried on the territory or other property belonging to the United States.

Thus Curry portrayed the Republicans as just as eager to disrupt the coastal slave trade as they were to ban slavery from the territories. Meanwhile, Mississippi's commissioner to Maryland, Alexander Handy, gave speeches in which he predicted that the Republicans would use the federal commerce power to abolish the entire interstate slave traffic, "thereby preventing the exportation of slaves from the old Southern States, until their increase shall become an evil, and compel their emancipation, and thus abolitionize those States." Mississippi's commissioner to Virginia, Fulton Anderson, said much the same thing, claiming that the Republicans intended to defy the Supreme Court, "and by the exertion of bare-faced power, to exclude slavery from the public Territory, the common property of all the States, and to abolish the internal slave trade between the States acknowledging the legality of the institution."[20]

Opponents of immediate secession challenged those claims, but with mixed success. In Maryland, Reverdy Johnson, in a complete reversal of the views he had expressed shortly after Lincoln's nomination, told a sympathetic audience that even if Lincoln held principles "fatal to Southern rights" he would be checked by Congress or by "a patriotic Judiciary." But Johnson argued that Lincoln in fact held no such fatal principles, and substantiated the point by quoting a series of questions posed by Stephen Douglas in the Lincoln-Douglas Debates of 1858 and the accompanying replies in which Lincoln said that he was not pledged to any of several antislavery actions, including banning the interstate trade. In Virginia, one delegate to the state's convention declared that it would be cowardly to renounce the Union just because an objectionable person had become President, and pointless too, since "we know that we have the protection of our common Constitution." Another delegate disagreed, however, claiming that the rise of the Republican party was but the latest in a long series of aggressions against slavery, and noting derisively that "the great splitter, who now occupies the presidential chair, who seems as good at splitting the Union as he formerly was at splitting rails . . . is not even certain that the abolition of the slave trade between the States is unconstitutional."[21]

Defenders of Lincoln's record of moderation received little help from the president himself, who, even after winning the election, declined to comment publicly on his precise intentions. A few weeks after the election, Lincoln wrote a passage for a speech by Lyman Trumbull saying that under a Republican administration the states would be left in complete control of their own affairs and free to protect property as they saw fit. The statement was immediately attacked from opposite directions, however, being condemned in the press both as a betrayal of Republican principles and as an attempt to hoodwink the South. Therefore, Lincoln resolved, he would not speak publicly. Behind the scenes, he did give private assurances to a few individuals. When congressman John A. Gilmer of North Carolina posed a list of questions about his intentions, Lincoln wrote back referring to his past statements, particularly those he made in the 1858 debates, and adding, "I have no thought of recommending the abolition of slavery in the District of Columbia, nor the slave trade among the slave states, even on the conditions indicated; and if I were to make such recommendation, it is quite clear Congress would not follow it." Lincoln marked his letter "strictly confidential," however, so it did nothing to quell the argument in the upper South over whether secession was necessary to prevent a Republican attack on the slave trade. A week later, Lincoln tried to get across the same message to former congressman Alexander H. Stephens of Georgia, saying, "Do the people of the South really entertain fears that a Republican administration would, *directly* or *indirectly*, interfere with their slaves, or with them, about their slaves? If they do, I wish to assure you, as once a friend, and still, I hope, not an enemy, that there is no cause for such fears." But Lincoln marked that letter "For your eye only," so it too had no public impact.[22]

A more important roadblock to secession in the upper South than either the loud propagandizing by Unionists and conditionalists or the private reassurances offered *sotto voce* by Lincoln, was the fear that the breakup of the Union might threaten the slave exports that were so essential to the prosperity of the region. It was well known that lower South extremists had been campaigning for years for the repeal of the federal law that had banned the importation of slaves from abroad. Because the 1808 clause of the Constitution only permitted and did not require Congress to outlaw slave importations as of 1808, a change in the federal law was all that was needed in order for states to resume importing slaves from Africa. Although the campaign to reopen the external slave trade had garnered little public support, it had been endorsed by some of the same people who now had surfaced as hardcore secessionists in the deep South. Consequently, there was much suspicion that if the deep South states left the Union they would soon reopen the Africa trade, with disastrous consequences for slave values in the upper South. A Cleveland newspaper even went so far as to charge that the desire to resume the Africa trade was the principal motive for secession in the lower South. The newspaper added that if the Africa trade were reopened, "it presumptively follows, that slaves, raised in the Border States, and now sold to the far South planters, at the exorbitant prices of $1000, to $1500 each, will then have to be sold at about what the imported African can be purchased for of the slave trader—say not over $100 to $200 each. . . . It would certainly seem plain enough, from this view, that the Border States are directly interested to *absolutely prevent* the secession of any state—*if they can.*" Many people in the upper South who were wary of secessionism no doubt reasoned similarly.[23]

On 20 December 1860, the same day that South Carolina seceded from the Union, Alabama's commissioner to North Carolina tried to reassure the citizens of the latter state that the slaveholders of the lower South had no desire "to depreciate the value of their own property, nor to demoralize their slaves by throwing among them savages and cannibals." On the contrary, "they will look, as heretofore, to the redundant slave population of the more Northern of their associated sister States of the South for such additions to their negroes as their wants may require." A week later, the governor of Kentucky, writing to the commissioner that Alabama had sent to his state, declared himself opposed to immediate secession and called instead for a southern convention. The Kentucky governor noted with regret that some lower South states were rumored to be considering banning slave imports from the upper South. "Such a course," he said, "is not only liable to the objection so often urged by us against the abolitionists of the North of an endeavor to prohibit the slave-trade between the States, but it is likewise wanting in that fraternal feeling which should be common to States which are identified in their institutions and interests. . . . It would certainly be considered an act of injustice for the border slave-holding States to prohibit, by their legislation, the purchase of the products of the cotton-growing States, even though it be founded upon the mistaken policy of protection to their own interests." That same day, the governor of Maryland received a communication from the Alabama commissioner to that state in which the commissioner argued that the Lincoln administration threatened the interstate slave trade, whereas his own home state was determined not to reopen the Africa trade.[24]

In February 1861 delegates from six seceded states — South Carolina, Georgia, Florida, Alabama, Mississippi, and Louisiana — met at Montgomery to found a new slaveholding nation, the Confederate States of America. The provisional constitution of the new confederation prohibited the importation of slaves from any foreign country except the United States, and it also empowered the Confederate Congress to prohibit "the introduction of slaves from any State not a member of this confederacy." From the point of view of the upper South, those provisions were polar opposites. Upper South slaveowners welcomed the news that the Confederate constitution outlawed the Africa trade, but they were alarmed that it raised the possibility of a ban on their own slave exports southward via the interstate trade.[25]

The lower South commissioners charged with the task of winning over to secession the reluctant state officials of the upper South did their best to emphasize the positive. The commissioner from Georgia to North Carolina trumpeted the fact that the Confederate Constitution explicitly banned slave imports from Africa but not from the upper South, and he ignored the sticky point that the constitution actually opened the way for a possible interruption of the interstate traffic should the Confederate Congress choose to exercise its new power to ban slave imports from the United States. In the "great movement" for southern independence, the Georgia commissioner explained, "we prefer the cordial co-operation of the border slave States to the doubtful profits of this commerce for all coming time. Go on, and continue to raise the supply of labor, and we will provide for our wants in your market. We could have influenced your action by prohibiting the introduction of your slaves into our midst. We could have increased them in your borders by this restrictive policy, until they would have become worse than valueless to you. We were unwilling to constrain the action of a free people. We were averse to inflicting loss and injury upon those who had never shown us aught but kindness."[26]

Georgia's commissioner to Virginia was more candid, as he defended rather than ignored the constitutional provision allowing the Confederate Congress to prohibit slave imports from the more northerly states. The object of that provision, he explained,

> was not to threaten you, but to save ourselves. If you should join the North, the mere instinct of self-preservation dictates that we ought to do all in our power to keep you a slave State as long as possible. And the best way to do that would be to prevent your citizens from selling their slaves to ours. And, I have no doubt, that they would be prevented from doing so. But there is no more reason for construing a power to authorize such prevention into a threat than there is for construing the power to tax imports into a threat. . . . Join us, and these clauses will all become harmless to you, for certainly in that case we would not have the will to use them against you, and if we would, we should not have the power for you with the other Border States that will go with you, will be 8,000,000 of people, whilst we shall be but 5,000,000.[27]

While misgivings about what might happen to the interstate slave trade clearly helped stiffen upper South resistance to secession, other factors were more fundamental. Most important, slavery in the upper South was not the absolute bedrock of the economy that it was in the cotton states. There were some areas, particularly in the Appalachian region, where slavery had never taken root, and other areas, particularly in the old tidewater, where it had long been in decline. Almost as important, it was obvious that in the event of civil war, the upper South states were vulnerable to invasion, and fighting and wartime destruction were likely to be concentrated on their soil. Consequently, most political leaders in the upper South were either outright Unionists or else hesitant secessionists. Most of the latter were conditionalists, who did not reject the possibility of their states seceding, if it came to that, but who hoped fervently that such drastic action might be avoided through a negotiated settlement that would restore the Union on the basis of new constitutional guarantees for the security of slavery. The effort to achieve such a settlement preoccupied the U.S. Congress from mid-December 1860 through mid-January 1861 and then had a last hurrah at the Washington Peace Conference in February.

Members of the U.S. House of Representatives introduced a score of proposals for dealing with the national crisis, most of them suggesting various constitutional amendments to protect slavery. Four of the plans included provisions that explicitly forbade the federal government to interfere with the interstate slave trade. Similar schemes were introduced in the Senate, the most notable being the work of Andrew Johnson of Tennessee, who suggested several amendments preventing Congress from interfering with slavery in any of the ways that had been suggested by abolitionists. One of Johnson's proposed amendments read, "Congress shall not touch the representation of three fifths of the slaves, nor the inter-State trade, coastwise or inland." His final amendment stated that all of his proposed amendments, once added to the Constitution, were to be unamendable. (Whether there could be such a thing as an unamendable amendment was uncertain, although there arguably was a precedent in that the Constitution itself had stated that certain of its provisions, among them the 1808 clause, were unamendable.) Both the House and the Senate appointed special committees—of thirty-three and thirteen members, respectively—to study the various plans and recommend a course of action.[28]

The House committee of thirty-three began its work by receiving plans for amendments to the Constitution from two of the committee members, Thomas R. Nelson of Tennessee and Miles Taylor of Louisiana. Nelson's scheme included an amendment saying, "No law shall be passed by Congress interfering with the slave trade" in the existing slave states, the territories, or any new states to be created south of the Missouri Compromise line. Taylor's proposal included a more broadly worded amendment saying, "Congress is interdicted from legislating on the subject of slavery in the District of Columbia, or in any other district, Territory, or place in which it may exercise authority or jurisdiction," which in his mind probably encompassed any use of the federal commerce power against the slave trade. Because the Republican members blocked the consideration of these proposals, however, the committee devoted most of a series of later meetings to wrangling over the issues of slavery in the territories and enforcement of the federal fugitive slave law. Meanwhile, the Senate committee of thirteen considered a plan introduced by John J. Crittenden of Kentucky on the Senate floor on 18 December 1860. Crittenden's plan is famous today primarily for its proposal to extend the Missouri Compromise line to the Pacific, allowing slavery in all territories south of the line. The plan also included several amendments to guarantee the security of slavery, however, including one reading, "Congress shall have no power to prohibit or hinder the transportation of slaves from one State to another, or to a Territory in which slaves are permitted to be held, whether that transportation be by land, navigable rivers, or by the sea."[29]

The "Crittenden Compromise" was more thorough and more carefully worded than any of the earlier schemes that had surfaced in Congress, and it quickly became the main focus of peacemakers in the House as well as the Senate. On 27 December, Congressman Nelson asked the House committee of thirty-three to substitute the Crittenden proposal for his own. The committee then considered the Crittenden plan, but the Republicans on the committee refused to accept it. On 3 January the committee passed a resolution submitted by W. McKee Dunn of Indiana which said, "That as there are no propositions from any quarter to interfere with slavery in the District of Columbia, or in places under the exclusive jurisdiction of Congress, and situate within the limits of States that permit the holding of slaves, or to interfere with the inter-State slave trade, this committee does not deem it necessary to take any action on those subjects." The Crittenden proposals also failed in the Senate committee of thirteen, again because of firm rejection by the Republicans. Following their leader, William Seward, the Republicans on the committee of thirteen did express their willingness to accept a constitutional amendment that would have made it impossible for any future constitutional amendment to interfere with slavery in the states, but they would not accept Crittenden's proposal to allow new slave territories or his perpetual guarantee against the use of federal powers, including the commerce power, to undermine slavery. Despite their rejection in committee, attempts were made to revive the Crittenden proposals both in the House and the Senate, but there too they were blocked by the Republicans.[30]

The refusal of the Republicans to accept the Crittenden plan appalled those who saw it as the last hope for avoiding civil war. On the Senate floor, Stephen Douglas excoriated the Republicans for their intransigence and questioned their motives. They were, Douglas noted, willing to amend the Constitution "so as to render it impossible, in all future time, for Congress to interfere with slavery in the States where it may exist under the laws thereof." That being the case,

> Why not insert a similar amendment in respect to slavery in the District of Columbia, and in the navy-yards, forts, arsenals, and other places within the limits of the slaveholding States, over which Congress has exclusive jurisdiction? Why not insert a similar provision in respect to the slave trade between the slaveholding States? The southern people have more serious apprehensions on these points than they have of your direct interference with slavery in the States.
>
> If their apprehensions on these several points are groundless, is it not a duty you owe to God and your country to relieve their anxiety and remove all causes of discontent? Is there not quite as much reason for relieving their apprehensions upon these points, in regards to which they are much more sensitive, as in respect to your direct interference in the States, where they know and you acknowledge that you have no power to interfere as the Constitution now stands? The fact that you propose to give the assurance on the one point and peremptorily refuse to give it on the others, seems to authorize the presumption that you do intend to use the powers of the Federal Government for the purpose of direct interference with slavery and the slave trade everywhere else, with the view to its indirect effects upon slavery in the States; or, in the language of Mr. Lincoln, with the view of its "ultimate extinction in all the States, old as well as new, north as well as south."

> If you had exhausted your ingenuity in devising a plan for the express purpose of increasing the apprehensions and inflaming the passions of the southern people, with the view of driving them into revolution and disunion, none could have been contrived better calculated to accomplish the object than the offering of that one amendment to the Constitution, and rejecting all others which are infinitely more important to the safety and domestic tranquillity of the slaveholding States.
>
> In my opinion, we have now reached a point where this agitation must close, and all the matters in controversy be finally determined by constitutional amendments, or civil war and the disruption of the Union are inevitable.[31]

The last, doomed effort at compromise was the Washington Peace Conference Convention of February 1861. Soon after Congress rejected the Crittenden compromise, the legislature of Virginia passed a resolution inviting every state to send delegates to a conference at Washington and suggesting that a settlement might be worked out based upon the Crittenden amendments modified so as to protect slavery in all territory south of 36° 30′ and also to "secure to the owners of slaves the right of transit with their slaves between and through the non-slave-holding States and Territories." The legislature of Tennessee passed a similar resolution, it too proposing that "slave property shall be rendered secure in transit through, or while temporarily sojourning in the non-slaveholding States or Territories, or in the District of Columbia." Thus both Virginia and Tennessee sought to add to the Crittenden guarantee against any use of the federal commerce power against the interstate slave trade a clause that would nullify northern personal liberty laws and allow slaveholders to travel through the free states without being deprived of their human property.[32]

The six slave states of the lower South that had already seceded and that were in the process of forming the Confederate States of America did not send delegates to the Washington Conference. Neither did Texas or Arkansas. Texas seceded a few days before the conference began. Arkansas sent no representatives even though it would not secede until May. All seven of the upper South and border slave states—Delaware, Maryland, Virginia, North Carolina, Kentucky, Tennessee, and Missouri—did send delegates, and so did fourteen northern states. At the conference, Kentucky joined Virginia and Tennessee in calling for slaveowners to be given the right of transit through the free states. Ohio and other northern states rejected the idea, however, and, in the end, the conference approved a proposed constitutional amendment that went only slightly beyond Crittenden, in that it created no general right of transit but did provide that slaveholders who were moving slaves from one slave state to another by water could touch along the shores of the free states and land on their soil in emergencies. As finally worded, the proposed amendment denied to the federal government "the power to prohibit the removal or transportation of persons held to labor or involuntary service in any State or Territory of the United States, to any other State or Territory thereof where it is established or recognized by law or usage; and the right during the transportation by sea or river, of touching at ports, shores, and landings, and landing in case of distress, shall exist; but not the right of transit in or through any State or Territory, or of sale or traffic, against the laws thereof." The measure was adopted by a vote of 12 to 7. The ayes came from all of the seven slave states in attendance, as well as Rhode Island, Pennsylvania, New Jersey, Ohio, and Illinois. The nays were cast by Maine, New Hampshire, Vermont, Massachusetts, Connecticut, Indiana, and Iowa. (The delegations from New York and Kansas were divided.)[33]

Three days before the Washington Conference began, Abraham Lincoln wrote William Seward that he would accept no compromise on the question of slavery in the territories but was more open-minded about other issues. "As to fugitive slaves, District of Columbia, slave trade among the slave states, and whatever springs of necessity from the fact that the institution is amongst us," Lincoln said, "I care but little, so that what is done be comely, and not altogether outrageous." Just where the dividing line between the comely and the outrageous was, Lincoln did not say. It appears, however, that the Washington Conference proposals, like the earlier guarantees for slavery in the Crittenden Plan, fell beyond the pale so far as he, Seward, and the other Republican leaders were concerned, for the Republican-dominated Congress promptly spurned them. The Senate rejected the Conference proposals by a vote of 34 to 3, while the Speaker of the House declined even to present them to that body. Thus the last effort at compromise came to an end.[34]

On 18 March, John C. Breckinridge, who only two weeks earlier had taken up the Senate seat formerly occupied by John J. Crittenden, made what amounted to a hail and farewell speech to his colleagues in the upper house. Strongly hinting that his home state of Kentucky would soon secede, Breckinridge echoed Stephen Douglas's earlier condemnation of the Republicans for spurning compromise: "They refused to recognize property in slaves, or to give it equal protection in all the Territories; then they refused to make an equitable division; then they refused to declare that they would not abolish slavery in this District; then they refused to declare that they would not abolish the inter-State slave trade. . . . Throughout, you have utterly refused to give any securities in regard to the District of Columbia, the inter-State trade, the rights of the South in the Territories, or any other aspect of the whole subject." For the time being, however, Kentucky held off its secessionists and remained neutral. Breckinridge stayed in his Senate seat throughout the spring and summer. In September, when the Kentucky legislature declared for the Union, he fled to Virginia. There he accepted a commission as a brigadier general in the Confederate army.[35]

Some historians have found it puzzling that the election of Lincoln resulted in secession and civil war, for Lincoln and his party offered no immediate menace to slavery. There is no puzzle, however, if it is understood that both the Republicans and the secessionists were concerned not just with the fractious present but also with the limitless future. The Republicans knew that the only compromise acceptable to the South was one that would ensure that for all time to come the South would be free to push for new slave territories while no federal pressure of any kind could ever be applied to undermine slavery. Lincoln believed that under such conditions, the South would soon demand the acquisition of Cuba or more of Mexico, as well as press for a "second Dred Scott" decision in which the Supreme Court would compel the free states to allow slavery on their soil. Secessionists, on the other hand, knew that the balance of political power in the nation was shifting against them, that if they did not act now when the outer defenses of slavery's citadel were under attack, then they would be too weak to resist when, at some future day, a North grown stronger and more hostile toward slavery would use federal power to undermine the institution and pave the way for its ultimate destruction.[36]

While emotion and irrationality certainly were present in the great crisis that ended in civil war, both Republican intransigence and southern secessionism were essentially rational, in that each side knew what was at stake and behaved accordingly. When Abraham Lincoln told Alexander Stephens that he had no intention of interfering with slavery either directly or indirectly, he knew full well that such an assurance for the short-term security of their human chattels could not satisfy southerners bent on perpetuating slavery for all time to come. For, Lincoln acknowledged, "You think slavery is *right* and ought to be extended; while we think it is *wrong* and ought to be restricted. That, I suppose, is the rub."[37] The territorial question was the paramount focus of conflict, but all of the constitutional provisions that might allow the federal government to undermine slavery also were crucial. The secessionists' apprehensions focused not on any particular one of those provisions but rather upon their overall conviction that the election of Lincoln preluded a series of steps by which the Republicans would weaken and eventually destroy slavery. The most important such provision in terms of its potential impact on the South was the interstate commerce power, by which the slave trade among the states might be burdened or even abolished. The slaveholders were determined to plug that constitutional loophole. The Republicans were determined to leave it open, in the hope that some future generation might use it in the great work of herding slavery toward its ultimate extinction.

8

The Friction and Abrasion of War

On 12 April 1861 the governor of South Carolina ordered shore batteries in Charleston harbor to open fire on the federal forces occupying Fort Sumter. After thirty-four hours of bombardment, the Stars and Stripes were lowered and the fort surrendered. In response, Abraham Lincoln declared that an insurrection existed and called for 75,000 volunteers to defend the integrity of the nation. Once Lincoln had made it clear that he intended to suppress secession by force of arms, four more southern states—Virginia, Arkansas, Tennessee, and North Carolina—seceded and joined the Confederacy. Four slave states remained within the Union, but of the four only Delaware was safe. The other three—Maryland, Kentucky, and Missouri—were internally divided and bitterly contested by their loyalist and secessionist elements. Lincoln knew that there would be little chance of restoring the Union militarily unless he could hold on to the latter three states with their manpower, resources, and strategic territory. In order to hold on to them, he had little choice but to proclaim that the North was fighting only to preserve the Union and not to destroy slavery. He adhered to that position for more than a year. As late as August 1862 he said in a public letter that his objective was solely to preserve the Union and that anything he did regarding slavery would be incidental to that goal.[1]

Behind the scenes, however, Lincoln was already maneuvering to undermine slavery. Although in the early months of the war he countermanded emancipation edicts issued on their own initiative by some of his generals, he did allow his commanders to treat escaped slaves as "contraband of war" instead of returning them to their masters. As the war went on, an ever-growing mass of fugitives accumulated behind Union lines, and it became increasingly evident that the contrabands had effectively freed themselves and could never be returned to bondage. In April 1862 Lincoln proposed and Congress approved a plan for compensated emancipation in the District of Columbia. Lincoln also appealed to the slave states still in the Union to embrace similar plans, promising them federal funding and urging them to accept the reality that slavery within their borders was doomed. "The incidents of war can not be avoided," Lincoln told the representatives of the loyal slave states. "If the war continue long, as it must, if the object be not sooner attained, the institution in your states will be extinguished by mere friction and abrasion—by the mere incidents of war. It will be gone, and you will have nothing valuable in lieu of it. Much of its value is gone already."[2]

Lincoln's argument made sense. Later that year Frederick Douglass reported in his newspaper that in Virginia the whole institution of slavery was falling apart. More and more blacks were fleeing to Union territory. Moreover, the fugitives were saying that in Confederate-held areas, while there was no longer a local market for slaves, kidnapers were roaming the countryside, stealing slaves and then taking them deeper into the Confederacy to sell. "This fact illustrates the morals of the rebels, and their proclivity for the slave trade," pronounced Douglass. He could not resist adding, although it was an exaggeration of the actual situation, that "the relation of master and slave does not exist, and it involves no one in the charge of Abolitionism to predict that there is hardly any likelihood of its ever being revived."[3]

But the border states were unwilling to face reality, and they firmly repulsed Lincoln's overtures. Given his lack of success in prodding the border states toward emancipation, it is understandable that Lincoln made no move against the interstate slave trade, for that might have severely tested the tenuous allegiance of the loyal slave states. Some congressmen, however, were less prudent. In the House of Representatives, on 24 March 1862, Isaac Arnold of Illinois, a former Free-Soiler now a Republican, introduced a bill "to render freedom national and slavery sectional." The bill prohibited slavery everywhere that the federal government had jurisdiction, including "In all vessels on the high seas, and on all national highways, beyond the territory and jurisdiction of each of the several States from which or to which the said vessels may be going." The wording is somewhat confusing, as vessels do not travel on highways, but Arnold appears to have believed that Congress possessed and should exercise the constitutional power to outlaw the interstate slave trade by land as well as by sea. Other congressmen were not so sure, however, and Arnold's Illinois colleague Owen Lovejoy later presented a substitute bill that dropped the reference to national highways. Lovejoy, an ardent abolitionist who had been in succession a Liberty man, a Free-Soiler, and a Republican, actually agreed with Arnold that Congress could and should ban the entire interstate slave trade, but he realized that opposition to the idea was too great, and so he made the tactical decision to water down the bill in order to give it more hope of passage. Later Lovejoy felt compelled to add still more water, and by the time the bill was enacted into law it applied only to the federal territories and said nothing at all about the slave trade, coastwise or inland.[4]

Meanwhile, in the newborn nation known as the Confederate States of America, the political leadership was interested in protecting rather than attacking the slave trade. The Confederacy's permanent constitution mostly copied word for word the U.S. Constitution of 1787 but added new safeguards for slavery. While it gave the Confederate Congress the power to regulate interstate commerce just as in the parent document, it provided elsewhere that Confederate citizens "shall have the right of transit and sojourn in any State of this Confederacy, with their slaves and other property; and the right of property in said slaves shall not be thereby impaired." It also included a broadened fugitive slave clause that declared not only that states must return escaped slaves but also that states could not free any slaves that had been "lawfully carried" into their territory from another state.[5] The new protections were scarcely necessary in a nation that had slavery as its bedrock, but the Confederate founding fathers were taking no chances.

While no one in the Confederacy had the audacity to propose banning the slave trade, there were some people, especially in religious circles, who did speak out against its nastiest feature, the willful destruction of slave families. By the time of the Civil War most southern clergy had long since come to accept the principle that slavery was ordained of God as the proper relationship between the races. But, like any good institution, it could be corrupted by sinful human behavior. Thus the clergy held that for slavery to be pure, both masters and slaves must behave in a manner that was consistent with biblical precepts, including the Ten Commandments and the teachings of Christ. Many religious leaders therefore thought that it was sinful for the owners of slaves to sell husbands away from their wives or children from their parents merely for the sake of profit. While preaching on that theme became uncommon once the interstate slave trade had solidified into an essential feature of the southern economy, it never entirely disappeared. For example, in 1840 Presbyterian minister Robert L. Dabney of Virginia insisted that slave marriages should be respected and that every black woman should be "mistress of her own chastity." Dabney was still at it a decade later, writing in both the *Richmond Enquirer* and in church periodicals that it was wrong to split husbands and wives. Some important lay people expressed similar views. Louisiana sugar planter Samuel Walker, disturbed by the Frémont vote in the 1856 presidential election, proposed that property in slaves be made inalienable. In 1858 Christopher Memminger, one of the most prominent politicians in South Carolina, headed an Episcopal church committee that advocated protection for slave relationships. That same year Thomas R. R. Cobb of Georgia published *An Inquiry into the Law of Negro Slavery,* in which he too favored protection, although he was rather at a loss as to how it might be provided. Cobb said that the "unnecessary and wanton" separation of slave couples ought to be prohibited by law, even though he claimed it occurred only "rarely, if ever." But because the slave system would become dysfunctional unless masters retained the right to sell off the occasional "vicious, corrupting negro" while keeping the blameless spouse, the law would have to distinguish somehow between the wanton separations and the necessary ones, and Cobb did not know how that could be done. He did think that a law could at least be passed making it public policy to sell slaves as family units when they were auctioned off by court order as a result of bankruptcies and estate settlements.[6] Cobb perhaps did not realize that such a policy would have been a gift to speculators. If slaves were sold by court order only in families as he proposed, then those potential buyers who needed only one slave would not enter the bidding. Consequently, an intact family would generally sell for less than the total price its members would have brought if auctioned individually. Traders could thus acquire such families at bargain prices and then break them up for resale, thereby pocketing money that otherwise would have gone to creditors and heirs.

When the war came, reform-minded southerners did not fall silent in deference to the Confederate struggle for survival. On the contrary, they pressed for change with even greater urgency. Tennessee educator John Berrien Lindsley said that the war was God's punishment for the South's failure to respect slave marriages. "Our divine master has most emphatically ordained the family relations as sacred," he declared, but "the legislatures of the Southern States have with equal emphasis repudiated these relationships as to four million of their people. The Legislatures of each of these states has thus absolutely *nullified* the law of Christ." The Episcopal *Church Intelligencer* argued that there was no longer any excuse for postponing reform, because southern secession had removed the abolitionist threat to slavery. Catholic bishop Augustin Verot of Georgia in *A Tract for the Times* (1861) said that it was a "grievous sin" for masters to neglect their duty to protect their servants' marital relationships and to prevent the sexual exploitation of women. Calvin H. Wiley, a Presbyterian of North Carolina, in his *Scriptural View of National Trials* (1863), said that slavery must be made biblical or God would destroy the Confederacy. The Reverend Isaac Tichnor warned the Baptist General Assembly of Alabama that God would grant victory only if abuses were rectified. "We have failed to discharge our duties to our slaves," he cried. "Marriage is a divine institution, and yet marriage exists among our slaves dependent upon the will of the master. 'What God has joined together, let no man put asunder,' yet this tie is subject to the passion, caprice or avarice of their owners." In Mississippi, Presbyterian minister James A. Lyon denounced as "an outrage upon the laws of God, both natural and revealed" the fact that state law neither recognized slave marriage nor prohibited "fornication, adultery, bigamy, incest, or even rape" among slaves. In 1865 Lyon drafted and presented to the state legislature a bill entitled "An act regulating the marriage and parental relations existing among slaves," which would have legalized marriages and prohibited the separation of children from their mothers.[7]

But, just as before the war, the calls for reform fell mostly on deaf ears. In Mississippi, the judiciary committee of the state senate had kind words for Lyon's bill but said the time was not opportune. Dismayed by that rebuff, Lyon doubted that slavery could survive without being purged of its abuses. "Perhaps," he mused, "God's intentions are to bring the institution to an absolute end." In retrospect, it seems evident that there never had been any real possibility of affording legal protection to slave families, because doing so would have been far too damaging to the material interest of the slaveholders. True, the interstate trade could have continued without any quantitative decrease even if the speculators had been compelled to deal only in family units rather than individuals. But the economic cost would have been enormous. A major reason that the slave-based southern economy was so productive is that its labor market was wonderfully efficient. Introducing any meaningful protection for the integrity of slave families would have destroyed that efficiency. A white family that desired to buy a cook would be severely inconvenienced if she could be had only along with her husband and children, whom the white family might neither need nor be able to afford. When a sugar planter required an additional field hand, he wanted to buy a strong young man. The man's wife, unless equally robust, would be of little use to such a buyer, and the couple's children of no use at all. The reformers' calls to protect the slave family bore no fruit because they were incompatible with the essence of slavery, which was, as Harriet Beecher Stowe had said, to treat a human being as a *thing*.[8]

It is somewhat paradoxical that while reform efforts were going nowhere in the South, and while the whole issue of the interstate slave trade was receiving only modest attention in the North, the American domestic slave trade was emerging as an important subject of debate in Great Britain. At the start of the war, the British government had proclaimed its neutrality. But few British people were neutral in sentiment. Some looked with sympathy on the Confederate cause, partly because it was obvious that a divided America would be less likely to rival Britain either economically or militarily. Moreover, the new southern republic because of its overwhelmingly agricultural economy could be expected to pursue a free trade policy. Thus it would offer an expanded market for British industrial products as well as continue to supply cotton to the mills of Lancashire. On the other hand, however, slavery had not existed in the British empire for a generation, and most Britons viewed it with disdain. Much of the debate in Britain therefore focused on the crucial question of whether the American Civil War was a battle over slavery or merely a southern effort to resist northern dominance and oppression. British public opinion was deeply divided on that question, and the division cut across class lines.[9]

Many of the most outspoken British supporters of Lincoln and the Union cause were people who had long been active in the antislavery crusade. Harriet Martineau, for one, had no doubt that slavery was the root cause of the war. In an article explicating "The Brewing of the American Storm," Martineau described her interview with James Madison during her 1835 tour of the United States. Madison, she recalled, "did not see any way back to decency"—meaning any way of ending slavery—other than by removing the black population through so-called colonization in Liberia or elsewhere. Yet he acknowledged that colonization efforts had achieved little and said that even his own slaves preferred being sold southward into continued bondage rather than emigrating to an uncertain freedom in Africa. Madison had feared that the American struggle over slavery would lead to a civil war, a contest that he knew the South could not win. "It was as painful as it was strange to listen to the cheerful old man," Martineau recalled. Martineau thus portrayed the American republic as tainted from birth by the original sin of human bondage, and she did not hesitate to allot to Madison, the last and greatest of the founding fathers, his full measure of responsibility: "The share he had in bringing on the conflict which he foresaw was, first, permitting a compromise about slavery to be introduced into the constitution; next, inviting confidence to a delusive scheme for getting rid of danger, by getting rid of negroes; and, again, keeping up the traffic in slaves, by sending his own to market." Martineau hailed the abolition of slavery in the District of Columbia as a great breakthrough, declaring that it meant that slavery was no longer a national institution in the

United States. In her zeal to promote the Union cause, she conveniently ignored the fact, certainly well known to her, that the Lincoln administration had made no move to suppress the interstate slave trade and that the coastal trade was still explicitly sanctioned by the federal law of 1807.[10]

The most important early English propagandist for the Confederacy was James Spence, a Liverpool businessman. In his book *The American Union,* first published in late 1861, Spence argued at length that the southern states had the constitutional right to secede. He argued too that it was economically imperative for Britain to back the South in order to restore the supply of cotton to its mills. It was inconceivable, he thought, that his countrymen "shall long continue dumb and passive when the most numerous of our industrial classes shall be pining in submissive destitution." Spence's book was soon countered by *The Slave Power* by John Elliott Cairnes, a professor of political economy and protégé of John Stuart Mill. Cairnes insisted that the American war was at bottom a struggle over slavery, and not, as Spence would have it, a contest over states' rights. And whereas Spence had not so much as mentioned the domestic slave trade of the United States, Cairnes laid great stress upon both its "barbarous inhumanity" and its critical role in sustaining the southern economy. Many writers, Cairnes said, had already told "the story of human beings, reared amidst the softening influences of civilization, who, so soon as they arrive at the maturity of their physical power, are, like so many cattle, shipped off to a distant region of tropical heat there to be worked to death — of husbands separated from their wives, children from their parents, brothers and sisters from each other — of exposure on the auction-block and transfer to new masters and strange climates — all this happening not to heathen savages, but to men and women capable of affection and friendship, and sensible to moral suffering."[11]

Cairnes said that the interstate slave trade brought stability and coherence to the southern economy. It did so both by supplying slaves to the "torrid regions," where a continual new supply was needed because of the "waste of human life" that occurred there, and by keeping slavery viable in the upper South, where it would otherwise "become unprofitable and disappear." He acknowledged that slaveowners in the upper South did not literally breed slaves like cattle. "It is perhaps true," he admitted, "that in no particular instance is a slave brought into the world for the purpose, distinctly conceived beforehand, of being sold to the South." But that hardly mattered, for "it is absolutely certain that the whole business of raising slaves in the Border states is carried on with reference to their price, and that the price of slaves in the Border states is determined by the demand for them in the Southern markets." Cairnes used 1850 census data to show that the slave population of the deep

South was increasing far more rapidly than that of the upper South. But he did not stop there. In order to demonstrate that it was commercial slave trading rather than just planter migration that accounted for the discrepancy, Cairnes ingeniously called attention to the fact that the demographic disparity between the upper and the lower South was not great for children and adolescents but was pronounced in the case of slaves who had reached young adulthood. "Now these are facts which no mere migration of population will account for," said Cairnes. "If a planter, with his family and its following of slaves, removed from Virginia to Arkansas, the young and old of both races would go together. . . . But where slave dealing prevails in connexion with slave-breeding, this cannot happen. . . . It is plain that nothing less than a regular and systematic traffic in human beings could produce such results as these in the vital statistics of a nation." The deep South demand for slaves was so voracious, Cairnes believed, that if the Confederacy succeeded in its war for independence, it would reopen the slave trade from Africa.[12]

Cairnes sent a copy of his book to Abraham Lincoln, who acknowledged receiving it "with more than ordinary pleasure" and praised its "intelligent sagacity" and "generous candor." Back in Britain, however, the book came under heavy attack from George McHenry, an American expatriate. Although McHenry was from Pennsylvania, he staunchly supported the South. "I am proud to call myself a Confederate-American," he declared, and he even tried to convince the Philadelphia Board of Trade that his native state should secede from the Union and join the Confederacy. In a series of letters to London newspapers, McHenry and Cairnes sparred over each other's claims and counterclaims. McHenry insisted that there was no such thing as an interstate slave trade, arguing that the disparities in slave population growth in the upper versus the lower South were entirely the result of planters migrating and taking their servants along with them. "It is," he said, "nonsense to be talking about 'slave-breeding' and 'slave-consuming' States." McHenry could never have gotten away with such brazen falsehood in America, where any visitor to the South was all too likely to have encountered a trader driving his chained coffle southward, but in Britain there were far fewer eyewitnesses to the scale and the cruelty of the American slave trade.[13]

Still, those who could testify did so. A published memoir by Francis Fedric, an ex-slave, told how his former master had paid off gambling debts by selling some of his people to a speculator, haggling over the prices in their presence. When one woman had been sold, Fedric recalled,

> She laid her child in one of the women's arms, and speaking low, said, "Take care of my child, if you please." The women were so terrified that they dared

> not say a word, for a few weeks earlier this very trader had given 1,000 dollars to Mr. W., a neighbouring planter. The slave had said it was hard for him to be carried away from his wife and children, [whereupon] the trader instantly beat him so unmercifully, that Mr. W. thought the poor slave would be killed, and said, "You are not going to throw away your money in that way, are you?" "I don't care," said the trader, "I have bought him, he is mine, and for one cent I would kill him. I never allow a slave to talk back to me after I have bought him." He had beaten the poor fellow so severely that he could not walk. The trader said to Mr. W. that he should be passing that way again in about a month, and if they would take care of the slave and cure him, he would pay the damage, and either call or send for him.[14]

John Hawkins Simpson spent five days writing down the testimony of Dinah, an escaped slave from Virginia who had somehow made her way to London. Simpson then published Dinah's story, which included a graphic account of how she had looked on as her master, who was also Dinah's own father, had sold ten-year-old Priscilla, who was Dinah's daughter and thus the master's own granddaughter, to a trader. Simpson coupled Dinah's story with an argument that Britain should pressure both the North and the South to outlaw all slave trafficking. He also said that England, France, and Germany all should resolve never again to receive and recognize an ambassador "sent by a country calling itself a Christian country, in which any laws remain unrepealed by which a slave-owner is permitted to buy and sell slaves in order that they may be carried against their will from the lands on which they were reared." Simpson appears to have been proposing that the slaves be made into serfs who could not be sold separately from the estates upon which they resided. He thought that his plan should win the backing of abolitionists because it was "a step in their own direction," but that it should appeal also to those who pitied the poor slave but doubted the feasibility of immediate emancipation. Simpson thought it obvious that the slave would benefit from becoming tied to the land: "His domestic ties will not be torn ruthlessly asunder in any state. Slave-rearing states will by degrees find it to be to their interest to educate and free their slaves, they yearly becoming less valuable after the Southern Slave Trade is closed. Slave-consuming states (*i.e.* slave importing, both from Border States and from Africa), unable to replace by purchase the frightful loss of human life which results from hard-driven labor in their cotton and rice swamps, will soon see that their prosperity depends very much on the degree of consideration and kindness, tending to prolong life, with which their slaves are treated."[15]

John Bright was the most outspoken Member of Parliament in support of the North. An advocate of a radically expanded franchise in Great Britain,

Bright was one of the few Englishmen who unreservedly admired American political practices and institutions. Bright appealed to English workers to identify with the victims of the American slave trade. After quoting excerpts from southern newspapers, he said, "Now I do not know whether there is any workingman here who does not fully or partly realize the meaning of these extracts." They mean, Bright said, that it would be a good thing if the English mill owner owned his employees, "that they should be to him capital, just the same as the horses are in his stable; that he should sell the husband South,—'South' in America means something very dreadful to the negro,—that they [*sic*] should sell the wife if they liked, that they should sell the children, that, in point of fact, they should do whatsoever they liked with them."[16]

In the end, Britain's wavering over whether to remain neutral or to intervene so as to compel the North to accept mediation was resolved not by the verbal conflict between the pro-Union and pro-Confederate propagandists at home, but by the bloody clashes between Blue and Gray on the battlefields of America. At Antietam on 17 September 1862 the southern forces sustained such heavy casualties that Robert E. Lee felt compelled to retreat from Maryland back to Virginia. Lincoln seized upon Lee's withdrawal as the good news he had been waiting for in order to issue his Preliminary Emancipation Proclamation. In it he announced his intention, unless the South gave up its struggle for independence, to declare on 1 January 1863 that all slaves residing in those areas still in rebellion were henceforth and forever free. When January came, he made good on his pledge. It took a while for the movers and shakers within the British government to fully grasp the import of what Lincoln had done. But once they did, those who had been drawn to the idea of British intervention in the war rapidly lost their enthusiasm. The British came to realize that the war was not going to end soon and that southern success was not a foregone conclusion. They also came to understand that the Emancipation Proclamation was not, as they had at first thought, just a cynical and cruel attempt to provoke servile insurrection, but a truly pivotal measure that had made the Union cause synonymous with the destruction of American slavery.[17]

With his eyes on the main prize of emancipation, Lincoln had little cause to concern himself with the interstate slave trade. But even after the Emancipation Proclamation had gone into effect and slavery was being pushed closer to oblivion with every advance of the Union army, some members of Lincoln's party still thought the slave trade issue worth pursuing. In January 1864, Israel Washburn of Maine published an article urging Congress to pass a law prohibiting the interstate slave trade. He repeated the old abolitionist argument that such a measure would be sanctioned by the Constitution because the commerce clause gave Congress the power to control all interstate commerce and the 1808 clause gave it power over internal migration. He noted that both Daniel Webster and John Quincy Adams had endorsed the idea that Congress could control the interstate slave trade. Outlawing that trade would, Washburn said, ensure the permanent annihilation of slavery. He pointed out that there was at present not a single person legally enslaved in South Carolina. The Emancipation Proclamation had seen to that. But so long as it was still lawful for a slaveholder from one of the loyal slave states to sell a slave to a resident of South Carolina, it remained possible that slavery could be reestablished there. Abolishing the interstate trade would ensure that bondage could never gain a new foothold in South Carolina: "Her laws may remain unaltered for a century, and the wishes of her people to hold slaves may be unchanged, and yet it will be impossible for a slave to be held in the state — unless, indeed, Congress should hereafter see fit to re-open the foreign or domestic slave trade, and thereby practically to establish slavery, an event which we can hardly regard as within the bounds of human probability." Once the southern states realized that slavery could never be reconstituted within their borders and consequently that their laws sanctioning the institution were inoperative and meaningless, they would repeal those laws. "And thus would be brought about, naturally and easily, the grand result to which the rebellion points, a Union of Free States."[18]

Washburn sent a copy of his article to Lincoln and in an accompanying letter asked him to "steal ten minutes from the country when the country will permit you to do so" in order to consider it. "Whether the prohibition of the domestic slave trade would accomplish all that I think it would, it could hardly fail to aid in the execution of any other measure looking to the suppression of the rebellion + the abolition of slavery," Washburn said. "The [Emancipation] Proclamation must be carried out — it is the shortest, most direct + easy + legal way to put an end to the cause of the Rebellion + so to put down the Rebellion. Assuming that this will be done, the importance of the inter-State prohibition is obvious." Last, and almost as an afterthought, Washburn remarked, "It seems a little inconsistent that while slaves in the rebel States have been emancipated, a law like that of 1807 regulating the slave trade coastwise, between the States, sh'd be in force." Although there is no record of a reply from Lincoln, he probably gave at least some thought to Washburn's proposal, if only because Washburn was such a prominent Republican. He was in fact the founder of the party at the national level. As a member of the House of Representatives in 1854, he had called a meeting of thirty-four anti-Nebraska congressmen and suggested that they form a new organization to be called the Republican Party. When he was elected governor of Maine in 1860, his victory had provided helpful momentum for Lincoln in the presidential contest later that year. In 1863 Lincoln had appointed him collector of customs at Portland. But whether Lincoln took Washburn's proposal seriously or not, nothing came of it.[19]

Instead of undermining bondage by banning the interstate slave trade, Lincoln was by now moving toward staking slavery through the heart by amending the Constitution to abolish it outright. In replying to the committee that notified him of his renomination for the presidency in 1864, Lincoln stated that such an amendment would be "a fitting, and necessary conclusion to the final success of the Union cause. Such alone can meet and cover all cavils. . . . In the joint names of Liberty and Union, let us labor to give it legal form, and practical effect." In April the proposed amendment had passed the Senate, but in June it failed to secure the necessary two-thirds majority in the House. Perhaps because the abolition amendment had been blocked for the time being, Charles Sumner then spearheaded an effort to secure congressional action against the slave trade. In March, Sumner had reported a bill from the Select Committee on Slavery and Freedmen that would have outlawed all commerce in slaves both by land and by water, but the Senate had refused to take it up. Sumner now tried to tack onto an appropriations bill a rider that would repeal the sections of the Act of 1807 that regulated the coastal slave trade. He said that he wished "to remove from the statute-book odious provisions in support of slavery," and that he was "at a loss to understand how at this moment, at this stage in our history, any senator can hesitate to unite with me in this work of expurgation and purification." But many senators did hesitate, and on 25 June Sumner's measure was defeated. Sumner did not give up. He urged his colleagues to consider that the Act of 1807 was the only remaining federal law that explicitly sanctioned human bondage. "It seems to me," he said, "this Congress will do wrong to itself, wrong to the country, wrong to history, wrong to our national cause, if it separates without clearing the statute-book of every support of slavery." The Senate heeded his plea. Only hours after first rejecting the measure by a vote of 13 yeas and 20 nays, Sumner's colleagues reversed themselves and, by a tally of 23 to 14, approved Sumner's provision declaring that the relevant sections of the 1807 law "are hereby repealed, and the coastwise slave trade prohibited for ever." Five days later, the House concurred, and on 2 July Lincoln signed the measure into law. Although the coastwise slave trade was now forbidden, interstate slave trading by land remained what it had always been, an activity neither explicitly sanctioned nor explicitly disallowed by federal statute. That would remain its legal status until, on 18 December 1865, the Thirteenth Amendment was at last declared ratified, thus legally abolishing all slavery in the United States and with it the domestic slave trade.[20]

Figure 8. Former slave pen at Alexandria. The Franklin and Armfield slave pen at Alexandria continued in use under various owners down to the Civil War. When Union forces captured the hastily abandoned facility in 1861, they found one elderly man still chained to a ring in the floor. The building was later used to house Confederate prisoners of war—a dramatic token of a southern world turned upside down. Courtesy National Archives and Records Administration, NWDNS-111-B-4687.

Interstate slave trading continued to go on in the seceded states throughout the war, in part because slavemasters in areas that were under imminent threat of invasion had considerable incentive to sell off their slaves to buyers in areas where such property was more secure. Southern newspapers sometimes expressed pleasure at the record high prices at which slaves were selling, attributing them to public confidence that the Confederate cause would prevail and Lincoln's emancipatory efforts come to nothing. Such reports ignored the fact that slave prices were rising only because inflation was eating away at the value of Confederate currency. In real terms, slave prices fluctuated along with southern fortunes on the battlefield, but the overall trend was markedly downward. Southerners continued to buy slaves with Confederate paper because they knew that the future value of both depended entirely upon the outcome of the southern thrust for independence. "If the cause fails," wrote a contributor to a

Georgia newspaper, "our right to property in slaves fails simultaneously. Confederate notes, bonds, stocks, and negroes will all go together." Thus business continued as usual, although on a reduced scale. As late as April 1864 a new firm of slave dealers announced its establishment in Montgomery, Alabama, promising to "keep constantly on hand a large and well selected stock such as families, house servants, gentlemen's body servants, seamstresses, boys and girls of all descriptions, blacksmiths, field hands." The firm asked newspapers in Atlanta and Savannah to copy its advertisement, which suggests that it was seeking to obtain "stock" from Georgia via the interstate trade. But not for long. In July the army commanded by William T. Sherman laid siege to Atlanta, and in September Atlanta fell. Sherman then began his march to the sea, laying waste to everything in his path. He was in Savannah by Christmas.[21]

In February 1865 Union forces recaptured Fort Sumter. As the Stars and Stripes fluttered once more above its ramparts, units of the Twenty-first United States Colored Troops landed on Charleston wharf, where their commanding officer accepted the surrender of the city. Charles Coffin, war correspondent for the *Boston Journal,* witnessed the scene, then walked to the city's abandoned slave mart. He took possession of the auction block steps and later sent them to William Lloyd Garrison as a souvenir. Another reporter, James Redpath of the *New York Tribune,* seized a cache of letters that had belonged to slave trader Ziba B. Oakes. The letters too went to Garrison. On the third of April, Union troops marched into Richmond. Charles Coffin was there and wrote gleefully of the failed efforts of trader Robert Lumpkin to escape with his stock of fifty slaves shortly before the arrival of the Yankees. At his jail, "within pistol-shot of Jeff Davis's window," Lumpkin hastily formed his slaves into a coffle and hurried them to the railroad depot. There he found that a multitude of citizens were trying desperately to get on a train but were being forced back by guards with fixed bayonets, "giving precedence to Davis and the high officials, and informing Mr. Lumpkin that his niggers could not be taken." Coffin rejoiced that Lumpkin's "sad and weeping fifty, in handcuffs and chains, was the last slave coffle that shall tread the soil of America." That was not quite true, however, for it is probable that at least a few coffles were still on the move in what remained of the crumbling Confederacy.[22]

No one knows exactly when and where the interstate slave trade came to an end. A few slaves may have been carried across state lines even after Robert E. Lee's surrender on 9 April 1865, for it took several weeks for news of the capitulation to reach the more remote regions of the South. Perhaps it was in some sleepy Texas border town that one last slave was brought over from Louisiana and sold. Whether it was there or elsewhere hardly matters. What does matter is that the slave trade was no more. All over the South auction rooms had fallen silent and traders' pens stood empty. No riverboats or coastal craft bore unwilling human cargo along the waterways. Weary captives no longer dragged their chains on country roads and mountain trails, cursing fate and weeping for the loss of loved ones left behind. The last droplets had drained away from that great jugular vein through which suffering human beings had flowed southward and westward in their hundreds of thousands. It was an epochal event but passed unnoticed amid a society shocked and shattered by the frictions and abrasions of war.

Notes

Chapter 1. A Continual Torment

1. John P. Parker, *His Promised Land: The Autobiography of John P. Parker, Former Slave and Conductor on the Underground Railroad,* ed. Stuart Seely Sprague (New York: W. W. Norton, 1996), especially pp. 26–27. On the harsher demands placed upon slaves in sugar as opposed to cotton production, see Michael Tadman, "The Demographic Cost of Sugar: Debates on Slave Societies and Natural Increase in the Americas," *American Historical Review* 105 (Dec. 2000): 1534–75.

2. Michael Tadman, *Speculators and Slaves: Masters, Traders, and Slaves in the Old South* (Madison: University of Wisconsin Press, 1989), 202–3, quoting Harriett Jarratt to Isaac Jarratt, 29 Oct. 1835 ("as long as you can get a negro to trade on"); Isaac Jarratt to Harriett Jarratt, 9 Nov. 1835 ("toiling for our wives and their little ones"); Isaac Jarratt to sister and cousin, 29 Dec. 1833 ("you lack the negroes"); Isaac Jarratt to Harriett Jarratt, 15 Feb. 1837 ("any Honest calling"), all in Jarratt-Puryear Family Papers, Duke University.

3. A[braham] Lincoln to Mary Speed, 27 Sept. 1841, *The Collected Works of Abraham Lincoln,* ed. Roy P. Basler, 9 vols. (New Brunswick, N.J.: Rutgers University Press, 1953–55), 1: 259–61 (quotations 260); Robert L. Kincaid, "Joshua Fry Speed—1814–1882: Abraham Lincoln's Most Intimate Friend," *Filson Club History Quarterly* 17 (Apr. 1943): 69–71; A[braham] Lincoln to Joshua F. Speed, 24 Aug. 1855, *Collected Works,* 2: 320–23 (quotations 320); William Wells Brown, *The Narrative of William W. Brown, a Fugitive Slave. And a Lecture Delivered before the Female Anti-Slavery Society of Salem, 1847,* 2d ed. (Boston: Anti-slavery Office, 1848; reprinted Reading, Mass.: Addison-Wesley, 1969), ed. Larry Gara, 17–18.

4. Benjamin Thomas, *Abraham Lincoln: A Biography* (New York: Alfred A. Knopf, 1952), 4, 7–8, 17–21; Michael Burlingame, *The Inner World of Abraham Lincoln* (Urbana: University of Illinois Press, 1994), 21–23; notes on interview of John Hanks by William H. Herndon in 1865–66, *Herndon's Informants: Letters, Interviews, and Statements about Abraham Lincoln,* ed. Douglas L. Wilson and Rodney O. Davis (Urbana: University of Illinois Press, 1998), 453–58 (quotation 453); Lincoln to Speed, 24 Aug. 1855, quotation 322.

5. Steven Deyle, " 'By Farr the Most Profitable Trade': Slave Trading in British Colonial North America," *Slavery and Abolition* 10 (Sept. 1989): 107–25, especially 115–16; Steven Deyle, "The Irony of Liberty: Origins of the Domestic Slave Trade," *Journal of the Early Republic* 12 (Spring 1992): 37–62; Allan Kulikoff, *The Agrarian Origins of American Capitalism* (Charlottesville: University Press of Virginia, 1992), 226–45; Tadman, *Speculators and Slaves,* 12–21; Frederic Bancroft, *Slave Trading in the Old South* (Baltimore: J. H. Furst, 1931; reprinted New York: Frederick Ungar, 1959), 1–44 and passim. Although poorly organized and somewhat antiquarian in its approach, Bancroft's pioneering study remains a gold mine of information on all aspects of the domestic slave trade; it is not entirely superseded by the more modern scholarship.

6. Kulikoff, *Agrarian Origins,* 248; Tadman, *Speculators and Slaves,* p. 12, table 2.1; Richard Follett, "Slavery and Plantation Capitalism in Louisiana's Sugar Country," *American Nineteenth Century History* 1 (Autumn 2000): 4.

7. Tadman, *Speculators and Slaves,* p. 12, table 2.1. James A. McMillin, *The Final Victims: Foreign Slave Trade to North America, 1783–1810* (Columbia: University of South Carolina Press, 2004), 48, suggests a high figure of 170,300 for slave importations and thereby implies that Tadman's figures for slaves entering the interstate trade between 1790 and 1810 are exaggerated. But McMillin's estimate of importations, while based upon vastly more hard evidence than earlier efforts, still involves much conjecture about such things as average ship capacity and sailing frequency.

For a set of estimates of interstate slave movements that are generally lower than Tadman's, calculated differently, and sorted by regions rather than individual states, see Peter D. McClelland and Richard J. Zeckhauser, *Demographic Dimensions of the New Republic: American Interregional Migration, Vital Statistics, and Manumissions, 1800–1860* (Cambridge: Cambridge University Press, 1982), table D-1, pp. 159–64. For interesting case studies of both planter migration southward and subsequent return northward to buy more slaves, see Tom Henderson Wells, "Moving a Plantation to Louisiana," *Louisiana Studies* 6 (Fall 1967): 279–89, and David O. Whitten, "Slave Buying in 1835 Virginia as Revealed by Letters of a Louisiana Negro Sugar Planter," *Louisiana History* 11 (Summer 1970): 231–44. Both of these cases have atypical aspects: The move described by Wells occurred at the unusually late date of 1854, and the planter whose purchasing trip northward is discussed by Whitten was a free man of color. (See also David O. Whitten, *Andrew Durnford: A Black Sugar Planter in the Antebellum South* [New Brunswick, N.J.: Transaction, 1995].) The ownership and exploitation of slaves by free blacks was not so rare as most historians have supposed. See David L. Lightner and Alexander M. Ragan, "Were African American Slaveholders Benevolent or Exploitative? A Quantitative Approach," *Journal of Southern History* 71 (Aug. 2005): 535–58.

8. Kulikoff, *Agrarian Origins,* 250–51; Jonathan B. Pritchett, "Quantitative Esti-

mates of the United States Interregional Slave Trade, 1820–1860," *Journal of Economic History* 61 (June 2001): 467–75. Pritchett applies regression analysis to both Tadman's estimates and the earlier, much lower ones presented in Robert W. Fogel and Stanley L. Engerman, *Time on the Cross: The Economics of American Negro Slavery* (Boston: Little, Brown, 1974). For the large literature on this issue that developed in the wake of *Time on the Cross,* see the list of references on pp. 474–75 of Pritchett's article. Recently Steven Deyle has surveyed the principal scholarship and sided with Tadman. See Steven Deyle, *Carry Me Back: The Domestic Slave Trade in American Life* (New York: Oxford University Press, 2005), appendix A (pp. 283–89), "Total Slave Migration, 1810–1860, and Percentage Attributable to the Interregional Slave Trade."

9. Walter Johnson, *Soul by Soul: Life Inside the Antebellum Slave Market* (Cambridge: Harvard University Press, 2000), 52; Frederic Bancroft, *The Life of William H. Seward,* 2 vols. (New York: Harper and Brothers, 1900), 2: 57; Bancroft, *Slave Trading,* 90.

10. Edward E. Baptist, "'Cuffy,' 'Fancy Maids,' and 'One-Eyed Men': Rape, Commodification, and the Domestic Slave Trade in the United States," *American Historical Review* 106 (Dec. 2001): 1619–50; Bancroft, *Slave Trading,* 58–64; E[than] A[llen] Andrews, *Slavery and the Domestic Slave-Trade in the United States. In a Series of Letters Addressed to the Executive Committee of the American Union for the Relief and Improvement of the Colored Race* (Boston: Light & Stearns, 1836; reprinted Detroit: Negro History Press, [1969?]), 135–43, describing visit to Armfield's pen on 24 July 1835; Donald M. Sweig, "Reassessing the Human Dimension of the Interstate Slave Trade," *Prologue* 12 (Spring 1980): 4–21; Robert H. Gudmestad, *A Troublesome Commerce: The Transformation of the Interstate Slave Trade* (Baton Rouge: Louisiana State University Press, 2003), 1–2; Wendell Holmes Stephenson, *Isaac Franklin: Slave Trader and Planter of the Old South* (Baton Rouge: Louisiana State University Press, 1938; reprinted Gloucester, Mass.: Peter Smith, 1968).

11. George W. Featherstonhaugh, *Excursion through the Slave States, from Washington on the Potomac to the Frontier of Mexico; with Sketches of Popular Manners and Geological Notices,* 2 vols. (London: John Murray, 1844), 1: 119–23, 166–70.

12. Pen Bogert, "'Sold for My Account': The Early Slave Trade between Kentucky and the Lower Mississippi Valley," *Ohio Valley History* 2 (Spring 2002): 3; William Calderhead, "The Role of the Professional Slave Trader in a Slave Economy: Austin Woolfolk, a Case Study," *Civil War History* 23 (Sept. 1977): 199–200; Bancroft, *Slave Trading,* 275–93; Tadman, *Speculators and Slaves,* 71–82. On shipment by water, see also Charles H. Wesley, "Manifests of Slave Shipments along the Waterways, 1808–1864," *Journal of Negro History* 27 (Apr. 1942): 155–74; Richard McMillan, "Savannah's Coastal Trade: A Quantitative Analysis of Ship Manifests, 1840–1850," *Georgia Historical Quarterly* 77 (Summer 1994): 339–59; Richard McMillan, "A Journey of Lost Souls: New Orleans to Natchez Slave Trade of 1840," *Gulf Coast Historical Review* 13 (Spring 1998): 49–59.

13. For an extensive treatment of this theme, see Deyle, *Carry Me Back,* chap. 8, "'The Nastiness of Life': African-American Resistance to the Domestic Slave Trade." On the select examples given here, see ibid., pp. 254–56; Howard Jones, "The Peculiar Institution and National Honor: The Case of the *Creole* Slave Revolt," *Civil War History* (Mar.

1975): 28–50; anecdote by Virginia ex-slave Fannie Berry, *Weevils in the Wheat: Interviews with Virginia Ex-Slaves,* ed. Charles L. Perdue et al. (Charlottesville: University Press of Virginia, 1976), 42; A. J. McElveen to Z. B. Oakes, n.p., 13 Aug. 1856, *"Broke by the War": Letters of a Slave Trader,* ed. Edmund L. Drago (Columbia: University of South Carolina Press, 1991), 128–29; McElveen to Oakes, Sumter Court House, S.C., 8 Sept. 1856, ibid., 130 (first quotation); John Hope Franklin and Loren Schweninger, *Runaway Slaves: Rebels on the Plantation* (New York: Oxford University Press, 1999), 119, citing Records of the Fifth District Court, New Orleans, John Henry Brown v. Alexander Hagan, 26 May 1855, case number 10,001, Suit records, reel 28, Louisiana Collections, New Orleans Public Library; McElveen to Oakes, Haynesville, Ala., 21 Oct. 1856, *"Broke by the War,"* 134 (second, third, and fourth quotations); McElveen to Oakes, Montgomery, Ala., 1 Nov. 1856, ibid. (fifth quotation); McElveen to Oakes, Sumter, S.C., 4 Nov. 1856, ibid., 135–36; McElveen to Oakes, Sumter Court House, S.C., 2 Dec. 1856, ibid., 137–38.

14. Charles Ball, *Slavery in the United States: A Narrative of the Life and Adventures of Charles Ball, a Black Man, Who Lived Forty Years in Maryland, South Carolina, and Georgia as a Slave,* ed. Isaac Fisher (New York: John S. Taylor, 1837), 16–17; James Redpath, *The Roving Editor: Or, Talks with Slaves in the Southern States* (New York: A. B. Burdick, 1859; reprinted New York: Negro Universities Press, 1968), 118.

15. On early southern white opposition, see Gudmestad, *Troublesome Commerce,* especially chap. 5, "Profits and Piety." On laws, see Winifred H. Collins, *The Domestic Slave Trade of the Southern States* (New York: Broadway, 1904), chap. 7, "Laws of the Southern States with Reference to Importation and Exportation of Slaves"; Bancroft, *Slave Trading,* 271–75; Gudmestad, *Troublesome Commerce,* 102–17; Deyle, *Carry Me Back,* 51–55, 306 note 22; Lacy Ford, "Reconsidering the Internal Slave Trade: Paternalism, Markets, and the Character of the Old South," in *The Chattel Principle: Internal Slave Trade in the Americas,* ed. Walter Johnson (New Haven: Yale University Press, 2004), 154–60. For the anecdotes mentioned in the text, see "Pigs for People," extract from *African Observer,* Jan. 1827, in *In the Hands of Strangers: Readings on Foreign and Domestic Slave Trading and the Crisis of the Union,* ed. Robert Edgar Conrad (University Park: Pennsylvania State University Press, 2001), 143; S. T. Robinson et al. to South Carolina Assembly, ca. 1843, *The Southern Debate over Slavery,* volume 1: *Petitions to Southern Legislatures, 1778–1864,* ed. Loren Schweninger (Urbana: University of Illinois Press, 2001), document 114, p. 187; Robert Russell, *North America, Its Agriculture and Climate* (Edinburgh: Adam and Charles Black, 1857), 300.

16. For a thorough account of the myth and how it developed, see Gudmestad, *Troublesome Commerce,* especially chap. 7, "Speculation Triumphant." The comparison of slave mothers to partridges is in Nehemiah Adams, *A South-Side View of Slavery; or, Three Months at the South, in 1854,* 3d ed. (N.p.: T. R. Marvin, 1854; reprinted Port Washington, N.Y.: Kennikat Press, 1969), 82–83.

17. James L. Huston, "The Experiential Basis of the Northern Antislavery Impulse," *Journal of Southern History* 56 (Nov. 1990): 609–40; Ebenezer Davies, *American Scenes and Christian Slavery: A Recent Tour of Four Thousand Miles in the United States* (London: John Snow, 1849; reprinted New York: Johnson Reprint Corporation, 1969),

23–24; Harriet Martineau, *Retrospect of Western Travel,* 2 vols. (London: Saunders and Otley, 1838; reprinted New York: Johnson Reprint Corporation, 1968), 1: 235–36.

Chapter 2. This Blind Mysterious Form of Words

1. Jack N. Rakove, *Original Meanings: Politics and Ideas in the Making of the Constitution* (New York: Alfred A. Knopf, 1996), 10, 9–10.

2. Debate of 21 Aug. 1787, James Madison's notes, *The Records of the Federal Convention of 1787*, ed. Max Farrand, revised ed., 4 vols. (New Haven: Yale University Press, 1937; reprinted 1966), 2: 364. The slave populations of South Carolina and Georgia had fallen sharply during the Revolutionary era, as slaves were removed to safer places by their owners, joined the British side, or simply ran away. Between 1775 and 1783, South Carolina's slave population fell by one quarter, from about 100,000 to 75,000, and Georgia's by two thirds, from 15,000 to 5,000. Meanwhile, the slave populations of Virginia and Maryland had increased, to the point that many planters had more hands than they needed. (Ira Berlin, *Many Thousands Gone: The First Two Centuries of Slavery in North America* [Cambridge: Belknap Press of Harvard University Press, 1998], 304, 264.)

3. Convention Journal, 25 Aug. 1787, Farrand, *Records of the Federal Convention*, 2: 408–9; debate of 25 Aug. 1787, ibid., 2: 415. Only eleven states participated because Rhode Island had never sent delegates to the convention while New York's delegation had already departed.

4. Debate of 29 Aug. 1787, ibid., 449; Luther Martin, "Genuine Information VII," *Baltimore Maryland Gazette*, 18 Jan. 1788, in *The Documentary History of the Ratification of the Constitution*, ed. Merrill Jensen, et al., 18 vols. (Madison: State Historical Society of Wisconsin, 1976–2001), 15: 413; debate of 29 Aug. 1787, Madison's notes, Farrand, *Records of the Federal Convention*, 2: 449–50; George Mason to Thomas Jefferson, Gunston Hall, 26 May 1788, in Jensen, *Documentary History of Ratification*, 18: 79; see also "George Mason's Account of Certain Proceedings in Convention," in the handwriting of Thomas Jefferson, in Farrand, *Records of the Federal Convention*, 3: 367. Pinckney's point was underlined by his South Carolina compatriot David Ramsay, who informed a Northern acquaintance that the leading men of South Carolina were agreed that the New Englanders "ought to be our carriers though a dearer freight should be the consequence," and added, "Your delegates never did a more political thing than in standing by those of South Carolina about negroes." David Ramsay to Benjamin Lincoln, Charleston, 29 Jan. 1788, in Jensen, *Documentary History of Ratification*, 15: 487.

For a detailed account of the gradual emergence of the "dirty compromise," as he terms it, see Paul Finkelman, *Slavery and the Founders: Race and Liberty in the Age of Jefferson* (Armonk, N.Y.: M. E. Sharpe, 1996), 22–28. On the important role of Connecticut delegates Roger Sherman and Oliver Ellsworth, see Christopher Collier, *All Politics Is Local: Family, Friends, and Provincial Interests in the Creation of the Constitution* (Hanover, N.H.: University Press of New England, 2003), 63–73.

5. Debate of 25 Aug. 1787, Madison's notes, in Farrand, *Records of the Federal Convention,* 2: 415–16 (quotation 415).

6. Walter Berns, "The Constitution and the Migration of Slaves," *Yale Law Journal* 78 (Dec. 1968): 198–228. This article is reprinted both in Kermit Hall, ed., *The Law of American Slavery: Major Historical Interpretations,* vol. 9, *United States Constitutional and Legal History* (New York: Garland, 1987), and in Walter Berns, *In Defense of Liberal Democracy* (Chicago: Regnery Gateway, 1984).

7. John Alvis, "The Slavery Provisions of the U.S. Constitution: Means for Emancipation," *Political Science Reviewer* 17 (Fall 1987): 253–59; Richard G. Stevens, "Liberal Democracy and Justice in the Constitution of Walter Berns," *Political Science Reviewer,* 22 (Fall 1993): 103–5; David Brion Davis, *The Problem of Slavery in the Age of Revolution* (Ithaca, N.Y.: Cornell University Press, 1975), 128–29 (quotation 129n); William M. Wiecek, *The Sources of Antislavery Constitutionalism in America, 1760–1848* (Ithaca, N.Y.: Cornell University Press, 1977), 75; Finkelman, *Slavery and the Founders,* 175n.

8. Committee of Detail working document in the hand of Edmund Randolph with emandations by John Rutledge, undated, in Farrand, *Records of the Federal Convention,* 2: 143; debate of 6 Aug. 1787, Madison's notes, ibid., 2: 183. Another undated working document of the committee, this one in the hand of James Wilson with emandations by Rutledge, used the wording "emigration or importation." (Ibid., 2: 169.) At the time, there was no clear distinction in usage between the words "immigration" and "emigration." (Davis, *Problem of Slavery in Age of Revolution,* 126n.) During the discussion of what became the 1808 clause, Roger Sherman of Connecticut opposed allowing a tax on slave imports because that would be "acknowledging men to be property, by taxing them as such under the character of slaves." James Madison also "thought it wrong to admit in the Constitution the idea that there could be property in men." (Debate of 25 Aug. 1787, Madison's notes, in Farrand, *Records of the Federal Convention,* 2: 416, 417.)

9. Berns, "Constitution and Migration," 217–18; debate of 25 Aug. 1787, Madison's notes, in Farrand, *Records of the Federal Convention,* 2: 417.

10. Pennsylvania debates, 3 Dec. 1787, in Jensen, *Documentary History of Ratification,* 2: 463; Martin, "Genuine Information VII," ibid., 15: 412.

11. "Letter from Massachusetts," *Connecticut Journal,* 24 Oct. 1787, in Jensen, *Documentary History of Ratification,* 3: 379; North Carolina debates, 26 July 1788, in *The Debates in the Several State Conventions, on the Adoption of the Federal Constitution, as Recommended by the General Convention at Philadelphia, in 1787 . . .* , ed. Jonathan Elliot, 2d ed., 5 vols. in 2 (Philadelphia: J. B. Lippincott, 1836–45; reprinted 1941), 4: 101, 102.

12. Pennsylvania debates, 28 Nov. 1787, in Jensen, *Documentary History of Ratification,* 2: 417; North Carolina debates, 26 July 1788, in Elliot, *Debates in the State Conventions,* 4: 101, 102; New Hampshire debates, undated fragment, ibid., 2: 203; Berns, "Constitution and Migration," 201.

13. Massachusetts debates, 18 Jan. 1788, in Elliot, *Debates in the State Conventions,* 2: 41; Berns, "Constitution and Migration," 205. It can be argued that ending slave importations in 1808 did eventually kill slavery, because the fact that slave importations into the South were choked off while white immigration into the North snowballed was the root cause of the shifting balance of political power that culminated in the Civil War. However, neither Dawes nor anyone else in 1788 foresaw that development. Rather,

Dawes probably was under the mistaken impression that the slave population could not sustain itself through natural increase. Such demographic failure was characteristic of most slave populations elsewhere, but not in the American South.

14. Tench Coxe, "An American Citizen IV: On the Federal Government," Philadelphia, ca. 21 Oct. 1787, *Addresses to the Citizens of Pennsylvania . . .* (Philadelphia, [1787]), in Jensen, *Documentary History of Ratification,* 13: 432; "Plain Truth to Timothy Meanwell," *Philadelphia Independent Gazateer,* 30 Oct. 1787, in Jensen, *Documentary History of Ratification* 14: 515.

15. Benjamin Rush to Jeremy Belknap, Philadelphia, 28 Feb. 1788, in Jensen, *Documentary History of Ratification,* 16: 250; Berns, "Constitution and Migration," 203; J. H. to Messrs. Hall & Sellers, *Pennsylvania Gazette,* 5 Mar. 1788, in Jensen, *Documentary History of Ratification,* supplementary microfiche 489 at frame 1947; William Rotch, Sr., to Moses Brown, Nantucket, 8 Nov. 1787, in Jensen, *Documentary History of Ratification,* 14: 520–21; James Pemberton to Moses Brown, Philadelphia, 16 Nov. 1787, ibid., 14: 524–25.

16. Pennsylvania debates, 4 Dec. 1787, ibid., 2: 499; Pennsylvania debates, 3 Dec. 1787, ibid., 463.

17. Pennsylvania debates, 3 Dec. 1787, ibid., 462, 463; Berns, "Constitution and Migration," 203.

18. Pennsylvania debates, 3 Dec. 1787, in Jensen, *Documentary History of Ratification,* 2: 463; Berns, "Constitution and Migration," 224–25.

19. Massachusetts debates, 30 Jan. 1788, in Elliot, *Debates in the State Conventions,* 2: 115–16.

20. Debate of 22 Aug. 1787, Madison's notes, in Farrand, *Records of the Federal Convention,* 2: 370; George Mason, "Suggested Revisions of Committee of Style Report," ca. 13 Sept. 1787, *Supplement to Max Farrand's The Records of the Federal Convention of 1787* (New Haven: Yale University Press, 1987), 269–71. Mason strongly endorsed ending the importation of slaves but never called for halting the interstate trade. His objection to importations was practical rather than moral; he argued that "such importations render the United States weaker, more vulnerable, and less capable of defence." ("*The Hon.* GEORGE MASON's *Objections to the New Constitution,*" *Massachusetts Centinel,* 21 Nov. 1787, in Jensen, *Documentary History of Ratification,* 14: 151.)

21. Publius [James Madison], "The Federalist 42," *New York Packet,* 22 Jan. 1788, in Jensen, *Documentary History of Ratification,* 15: 429; Berns, "Constitution and Migration," 215.

22. Madison, "Federalist 42"; Berns, "Constitution and Migration," 215–16.

23. U.S. House of Representatives, Mar. [*sic;* actually 12 Feb.] 1790, in Elliot, *Debates in the State Conventions,* 4: 408; Berns, "Constitution and Migration," 209n.

24. James Madison to Robert Walsh, Montpellier, 27 Nov. 1819, in Farrand, *Records of the Federal Convention,* 3: 437; James Madison to Joseph C. Cabell, 13 Feb. 1829, draft copy, James Madison Papers, Library of Congress, microfilm. Madison struck from his 1829 letter about two hundred words that originally followed the word "lodged." In the cancelled passage, he said that the interstate commerce power was couched in general terms because of "the notoriety of its object, and a confidence that it would not in practice be extended to local interferences obnoxious to the States authorities & to this explana-

tion may be added the difficulty of so defining & qualifying the power, as to retain the use, and guard ag[st]. the abuse of it: a difficult[y] that will be felt by whoever makes the attempt."

25. Harriet Martineau, *Retrospect of Western Travel,* 2 vols. (London: Saunders and Otley, 1838, reprinted New York: Johnson Reprint Corporation, 1968), 1: 193.

26. Debate of 22 Aug. 1787, Madison's notes, in Farrand, *Records of the Federal Convention,* 2: 371.

27. Civis [David Ramsay], "To the Citizens of South Carolina," Charleston *Columbian Herald,* 4 Feb. 1788, in Jensen, *Documentary History of Ratification,* 16: 25.

28. Virginia debates, 17 June 1788, in Jensen, *Documentary History of Ratification,* 10: 1341; Virginia debates, 24 June 1788, ibid., 1476; Virginia debates, 17 June 1788, ibid., 1341–42 (quotation). Edmund Randolph made much the same point as Nicholas, saying that the 1808 clause "is an exception from the power of regulating commerce, and the restriction is only to continue till 1808. Then Congress can, by the exercise of that power, prevent further importations, but does it affect the existing state of slavery?" It seems evident that Randolph too had no idea that Congress might have power to attack the domestic slave trade. (Virginia debates, 24 June 1788, ibid., 1483.)

29. It is doubtful that anybody in the 1780s would have thought that a planter's moving along with his own slaves from one state to another would constitute "commerce." Although the interstate slave trade proper was increasing by the late 1780s, it was still small and mostly involved slaves who were being sold directly from one planter to another rather than through an intermediary. It was not until the nineteenth century that professional slave traders dominated the market. (Steven Deyle, "The Irony of Liberty: The Origins of the Domestic Slave Trade," *Journal of the Early Republic* 12 [Spring 1992]: 59.)

30. Pennsylvania Abolition Society, "To the Hon. the CONVENTION of the United States of America, now assembled in the City of Philadelphia," 2 June 1787, *Pennsylvania Gazette,* 5 Mar. 1788, in Jensen, *Documentary History of Ratification,* supplementary microfiche 489 at frames 1947–49; New-York Manumission Society petition to New York legislature, draft copy, Feb. 1786, John Jay Papers, Rare Book and Manuscript Library, Columbia University. The Pennsylvania Abolition Society petition was not actually presented to the Convention because Tench Coxe and Benjamin Franklin thought it would be counterproductive. (Tench Coxe to James Madison, Philadelphia, 31 Mar. 1790, in Farrand, *Records of the Federal Convention,* 3: 361.) A slightly different version of the petition to the New York legislature appears in Jay's manuscript history of the New-York Manumission Society (handwritten fragment), minutes of 4 May 1786, Boston Public Library. The New-York Manumission Society decided on 16 August 1787 to submit an antislavery petition to the Constitutional Convention, and Jay actually drafted it, but on the advice of Alexander Hamilton at a meeting the next day, the idea was abandoned. (Richard B. Morris, *Witnesses at the Creation: Hamilton, Madison, Jay, and the Constitution* [New York: Holt, Rinehart and Winston, 1985], 193.)

31. Debate of 11 July 1787, Madison's notes, in Farrand, *Records of the Federal Convention,* 1: 580–81.

32. Debate of 22 Aug. 1787, Madison's notes, Farrand, *Records of the Federal Convention,,* 2: 371; "Truth et Justice," *New Jersey Gazette,* 11 Apr. 1781, quoted in Arthur

Zilversmit, *The First Emancipation: The Abolition of Slavery in the North* (Chicago: University of Chicago Press, 1967), 146. The theme of property rights as a barrier to emancipation permeates Zilversmit's fine study; see especially pp. 199–200. See also Shane White, *Somewhat More Independent: The End of Slavery in New York City, 1770–1810* (Athens: University of Georgia Press, 1991), 46–47.

About four hundred slaves resided in Philadelphia at the time of the Constitutional Convention. Pennsylvania's gradual abolition law, the first in the nation, had freed only those slaves born after 1 March 1780 and then only when they reached age twenty-eight. Thus no slave was freed by the law until 1808, and total abolition was not achieved until 1848. (Gary B. Nash, *Forging Freedom: The Formation of Philadelphia's Black Community, 1720–1840* [Cambridge: Harvard University Press, 1988], 63–65.)

Chapter 3. Are They Not the Lord's Enemies?

1. *Annals of Congress,* 1 Cong., 2 sess., House, 1133 (11 Feb. 1790), 1197–98 (12 Feb. 1790); facsimiles of the manuscript petitions printed in *National State Papers of the United States, 1789–1817,* 35 vols. (Wilmington, Del.: Michael Glazier, 1985), part 2: *Texts of Documents, Administration of George Washington,* 3: 422–29, document 34; Howard A. Ohline, "Slavery, Economics, and Congressional Politics, 1790," *Journal of Southern History* 46 (Aug. 1980): 345, citing "Friends Remarks to the Committee of Congress at New York," February 1790, James Pemberton Papers, Historical Society of Pennsylvania, Philadelphia.

2. *Annals,* 1 Cong., 2 sess., House, 1204 (12 Feb. 1790).

3. Ibid., 1186 (quotation from Aedemus Burke, 11 Feb. 1790). Most of the points mentioned were made repeatedly during the debates. For good examples of each, see ibid., 1186 (meddling), 1458 (no remedy), 1185 (undermines value), 1198 (false hopes), 1452 (humane treatment), 1455 (inferior race), 1198 (enlightened men), 1200 (history), 1187 (Bible), 1463 (economy), 1198 (civil war).

4. William C. diGiacomantonio, "For the Gratification of a Volunteering Society: Antislavery Pressure Group Politics in the First Federal Congress," *Journal of the Early Republic* 15 (Summer 1995): 177; *Annals,* 1 Cong., 2 sess., House, 1414 (committee report, 8 Mar. 1790), 1454 (William L. Smith, 17 Mar. 1790). The committee had seven members: Abiel Foster (N.H.), Elbridge Gerry (Mass.), Benjamin Huntington (Conn.), John Laurence (N.Y.), Thomas Sinnickson (N.J.), Thomas Hartley (Pa.), and Josiah Parker (Va.). (diGiacomantonio, "For the Gratification," 178n.)

5. *Annals,* 1 Cong., 2 sess., 1414, 1415 (8 Mar. 1790).

6. *A Necessary Evil? Slavery and the Debate over the Constitution,* ed. John P. Kaminski (Madison, Wisc.: Madison House, 1995), 226–28. Scott's speech was not printed in the *Annals of Congress.* (Cf. *Annals,* 1 Cong., 2 sess., House, 1466 [22 Mar. 1790].)

7. Richard S. Newman, "Prelude to the Gag Rule: Southern Reaction to Antislavery Petitions in the First Federal Congress," *Journal of the Early Republic* 16 (Winter 1996): 571–99, provides a good description of how the deep South congressmen bullied many upper South and some Northern representatives into supporting their demands.

8. Edward Needles, *An Historical Memoir of the Pennsylvania Society, for Promoting the Abolition of Slavery; the Relief of Free Negroes Unlawfully Held in Bondage, and for*

Improving the Condition of the African Race Compiled from the Minutes of the Society and Other Official Documents (Philadelphia: Merrihew and Thompson, 1848), 43; *Annals,* 4 Cong., 2 sess., 2015–24 (quotation 2015); *The Black Presence in the Era of the American Revolution,* ed. Sidney Kaplan and Emma Nogrady Kaplan, rev. ed. (Amherst: University of Massachusetts Press, 1989), 272–76 (quotations 275–76).

9. *Annals,* 5 Cong., 2 sess., House, 1957 (16 June 1798), 1979 (19 June 1798); Henry Adams, *The Life of Albert Gallatin* (Philadelphia: J. B. Lippincott, 1879; reprinted New York: Peter Smith, 1943), 86, 209; *Annals,* 5 Cong., 2 sess., House, 2009 (first quotation, 21 June 1798), 1963 (second quotation, 16 June 1798), 1969 (16 June 1798), 1996 (19 June 1798), 2009 (21 June 1798). Another Republican, Robert Williams, said that "migration" could not refer to slaves because "they were not imported according to their free will. It must apply to emigrants, not only from foreign countries, but from one State to another." Williams thus asserted that the 1808 clause applied to the interstate movement as well as to the immigration of whites. Probably he did not realize that his words carried a dangerous implication. For if "migration" meant what he said it did, then perhaps "importation" encompassed the bringing of slaves into a state from other states as well as from abroad. In other words, Williams appeared to imply that the federal government would possess authority over the interstate slave trade beginning in 1808. (*Annals,* 5 Cong., 2 sess., House, 1964 [16 June 1798].)

10. *Annals,* 5 Cong., 2 sess., House, 1991 (quotation, 19 June 1798), 1959 (16 June 1798), 1967 (16 June 1798), 1990 (19 June 1798).

11. Ibid., 1968–69 (16 June 1798), 1993 (19 June 1798), 2003 (21 June 1798).

12. Ibid., 2004–5 (Jonathan Dayton, 21 June 1798), 1979 (Albert Gallatin, 19 June 1798). The publication of James Madison's notes on the Constitutional Convention would later make clear that Baldwin was correct. When the 1808 clause was being considered in 1787, Gouverneur Morris pointed out that its wording implied that Congress could tax freemen who were imported. George Mason then said that the provision could be used to block the importation of convicts. (Debate of 25 Aug. 1787, James Madison's notes, *The Records of the Federal Convention of 1787,* ed. Max Farrand, 4 vols. [New Haven: Yale University Press, 1937; reprinted New Haven: Yale University Press, 1966], 2: 417.)

13. Thomas Jefferson, Kentucky Resolutions, 16 Nov. 1798, *Documents of American History,* ed. Henry Steele Commager, 7th ed., 2 vols. (New York: Appleton-Century-Crofts, 1963), 1: 179–80.

14. Everett S. Brown, "The Senate Debate on the Breckinridge Bill for the Government of Louisiana, 1804," *American Historical Review* 22 (Jan. 1917): 340–64. The Louisiana Purchase probably was a major factor in South Carolina's decision to resume slave imports from Africa. See Jed Handelsman Shugerman, "The Louisiana Purchase and South Carolina's Reopening of the Slave Trade in 1803," *Journal of the Early Republic* 22 (Summer 2002): 263–90.

15. *Annals,* 9 Cong., 1 sess., 346–51, 358–75, 434–40 (quotation 439–40), 442–46.

16. Ibid., 2 sess., 271 (8 Jan. 1807).

17. For the final wording of this provision, which became sections 9 and 10 of the law, see p. 1270 of "An Act to prohibit the importation of slaves . . . ," *Annals,* 9 Cong., 2 sess., appendix, 1266–70. The original version of the bill proposed a limit of fifty tons, but the Senate lowered it to forty tons and the House acquiesced.

18. *Annals,* 9 Cong., 2 sess., House, 484 (Peter Early, 12 Feb. 1807), 527 (David R. Williams, 18 Feb. 1807), 528 (John Randolph, 18 Feb. 1807).

19. Robert H. Gudmestad, *A Troublesome Commerce: The Transformation of the Interstate Slave Trade* (Baton Rouge: Louisiana State University Press, 2003), 35–40; Russell Kirk, *Randolph of Roanoke: A Study in Conservative Thought* (Chicago: University of Chicago Press, 1951), 108–10, 129–30 (first quotation), 133; *Annals,* 9 Cong., 2 sess., House, 528 (second quotation).

20. *Annals,* 9 Cong., 2 sess., Senate, 87 (25 Feb. 1807); ibid., House, 626–27 (26 Feb. 1807).

21. Ibid., House, 636–37 (27 Feb. 1807).

22. Ibid., 15 Cong., 2 sess., House, 1166 (James Talmadge, Jr., 13 Feb. 1819; the *Annals* report that "an interesting and pretty wide debate" took place at this time, but no details are provided); ibid., 1170–79 (John W. Taylor, 15 Feb. 1819).

23. Ibid., 1179–84 (quotation 1184).

24. "The Substance of Two Speeches on the Missouri Bill Delivered by Mr. King in the Senate of the United States," *The Life and Correspondence of Rufus King, Comprising His Letters, Private and Official, His Public Documents, and His Speeches,* ed. Charles R. King, 6 vols. (New York: G. P. Putnam's Sons, 1894–1900), 6: 690–703 (quotations 691, 701, 702). This document was published also, in slightly different form, in Rufus King, "The Missouri Question," *Niles' Register* 17 (4 Dec. 1819), 215–21. See also Robert Ernst, "Rufus King, Slavery, and the Missouri Crisis," *New-York Historical Society Quarterly* 46 (Oct. 1962): 357–82.

25. *Annals,* 15 Cong., 2 sess., House, 1204, 1207, 1210 (16 Feb. 1819).

26. Glover Moore, *The Missouri Controversy, 1819–1821* (Lexington: University of Kentucky Press, 1953), 65–79; John Jay to Elias Boudinot, Bedford, 17 Nov. 1819, *The Correspondence and Public Papers of John Jay,* ed. Henry P. Johnston, 4 vols. (New York: Putnam's, 1890–93), 4: 430–31, also draft copy in John Jay Papers, Rare Book and Manuscript Library, Columbia University; Frank Monaghan, *John Jay: Defender of Liberty . . .* (New York: Bobbs-Merrill, 1935), 284.

27. *A Memorial to the Congress of the United States, on the Subject of Restraining the Increase of Slavery in New States to Be Admitted into the Union* (Boston: Sewell Phelps, 1819), 9–10, 21. Webster's name appears first on the list of the committee members who submitted the memorial to a public meeting held in the State House on 3 December 1819. The others were George Blake, Josiah Quincy, James T. Austin, and John Gallison. Of course Webster's primacy may reflect merely his personal prestige rather than authorship of the document.

28. Philadelphian [pseud. Robert Walsh], *Free Remarks on the Spirit of the Federal Constitution, the Practice of the Federal Government, and the Obligations of the Union, Respecting the Exclusion of Slavery from the Territories and New States* (Philadelphia: A. Finley, 1819), 17–18, 19, 19n, 20.

29. Ibid., 20–23 (quotation 21), 112 endnote F.

30. Ibid., 14–15, 17; James Madison to Robert Walsh, Montpellier, 27 Nov. 1819, in Farrand, ed., *Records of the Federal Convention,* 3: 436–38 (appendix A, document 332). Because Walsh in his *Free Remarks* quotes Jay's 17 Nov. 1819 letter to Boudinot, he almost certainly had received this letter from Madison before publishing the pamphlet. In a later letter to Walsh, Madison pointed out that in his "Federalist" essay he had ridiculed

the idea that Congress would want to interfere with *beneficial* emigrations from Europe to America after 1808; he had not said that Congress would possess no power over white immigration. (Madison to Walsh, Montpellier, 11 Jan. 1820, in Farrand, *Records of the Federal Convention,* 3: 438 [appendix A, document 333].)

31. Senator William Plumer, Jr., wrote his father that Randolph gave an address of great length on 2 February and that Clay did the same on 8 February, but neither speech was printed in the *Annals.* (*The Missouri Compromises and Presidential Politics, 1820–1825, from the Letters of William Plumer, Junior,* ed. Everett Somerville Brown [St. Louis: Missouri Historical Society, 1926, reprinted New York: Da Capo Press, 1970], 6, 8.) The Adams quotation is from *Memoirs of John Quincy Adams Comprising Portions of His Diary from 1795 to 1848,* ed. Charles Francis Adams, 12 vols. (Philadelphia: J. B. Lippincott, 1874–77), 4: 529 (diary entry for 23 Feb. 1820). See also John Quincy Adams to William Plumer, Jr., Washington, 26 July 1824, in Brown, *Missouri Compromises and Presidential Politics,* 117–19, enclosing a copy of the same diary entry.

32. On "new states," see *Annals,* 16 Cong., 1 sess., Senate, 211–12 (James Burrill, Jr., of Rhode Island, 20 Jan. 1820), 281 (Benjamin Ruggles of Ohio, 27 Jan. 1820); ibid., House, 1127–28 (Joseph Hemphill of Pennsylvania, 5 Feb. 1820). David Morrill of New Hampshire said at one point that Congress could prohibit the internal migration of slaves into "any State or territory, except those within the jurisdiction of the original States, which admitted slavery at the time of the adoption of this Constitution." He appears to have forgotten momentarily that in 1808 even the original states had lost their guarantee against any such congressional interference in the interstate slave trade. (Ibid., Senate, 139 [17 Jan. 1820].) On distinct meanings of "migration" and "importation," see ibid., Senate, 212 (Burrill, 20 Jan. 1820, mentioning "sin of tautology"); ibid., House, 959 (John W. Taylor of New York, 27 Jan. 1820), 1127 (Hemphill, 5 Feb. 1820), 1197 (John Sergeant of Pennsylvania, 9 Feb. 1820). On Acts of 1804 and 1807, see ibid., Senate, 126 (Jonathan Roberts of Pennsylvania, 19 Jan. 1820), 179 (Prentiss Mellen of Massachusetts, 19 Jan. 1820), 212 (Burrill, 20 Jan. 1820); ibid., House, 1200 (Sergeant, 9 Feb. 1820).

33. Ibid., House, 941 (Samuel Smith of Maryland, 28 Jan. 1820). John Sergeant of Pennsylvania pounced on Smith's statement. Sergeant argued that because the 1808 clause did not in fact make any such distinction between slaves born at home versus abroad, Smith had really provided support for the northern view. (Ibid., 1197 [Sergeant, 9 Feb. 1820].) On migration referring only to whites, see ibid., Senate, 130 (John Elliott of Georgia, 17 Jan. 1820), 198 (Walter Leake of Mississippi, 19 Jan. 1820), 306 (Nicholas Van Dyke of Delaware, 28 Jan. 1820); ibid., House, 1164 (Louis McLane of Delaware, 7 Feb. 1820), 1335–37 (Christopher Rankin of Mississippi, 15 Feb. 1820), 1501 (John Scott, nonvoting delegate from Missouri territory, 25 Feb. 1820). On taxing only importations, see ibid., Senate, 131 (Elliott, 17 Jan. 1820), 230–31 (Nathaniel Macon of North Carolina, 20 Jan. 1820), 318 (James Barbour of Virginia, 1 Feb. 1820). For comments of Hardin and Reid, see ibid., House, 1078 (Benjamin Hardin, Jr., of Kentucky, 4 Feb. 1820), 1026–27 (Robert Raymond Reid of Georgia, 1 Feb. 1820).

34. Ibid., Senate, 166–67 (Freeman Walker of Georgia, 19 Jan. 1820).

35. Ibid., House, 1365 (James Johnson of Virginia, 16 Feb. 1820). On slaves as family members, see ibid., 319–20 (Barbour, 1 Feb. 1820); 942 (Samuel Smith , 26 Jan. 1820),

1080 (Hardin, 4 Feb. 1820), 1163 (McLane, 7 Feb. 1820). On commerce clause intended to promote free trade, see ibid., Senate, 320 (Barbour, 1 Feb. 1820); ibid., House, 996 (Alexander Smyth of Virginia, 28 Jan. 1820), 1162 (McLane, 7 Feb. 1820), 1317 (Charles Pinckney of South Carolina, 14 Feb. 1820). On claim that southern states would not have ratified, see ibid., Senate, 230–31 (Macon, 20 Jan. 1820), 262 (William Smith of South Carolina, 26 Jan. 1820); ibid., House, 1365–66 (Johnson, 16 Feb. 1820). On claim that nor would northern states, see ibid., Senate, 262 (William Smith, 26 Jan. 1820). On no preferential treatment allowed, see ibid., 320 (Barbour, 1 Feb. 1820); ibid., House, 996 (Smyth, 28 Jan. 1820), 1161–62 (McLane, 7 Feb. 1820), 1317–18 (Pinckney, 14 Feb. 1820), 1501 (Scott, 25 Feb. 1820). Article I, Section 9, Clause 6 of the Constitution says, "No Preference shall be given by any Regulation of Commerce or Revenue to the Ports of one State over those of another."

36. Moore, *Missouri Controversy,* 99–103; Thomas Jefferson to John Holmes, 22 Apr. 1820, Thomas Jefferson Papers, Library of Congress, quoted in Stuart Leibiger, "Thomas Jefferson and the Missouri Crisis: An Alternative Interpretation," *Journal of the Early Republic* 17 (Spring 1997): 124. Leibiger argues that Jefferson's statement was made at least partly for political effect. Holmes, a congressman representing the Maine district of Massachusetts, had been a leader of the northern "doughfaces" (an epithet coined at that time by John Randolph) who had backed the compromise. Jefferson's endorsement helped Holmes mollify his antislavery constituents.

37. *Annals,* 18 Cong., 1 sess., House, 1296–1307, quotation 1299 (30 Jan. 1824). Henry Adams considered this Randolph's greatest speech. (Henry Adams, *John Randolph* [Boston: Houghton, Mifflin, 1882], 272–73.)

38. James Jones, "The President's address to the eighth convention of the Manumission Society of Tennessee; held at Friends meeting house, Lost Creek, Jefferson county, on the 12th and 13th days of the eighth month, (August) 1822," *Genius of Universal Emancipation* 2 (July 1822): 21–23 (quotations 22).

39. Needles, *Historical Memoir,* 78; *The American Convention for Promoting the Abolition of Slavery and Improving the Condition of the African Race* . . . , 3 vols. (New York: Bergman, 1969), 3: 811, 877–78 (quotation 878), 989–90 (quotation).

40. *American Convention,* 2: 542, 628; ibid., 3: 931–32, 1001–02.

41. Ibid., 3: 909 (quotation), 1070 (quotation). On the Convention's ineffectual ditherings, see ibid., 825, 828, 843, 912, 944, 959, 965, 976–77, 1026, 1033–36, 1095, 1116.

42. "Plan for the Abolition of Slavery," *Genius of Universal Emancipation* 2 (Jan. 1823): 97–102 (quotations 98, 99); Merton L. Dillon, *Benjamin Lundy and the Struggle for Negro Freedom* (Urbana: University of Illinois Press, 1966), 3–6, quoting *Genius of Universal Emancipation* 13 (Nov. 1832), 8; "United States' Slave Trade," *Genius of Universal Emancipation* 3 (Dec. 1823): 82; "Note by the Editor," *Genius of Universal Emancipation* 3 (Nov. 1823): 70.

43. Dillon, *Benjamin Lundy,* 118, quoting *Genius of Universal Emancipation and Baltimore Courier* 2 (2 Jan. 1827): 110, and ibid. (24 Feb. 1827): 174; A.O.B. to editor of *Boston Courier,* 12 Aug. 1828, *The Letters of William Lloyd Garrison,* 6 vols. (Cambridge: Belknap Press of Harvard University Press, 1971–81), 1: 66–68; Paul Finkelman, *Slavery in the Courtroom: An Annotated Bibliography of American Cases* (Washington, D.C.: Library of Congress, 1985), 161–64.

44. Paul Goodman, *Of One Blood: Abolitionism and the Origins of Racial Equality* (Berkeley: University of California Press, 1998), chap. 3, "The Black Struggle for Racial Equality, 1817–1832," and chap. 4, "The Conversion of William Lloyd Garrison;" C. Peter Ripley, *The Black Abolitionist Papers,* 5 vols. (Chapel Hill: University of North Carolina Press, 1985–92), 3: 3–69; William Grimes, *Life of William Grimes, the Runaway Slave* (New York: the author, 1825), 8 (quotations), 22–23; Solomon Bayley, *A Narrative of Some Remarkable Incidents in the Life of Solomon Bayley, Formerly a Slave in the State of Delaware, North America* (London: Harvey and Darton, 1825), 1–3, 17–18, 25–27, 32. These two and the many later slave narratives are accessible on the University of North Carolina website www.docsouth.unc.edu.

45. *Freedom's Journal,* 10 Aug. 1827, p. 86 (second quotation, "Virginia is now the greatest seat"); 15 Feb. 1828, pp. 185–86; 26 Sept. 1828, p. 211; 17 Oct. 1828, pp. 234–35 (first quotation, "harrow up the feelings," and final, block quotation); 31 Oct. 1828, p. 254; 7 Nov. 1828, p. 259; 14 Nov. 1828, p. 268, copying *Georgetown Columbian* (third quotation, "they are *black*"); 12 Dec. 1828, p. 292; 16 Jan. 1829, p. 329. *Freedom's Journal* may be accessed on the Historical Society of Wisconsin website www.wisconsinhistory.org.

46. *Walker's Appeal, in Four Articles; Together with a Preamble, to the Coloured Citizens of the World, But in Particular, and Very Expressly, to Those of the United States of America, Written in Boston, State of Massachusetts, September 28, 1829,* 3d ed. (Boston: David Walker 1830), reprinted in Herbert Aptheker, *"One Continual Cry": David Walker's Appeal to the Colored Citizens of the World (1829–1830): Its Setting and Its Meaning* (New York: Humanities Press, 1965), 86–90.

Chapter 4. Different Opinions at Different Times

1. While this chapter derives primarily from my own analysis of the official reports of the relevant Supreme Court cases, I have benefited greatly from the factual detail and explication of legal complexities in G. Edward White, *The Marshall Court and Cultural Change, 1815–35,* Oliver Wendell Holmes Devise History of the Supreme Court of the United States, vols. 3–4 (New York: Macmillan, 1988), and in Carl B. Swisher, *The Taney Period, 1836–64,* ibid., vol. 5 (New York: Macmillan, 1974). Equally helpful was Charles Warren, *The Supreme Court in United States History,* rev. ed., 2 vols. (Boston: Little, Brown, 1937), which remains unsurpassed in its attention to the political context of the Court's decision-making.

2. *Gibbons v. Ogden,* 22 U.S. (9 Wheaton) 1 (1824); Swisher, *Taney Period,* 378–82; Warren, *Supreme Court,* 1: 623–27. Johnson nullified the South Carolina law in *Elkison v. Deliesseline,* 8 Federal Cases 493 (1823). The South Carolina governor's message, 1 Dec. 1824, is quoted in Warren, *Supreme Court,* 1: 627.

3. Marshall to Story, 26 Sept. 1823, Joseph Story Papers, Massachusetts Historical Society. The Circuit Court case in which Marshall confronted the Virginia law was *The Brig Wilson,* 1 Brock 423, according to Warren, *Supreme Court,* 1: 624n.

4. *Gibbons v. Ogden,* 33–159 (quotation from argument of Thomas Emmet, 119).

5. Ibid., 9–10, 14, 26.

6. Ibid., 186–222 (quotations 216–17, 196, 209). On the doubtful conflict between the New York statute and the federal license, see White, *Marshall Court,* 570.

7. *Gibbons v. Ogden,* 222–31 (quotation 227).

8. Draft of Taney's unpublished advisory opinion, 28 May 1832, quoted in Carl Brent Swisher, "Mr. Chief Justice Taney," in Allison Dunham and Philip B. Kurland, eds., *Mr. Justice,* rev. and enl. ed. (Chicago: University of Chicago Press, 1964), 43.

9. *City of New York v. Miln,* 36 U.S. (11 Peters) 102 (1837), 109.

10. Ibid., 119, 119–20.

11. Ibid., 132, 139, 152–53, 157, 158. It is possible that Story wrote the judgment of the court in *Gibbons v. Ogden,* or at least a preliminary version of it, while Marshall was incapacitated by injuries suffered when he stumbled over a cellar door at the boarding-house where the justices resided. (White, *Marshall Court,* 573n.) In his *Miln* ruling, Barbour stated—in startling contrast to what Marshall had said in *Gibbons v. Ogden*—that commerce involved only the carrying of goods and not of people. Although Barbour's assertion was published in an official ruling of the court, it took the other majority justices by surprise and had not been approved by them. Consequently, it was not treated as a valid precedent in later cases. (Even if it had been, it seems likely that slaves would still have been regarded as merchandise and thus subject to the commerce power, even if other people were not.) Justice Wayne brought this messy matter to light in his concurring opinion in the *Passenger Cases* 48 U.S. (7 Howard) 283 (1849), 429–37. Wayne said, much to the annoyance of Story, that Story had been the only other justice who had agreed with Barbour.

12. Swisher, *Taney Period,* 365–67; Warren, *Supreme Court,* 2: 67–70. For the newspaper reporting about the ladies and Senators, Warren cites the *New York Express,* 19 and 23 Feb. 1841. Meredith Lang, *Defender of the Faith: The High Court of Mississippi, 1817–1875* (Jackson: University Press of Mississippi, 1977), 52, claims—but presents no evidence to prove—that one motive for the 1832 constitutional clause was to "soothe the public conscience" by differentiating "good" slaveowners from "bad" traders. Lang adds that fear of insurrections was another and perhaps stronger motive.

13. *Groves v. Slaughter,* 40 U.S. (15 Peters) 449 (1841), quotations 468, 468, 465, 465.

14. Robert J. Walker, *Argument of Robert J. Walker, Esq., before the Supreme Court of the United States, on the Mississippi Slave Question, at January Term, 1841. Involving the Power of Congress and of the States to Prohibit the Inter-state Slave Trade* (Philadelphia: John C. Clark, 1841), 49, 51, 58, 88; R. J. Walker to Martin Van Buren, Washington, 31 Aug. 1842, Martin Van Buren Papers, Library of Congress, Washington, D.C.; John Quincy Adams diary, 19 Feb. 1841, in Charles Francis Adams, ed., *Memoirs of John Quincy Adams Comprising Portions of His Diary from 1795 to 1848,* 12 vols. (Philadelphia: J. B. Lippincott, 1874–77), 10: 426–27.

15. *Groves v. Slaughter,* 477 (here Walter Jones labels his fellow counsel Ajax and Achilles), 489.

16. Ibid., 488.

17. Ibid., 495.

18. Ibid., 457, 503.

19. Ibid., 503, 506, 506, 508, 508. John Quincy Adams recorded that "Judge McLean

took from his pocket and read a counter-opinion, unexpectedly to the other Judges." Adams evidently erred, however, in reporting that this happened just after the opinion of the court had been read by "the Chief Justice," for the official report indicates that Thompson, not Taney, delivered the court's ruling. (John Quincy Adams diary, 10 Mar. 1841, *Memoirs of John Quincy Adams,* 10: 442.)

I disagree with William Wiecek, who says that McLean delivered "a semi-abolitionist opinion, arguing that federal commerce power over the interstate slave trade was exclusive." In fact, McLean stated explicitly that although he believed that the federal commerce power was exclusive, Congress nevertheless could *not* regulate "the transfer and sale of slaves from one state to another." It is true that abolitionists must have welcomed McLean's message that the federal government had no power to promote slavery or to compel the free states to tolerate it. But abolitionists cannot have liked McLean's equally clear message that the federal government could not lift a finger against slavery in the states where it existed, such as by interfering with the slave trade. Indeed, McLean's opinion may have won more favor in proslavery than in antislavery circles. "All the abolitionists who respect the unanimous opinion of the Supreme Court will now abandon so much of their petitions as call on Congress to regulate or prohibit the transportation of slaves," crowed a Mississippi newspaper after the announcement of the court's decision in *Groves v. Slaughter.* "One point of the abolition controversy (and that the most important) is solemnly settled in favor of the South." (William M. Wiecek, "Slavery and Abolition Before the United States Supreme Court, 1820–1860," *Journal of American History* 65 (June 1978): 52; *Groves v. Slaughter,* 506; *Columbus Democrat,* 8 May 1841, quoted in Warren, *Supreme Court,* 2: 72.)

20. *Groves v. Slaughter,* 508, 515, 516.

21. Ibid., 510, 516.

22. Warren, *Supreme Court,* 2: 168–70; ibid., 170, quoting *Richmond Enquirer,* 4 Mar. 1841. Paul Finkelman, *An Imperfect Union: Slavery, Federalism, and Comity* (Chapel Hill: University of North Carolina Press, 1981), is a superb account of the breakdown of comity among the states.

23. Swisher, *Taney Period,* 378–82.

24. Ibid., 370–77, quoting (on p. 371) *Charleston Courier,* 5 Feb. 1845.

25. D[aniel] Webster to Fletcher Webster, Washington, 16 June 1849, *The Private Correspondence of Daniel Webster,* 2 vols. (Boston: Little, Brown, 1857), 2: 327; Swisher, *Taney Period,* 2: 382–84; *Passenger Cases,* 331, 374.

26. Swisher, *Taney Period,* 384–85; Warren, *Supreme Court,* 2: 175–78; *Speech of Daniel Webster* [26 Jan. 1830], *in Reply to Mr. Hayne, of South Carolina: The Resolution of Mr. Foot, of Connecticut, Relative to the Public Lands, Being under Consideration* (Washington, D.C.: Gales and Seaton, 1830; microfiche, Louisville, Ky.: Lost Cause Press, 1978); D[aniel] Webster to Richard Milford Blatchford, 3 Feb. 1849, *The Papers of Daniel Webster: Legal Papers,* ed. Alfred S. Konefsky and Andrew J. King, 3 vols. (Hanover, N.H.: University Press of New England for Dartmouth College, 1982), vol. 3, part 2, pp. 727–28.

27. *Passenger Cases,* 326, 349, 377, 305–06, 382 (quotation).

28. Swisher, *Taney Period,* 388; *Passenger Cases,* 283 (quotation).

29. *Passenger Cases,* 396, 406.

30. Ibid., 410, 428–29 (quotation).

31. Ibid., 452, 455, 456 (quotation), 462 (quotation), 464.

32. Ibid., 471, 474 (quotations), 476 (quotation), 518.

33. Ibid., 498 (quotations), 511 (quotation).

34. Ibid., 542, 528, 526, 572. The Latin is from the classical author Locanus (Marcus Annaeus Lucan), *Pharsalia,* Book 7, line 580.

35. *Charleston Mercury,* 14 Feb. 1849, copied in *Boston Courier,* 21 Feb. 1849, quoted in Warren, *Supreme Court,* 2: 182.

36. *Cooley v. Board of Wardens of the Port of Philadelphia,* 53 U.S. (12 Howard) 299 (1852), quotation on 319; Swisher, *Taney Court,* 404–7. McLean upheld exclusive federal commerce power but made no mention of the interstate slave trade question (*Cooley,* 321–25), while Wayne dissented without writing an opinion. Since the *Passenger Cases* decision, Curtis had replaced Levi Woodbury. John McKinley was still on the court but was too ill to participate in *Cooley.* McLean not only dissented from the *Cooley* decision; he subsequently ignored it. On circuit later that year, he said, "That the exclusive power to regulate commerce among the states, is vested in congress, in my judgment, is not now a debatable question." (*Rogers v. Cincinnati* [1852], 20 Federal Cases 1111, quoted in Swisher, *Taney Court,* 407.)

37. *Dred Scott v. Sandford,* 60 U.S. (19 Howard) 393 (1857), quotations 450, 452, 490, 500, 516.

38. Ibid., 518, 527, 536–37 (quotation), 457–69.

39. Abraham Lincoln, "House Divided" speech, Springfield, Ill., 16 June 1858, *The Lincoln-Douglas Debates of 1858,* ed. Robert W. Johannsen (New York: Oxford University Press, 1965), 19–20; Lincoln's reply, fifth joint debate, Galesburg, 7 Oct. 1858, ibid., 230, 231.

40. William E. Nelson, "The Impact of the Antislavery Movement upon Styles of Judicial Reasoning in Nineteenth Century America," *Harvard Law Review* 87 (Jan. 1974): 546–47; Finkelman, *Imperfect Union,* 296–310, 314–15. For an imaginative but well-grounded explanation of how the Taney court might have made this dire prediction come true, see Paul Finkelman, "The Nationalization of Slavery: A Counter-factual Approach to the 1860s," *Louisiana Studies* 14 (1975): 213–40.

Chapter 5. The Door to the Slave Bastille

1. "To the Public," *Liberator,* 1 Jan. 1831, p. 1 (quotation); C. Peter Ripley, ed., *The Black Abolitionist Papers,* 5 vols. (Chapel Hill: University of North Carolina Press, 1985–92), 3: 9. The contrast between the old and the new forms of antislavery is illuminated in Richard S. Newman, *The Transformation of American Abolitionism: Fighting Slavery in the Early Republic* (Chapel Hill: University of North Carolina Press, 2002).

2. Aileen S. Kraditor, *Means and Ends in American Abolitionism: Garrison and His Critics on Strategy and Tactics, 1834–1850* (New York: Pantheon Books, 1969), 119; James Brewer Stewart, *Holy Warriors: The Abolitionists and American Slavery* (New York: Hill and Wang, 1976), 94; "Political Action," *Voice of Freedom* (variant title for *Emancipator*), May 1836, p. 2, cols. 1–2.

3. Circular calling for antislavery convention, *Liberator,* 5 Oct. 1833, p. 159; AA-SS

Constitution, Article II, in *Proceedings of the Anti-Slavery Convention, Assembled at Philadelphia, December 4, 5, and 6, 1833* (New York: Dorr & Butterfield, 1833), 6–7; "Declaration of Sentiments," ibid., 15.

4. Jay's primacy in calling for a ban on the interstate slave trade is implied in Bayard Tuckerman, *William Jay, and the Constitutional Movement for the Abolition of Slavery* (New York: Dodd, Mead, 1893), xi–xii, 45–52, and in John Jay [son of William Jay], *The Constitutional Principles of the Abolitionists, and Their Endorsement by the American People. A Letter to the American Anti-Slavery Society, on the 30th Anniversary of Its Foundation in Philadelphia, the 30th of December, 1833* (New York, 1864), 7, 10–11. Jay's 1826 activity is mentioned in Frederick Douglass, *Eulogy of the Late Hon. Wm. Jay . . . Delivered on the Invitation of the Colored Citizens of New York City, in Shiloh Presbyterian Church, New York, May 12, 1859* (Rochester: A. Strong & Co., 1859), 24, and in William Jay to Aaron Brown, 22 Mar. 1830, draft copy, Jay Family Papers, Rare Book and Manuscript Library, Columbia University. "I early imbibed my Father's hostility to slavery," wrote William Jay in a letter to Joseph C. Hornblower, 17 July 1850, typed copy in Jay Family Papers. Jay's correspondence with Tappan and May is discussed in Tuckerman, *William Jay,* 45–52 (quotation 45–46).

Despite his antislavery convictions, Jay was reluctant to become publicly involved in radical abolitionism. In September 1833 he refused to sign an abolitionist manifesto sent to him by Amos A. Phelps. Only in March 1834 was Elizur Wright, Jr., able to report that Jay had made a donation of fifty dollars and was "much more decidedly with us than at the time of the convention." (Jay to Phelps, 7 Sept. 1833, and Wright to Phelps, 3 Mar. 1834, both in Rare Books Department, Boston Public Library, Courtesy of the Trustees.)

5. Tuckerman, *William Jay,* 51; John G. Whittier, "The Antislavery Convention of 1833," *Atlantic Monthly* 33 (Feb. 1874), 169 (quotation). Receipt of Jay's letter is mentioned but its text is not printed in the *Proceedings of the Anti-Slavery Convention.*

6. David Lee Child, *The Despotism of Freedom: Or the Tyranny and cruelty of American Republican Slave-masters shown to Be the Worst in the World; in a Speech delivered at the first anniversary of the New England anti-slavery society, 1833* (Boston: Young Men's Anti-Slavery Association, 1833), 51; A. Neuter (claiming to report a conversation he has overheard), "Dialogue between C, a Colonizationist, and A, an Abolitionist, on the Subject of the Anti-Slavery Society," part 2, *The Abolitionist: Or Record of the New-England Anti-Slavery Society* 1 (Sept. 1833): 132; *Liberator,* 5 Oct. 1833, pp. 157–58. Among the resolutions adopted at the meeting at which Child delivered his speech were one declaring that Congress ought to abolish slavery in the District of Columbia and another, moved by Garrison, calling for the organization of a national antislavery society. No resolution regarding the interstate slave trade was considered. (*The Abolitionist: Or Record of the New-England Anti-Slavery Society* 1 [Feb. 1833]: 1, 20.)

7. La Roy Sunderland, *Anti-Slavery Manual, Containing a Collection of Facts and Arguments on American Slavery* (New York: Piercy & Reed, 1837; reprinted New York: Negro Universities Press, 1969), 123, 121, copying portions of Henry B. Stanton to "Brother Leavitt," 22 Apr. 1834, printed in *Liberator,* 17 May 1834, p. 77, and 24 May 1834, p. 83, copying *New York Evangelist.*

8. David Lee Child et al., "Report on the Slave Trade," *Liberator,* 7 June 1834, pp. 89–91.

9. William Jay, *An Inquiry into the Character and Tendency of the American Colonization and American Anti-Slavery Societies* (New York: Leavitt, Lord & Co., 1835), 136 (quotation), and chap. 5 (pp. 149–57), "Slavery under the Authority of Congress"; David M. Reese, *Letters to the Hon. William Jay, Being a Reply to His "Enquiry into the American Colonization and American Anti-slavery Societies"* (New York: Leavitt, Lord & Co., 1835), 100. John Rankin to Amos A. Phelps, 16 Apr. 1835 (Rare Books Department, Boston Public Library, Courtesy of the Trustees) reported that "Judge Jay's book is helping us considerably" and that a new edition of five thousand copies was to appear the following week. For a dismissive response by an anonymous "gentleman, writing from Pittsburgh" to the Reese *Letters* "so ostentatiously recommended" by colonizationists, see "Judge Jay and His Opponent," *Emancipator,* Aug. 1835, p. 4, col. 4. Jay himself regarded Reese's book as "a very dishonest one" but felt that his own work "must, + will speak for itself." (William Jay to Peter Augustus Jay [his brother], Bedford, N.Y., 11 June 1835, Jay Family Papers, Rare Book and Manuscript Library, Columbia University.)

10. Mrs. [Lydia M.] Child, *An Appeal in Favor of That Class of Americans Called Africans* (New York: John S. Taylor, 1836), 216; John G. Whittier to Edward Everett, Governor of Massachusetts, n.d., *Liberator,* 20 Feb. 1836, p. 29; "Anti-Slavery Meeting at Pittsburgh" [reporting John Rankin speech, 30 May 1836], *Emancipator,* 16 June 1836, p. 2, cols. 4–6. Lydia Child also ignored the interstate slave trade issue in her less famous *Anti-Slavery Catechism* (Newburyport: Charles Whipple, 1836), 33.

11. *Remarks on the Constitution, by a Friend of Humanity, on the Subject of Slavery* (Philadelphia: Evening Star, 1836), 2 (quotation), 3, 12 (quotation). In 1836 Walsh was still living in Philadelphia and was writing on many topics. In the following year he retired and moved to Paris, where he resided until his death in 1859. (*Dictionary of American Biography* [New York, 1936], 19: 391–92.)

12. Alvan Stewart, "Address to the Abolitionists of the State of New York. As Reported By a Committee appointed by the first Annual Meeting of the New York State Anti-Slavery Society, of which Committee Alvan Stewart, Esq., was Chairman. and which was unanimously adopted, October, 1836," *Writings and Speeches of Alvan Stewart, on Slavery,* ed. Luther R. Marsh (New York: A. B. Burdick, 1860), 86–107 (quotations 100–101, 101).

13. Ibid., quotations 102–3, 106, 107.

14. Drew R. McCoy, *The Last of the Fathers: James Madison and the Republican Legacy* (Cambridge: Cambridge University Press, 1989), 255–60. After Madison's death in 1836, his widow sold slaves to traders singly and without the slaves' consent, despite the fact that Madison's will had explicitly forbidden it. (Ibid., 318–22.) Capital gains were important to slaveowners in the lower South too, but there they were not so endangered by the prospect of a ban on the interstate trade. See Richard Sutch, "The Profitability of Ante-Bellum Slavery—Revisited," *Southern Economic Journal* 31 (Apr. 1965), table viii, p. 376, and Gavin Wright, *The Political Economy of the Cotton South: Households, Markets, and Wealth in the Nineteenth Century* (New York: W. W. Norton, 1978), 16–17, 139–44. On the rigors of the cane fields, see Michael Tadman, "The Demographic Cost of Sugar: Debates on Slave Societies and Natural Increase in the Americas," *American Historical Review* 105 (Dec. 2000): 1534–75.

15. Michael Tadman, *Speculators and Slaves: Masters, Traders, and Slaves in the Old*

South (Madison: University of Wisconsin Press, 1989), p. 12, table 2.1. According to one contemporary account, in 1836 "the public highways to Mississippi became lined—yea literally crowded—with slaves. When they arrived, the immense number (swelling the rise of 40,000) made the callous hearts of all the traders ache." ("Startling Developments. The Domestic Slave Trade," *Massachusetts Abolitionist,* 2 Apr. 1840, p. 25, copying *Philanthropist,* copying *United States Gazette* [Philadelphia].) Another source makes the utterly implausible assertion that 250,000 slaves were carried into Mississippi, Alabama, Louisiana, and Arkansas during the year 1836. (Sunderland, *Anti-Slavery Manual,* 135, citing *Natchez Courier.*)

Stewart's claim that the annual volume of the interstate slave trade was twice that ever attained by the slave trade from Africa is not so farfetched as one might suppose. Of the approximately ten million Africans who were carried across the Atlantic between 1630 and 1810, an estimated 661,000 came to what is now the United States. The largest number to arrive in any ten-year period was the 143,000 who came in the decade 1800–1809. (Robert W. Fogel, *Without Consent or Contract: The Rise and Fall of American Slavery* [New York: W. W. Norton, 1989], p. 19, fig. 1; Robert W. Fogel, Ralph A. Galantine, and Richard L. Manning, ibid., supplemental volume *Evidence and Methods* [New York: W. W. Norton, 1992], p. 55, table 42; for alternative estimates, see James A. McMillin, *The Final Victims: Foreign Slave Trade to North America, 1783–1819* [Columbia: University of South Carolina Press, 2004].)

16. On the political power of the slaveholders, see Leonard L. Richards, *The Slave Power: The Free North and Southern Domination, 1780–1860* (Baton Rouge: Louisiana State University Press, 2000), and Don E. Fehrenbacher, *The Slaveholding Republic: An Account of the United States Government's Relations to Slavery* (Oxford: Oxford University Press, 2001). On the circumvention of laws by traders, see Robert H. Gudmestad, *A Troublesome Commerce: The Transformation of the Interstate Slave Trade* (Baton Rouge: Louisiana State University Press, 2003), 102–13, and Steven Deyle, *Carry Me Back: The Domestic Slave Trade in American Life* (New York: Oxford University Press, 2005), 51–55. A ban on the interstate trade might have resulted in a situation somewhat like that of the West Indies, where British restrictions on the inter-island slave trade seriously retarded economic expansion. See Seymour Drescher, *Econocide: British Slavery in the Era of Abolition* (Pittsburgh: University of Pittsburgh Press, 1977), and Hilary McD. Beckles, "'An Unfeeling Traffick': The Intercolonial Movement of Slaves in the British Caribbean, 1807–1833," in *The Chattel Principle: Internal Slave Trades in the Americas,* ed. Walter Johnson (New Haven: Yale University Press, 2004), 256–74.

17. Stewart, *Holy Warriors,* 69–71; "Report on that portion of the President's Message which related to the adoption of efficient measures to prevent the circulation of incendiary Abolition Petitions through the Mail, February 4th, 1836," *Works of John C. Calhoun,* ed. Richard K. Crallé, 6 vols. (New York: Appleton, 1851–56; reprinted New York: Russell and Russell, 1968), 5: 190–208 (quotations 199); Harold W. Thatcher, "Calhoun and Federal Reinforcement of State Laws," *American Political Science Review* 36 (Aug. 1942): 873–80. I am indebted to Don Fehrenbacher for the observation that Calhoun "did not want a federally imposed censorship that might indirectly encourage those advocating a federal prohibition of the interstate slave trade." (Fehrenbacher, *Slaveholding Republic,* 302.) For an abolitionist response to Calhoun, see "Freedom's Defence," *Voice of Freedom* [variant title of *Emancipator*], May 1836, p. 4, cols. 1–6.

18. Millard Fillmore to James Brooks, Albany, 13 Sept. 1848, printed in "Protection to Southern Trade," *National Anti-Slavery Standard,* 28 Sept. 1848, p. 71, col. 3; Millard Fillmore to chairman of a committee appointed by the Anti-Slavery Society of the County of Erie, Buffalo, 17 Oct. 1838, printed in *National Anti-Slavery Standard,* 25 July 1850, p. 34, col. 6. For numerous letters from Massachusetts political candidates replying to abolitionist queries, see *Liberator,* 10 Nov. 1837. Most of the replies agree that Congress should abolish the interstate slave trade, although one respondent says that he is not sure that Congress possesses that power: "I hope, but on this point I have some doubt." (Thomas Mandell to Andrew Robinson, President of Bristol County Anti-Slavery Society, 28 Oct. 1837, ibid.)

19. Sarah Lewis et al., "Circular of the Anti-slavery Convention of American Women," appendix (pp. 32–33) to Boston Female Anti-Slavery Society, *Annual Report* (sixth, 1839), 33.

20. Sarah and Angelina Grimké to [Thomas] Clarkson, [ca. 1 Mar. 1837], *Friend of Man,* 6 Apr. 1837, reprinted in *Letters of Theodore Dwight Weld, Angelina Grimké Weld, and Sarah Grimké, 1822–1844,* ed. Gilbert H. Barnes and Dwight L. Dumond, 2 vols. (New York: D. Appleton-Century, 1934), 1: 365–72 (quotation 370); *Proceedings of the Anti-slavery Convention of American Women, Held in the City of New-York, May 9th, 10th, 11th, and 12th, 1837* (New York: William S. Dorr, 1837), 8. A similar call was issued in 1839. See "Circular of the Anti-slavery Convention of American Women," pp. 25–28 of *Proceedings of the Anti-Slavery Convention of American Women, Held in Philadelphia, May 1st, 2nd and 3d, 1839* (Philadelphia: Merrihew and Thompson, 1839), 26. The Mary Parker quotation is from Anti-Slavery Convention of American Women, *Circular to the Societies of Anti-Slavery Women in the United States* ([Boston?] [1837?]), copy in Boston Public Library. See also *An Appeal to the Women of the Nominally Free States, Issued By an Anti-slavery Convention of American Women, Held by Adjournments from the 9th to the 12th of May 1837* (New York: William S. Dorr, 1837), 58, saying all women ought to sign such petitions. The AA-SS circular quotations are from "Petitions! Petitions!" *Liberator,* 23 June 1837, 102. This effort was repeated in 1839. See AA-SS circular dated 9 Sept. 1839, *Massachusetts Abolitionist,* 3 Oct. 1839, 129.

21. *Correspondence Between the Hon. F. H. Elmore, One of the South Carolina Delegation in Congress, and James G. Birney, One of the Secretaries of the American Anti-Slavery Society,* Anti-Slavery Examiner, no. 8 (New-York: American Anti-Slavery Society, 1838), 65, app. G; Dwight L. Dumond, *Antislavery: The Crusade for Freedom in America* (Ann Arbor: University of Michigan Press, 1961), 245–46; William Lee Miller, *Arguing About Slavery: The Great Battle in the United States Congress* (New York: Alfred A. Knopf, 1996), 305–6. For hundreds of petitions calling for various measures including the banning of the interstate slave trade that were introduced (before the gag rule was reenacted for that session) by John Quincy Adams and others, see U.S. Congress, *House Journal,* 18 Feb. 1839, pp. 574–604.

22. William Jay, "Slavery and the Slave Trade Under the Authority of Congress," *Anti-Slavery Record* 3 (Nov. 1837), 121–32; William Jay, *A View of the Action of the Federal Government, in Behalf of Slavery* (New York: J. S. Taylor, 1839), 185–86 (The original reads "the Senate's coasting trade." Although the word "Senate's" seems to be included by mistake, it appears also in an 1844 edition of the same work); H. B. Stanton, "Mr.

Stanton's Speech at the Anniversary of the American Anti-Slavery Society [7 May 1839]," *Massachusetts Abolitionist,* 23 May 1839, p. 14, copying *New York Evangelist* (Later, as AA-SS Corresponding Secretary, Stanton put out a circular calling for petitions to Congress demanding abolition in the District of Columbia, abolition in Florida Territory, and prohibition of "the traffic in slaves between the states." See AA-SS circular dated 9 Sept. 1839, *Massachusetts Abolitionist,* 3 Oct. 1839, 129); Alvan Stewart to Messrs. Lundy, Scott, Parish, Gunn, and Jones, 22 Jan. 1837, in *Proceedings of the Pennsylvania Convention to Organize a State Anti-Slavery Society, at Harrisburg, on the 31st of January and 1st, 2d and 3d of February 1837* (Philadelphia: Merrihew & Gunn, 1837), 21–22 (For the convention's favorable response, see ibid., 40–43, 59–61, 84); Alvan Stewart, "Report of a Speech Delivered Before a Joint Committee of the Legislature of Vermont, Raised to inquire into the propriety of reporting and passing Resolutions addressed to Congress, praying that body to abolish the internal Slave Trade between the States, Slavery in the District of Columbia, and in the Territories of the United States, and to prevent the admission of new Slave States, and Texas into the Union, by special request and invitation from the Vermont State A.S. Society, on the 25th, 26th, and 27th of October, 1838," in Stewart, *Writings and Speeches,* 160–85 (quotations 176–77).

23. Samuel J. May, "Slavery and the Constitution," *Quarterly Anti-Slavery Magazine* 2 (Oct. 1836): 73–90, and 2 (Apr. 1837): 226–38 (quotations 223, 238); "Domestic Slave Trade," *Quarterly Anti-Slavery Magazine,* 2 (July 1837): 409–12 (quotation 411–12) [This unsigned article was presumably by Wright, who was then editor]; James G. Birney to F. H. Elmore, 8 Mar. 1838, *Correspondence Between Elmore and Birney,* 30; Myron Holley, "Address of the Warsaw [N.Y.] Convention," *Massachusetts Abolitionist,* 16 Jan. 1840, pp. 189–90; ibid., 23 Jan. 1840, p. 193 (quotation); ibid., 30 Jan. 1840, p. 197; ibid., 6 Feb. 1840, p. 201; ibid., 13 Feb. 1840, p. 205; *Address of Scipio* [N.Y.] *Quarterly Meeting of Friends* [13 Apr. 1837] *on the Subject of Slavery, to Its Members* (Skaneateles: M. A. Kinney, [1837?]), 7–8; *Address to the Citizens of the United States of America on the Subject of Slavery, from the Yearly Meeting of the Religious Society of Friends, (called Quakers) held in New-York* [29 May–2 June 1837] (New York: New York Yearly Meeting of Friends; Mahlon Day, printer, 1837), 8; *Slavery and the Domestic Slave Trade in the United States. By the Committee Appointed by the Late Yearly Meeting of Friends Held in Philadelphia, in 1839* (Philadelphia: Merrihew and Thompson, 1841), 24–25; *Free and Friendly Remarks, on a Speech Lately Delivered to the Senate of the United States, by Henry Clay, of Kentucky, on the Subject of the Abolition of North American Slavery* (New York: Mahlon Day & Co., 1839), 22, 20.

24. Robert H. Abzug, *Passionate Liberator: Theodore Dwight Weld and the Dilemmas of Reform* (New York: Oxford University Press, 1980), 210–14.

25. [Theodore Dwight Weld, Angelina Grimké Weld, and Sarah Grimké], *American Slavery As It Is: Testimony of a Thousand Witnesses* (New York: American Anti-Slavery Society, 1839; reprinted New York: Arno Press and the New York Times, 1968), 7, 76 (quotation), 180, 89 (quotation).

26. Ibid., 164–67 (quotations 167, 166).

27. Ibid., 166–67, 69, 72.

28. Ibid., 89 (quotation), 50, 97 (quotation).

29. On Vermont, see Wilbur H. Siebert, *Vermont's Anti-Slavery and Underground*

Railroad Record [Columbus, Ohio: Spahr and Glenn, 1937], 48–49, 51, citing Vermont *Acts and Resolves,* Oct. sess. 1836, p. 53; Oct. sess. 1837, pp. 60, 106–7; Oct. sess. 1838, p. 23. See also *Correspondence Between Elmore and Birney,* 43. The 1837 resolutions included declarations opposing the annexation of Texas, opposing the admission of any more slave states, and endorsing the power of Congress to ban slavery in the District of Columbia and in the territories. The resolution on the interstate slave trade passed the lower but not the upper house of the legislature. On Massachusetts, see "RESOLVES Relating to the Slave Trade between the States," Massachusetts General Court, 1838 sess., Senate Document No. 87, *Report on the Powers and Duties of Congress upon the Subject of Slavery and the Slave Trade* [hereinafter cited as *1838 Massachusetts Report*], 35; "The Slave Trade Between the States," ibid., 22–31 (quotation 22). Massachusetts issued another call for a ban on the interstate trade in 1840. See Commonwealth of Massachusetts, "Resolves relating to Slavery & the Slave Trade & the admission of new states into the union, and copy of a Correspondence between Edmund Jackson & Hon. Robt. C. Winthrop in 1840," Massachusetts Anti-Slavery Society mss., New-York Historical Society; "Report on Slavery and the Slave Trade," *Massachusetts Abolitionist,* 26 Mar. 1840, p. 24. Vermont did the same in 1842. See Siebert, *Vermont's Anti-Slavery,* 54–55, citing Vermont *Acts and Resolves,* 1842, p. 97. On Rhode Island, see William Sprague to Oliver Johnson, Corresponding Secy. of RIA-SS, 28 Mar. 1838, *Correspondence Between Elmore and Birney,* 56–57.

30. According to *Massachusetts Abolitionist,* 7 Feb. 1839, John Quincy Adams said in the House on 21 Jan. 1839 that of all the measures called for in abolitionist petitions, "it is only those against the annexation of Texas . . . and those which call for the prohibition of the internal slave trade between the States, which I have been willing to vote for." Adams's allusion to the interstate trade was not recorded by the *Globe* reporter in his brief summary of the same speech. (*U.S. Congressional Globe,* 25 Cong., 3 sess., House, 130.) For Webster's speech, 6 Feb. 1837, see *Globe,* 24 Cong., 2 sess., Senate, 163. Jonathan H. Earle, *Jacksonian Antislavery and the Politics of Free Soil, 1824–1854* (Chapel Hill: University of North Carolina Press, 2004), 45, says that one of Morris's resolutions would have "put an end to the interstate slave trade." For Calhoun's comment, see *Globe,* 25 Cong., 2 sess., Senate, 676 (29 Dec. 1837).

31. *Globe,* 25 Cong., 3 sess., House, 21–22 (11 Dec. 1838), quotations from first, third, and fifth resolutions.

32. Henry Clay, "On Abolition," speech in Senate, 7 Feb. 1839, in *Works of Henry Clay Comprising His Life, Correspondence and Speeches,* ed. Calvin Colton, 7 vols. (New York: Henry Clay Publishing Company, 1897), 6: 139–59, see especially 149; [Francis Philpot], *Facts for White Americans, with a Plain Hint for Dupes, and a Bone to Pick for White Nigger Demagogues and Amalgamation Abolitionists, including the Parentage, Brief Career, and Execution, of Amalgamation Abolitionism, Whose Funeral Sermon was Preached at Washington on the 7th of February, 1839* (Philadelphia: Published for the author, 1839). For an earlier consideration and refutation of the point raised by Clay, see *1838 Massachusetts Report,* 24–26. For replies to Clay, see *Letter of Gerrit Smith to Hon. Henry Clay,* Anti-Slavery Examiner, no. 9 (New York, 1839); *Speech of the Hon. Thomas Morris, of Ohio, in Reply to the Speech of the Hon. Henry Clay, in Senate, February 9, 1839,* Anti-Slavery Examiner, no. 10 (New York, 1839);

William E. Channing, *Remarks on the Slavery Question, in a Letter to Jonathan Phillips, Esq.* (Boston, 1839); and the previously-cited *Free and Friendly Remarks.* John Quincy Adams said of Channing's effort, "He demolishes all the argument of Clay's speech. . . . The remark of Junius, that the arguments of tyranny are as despicable as its power is dreadful, applies especially to all arguments in behalf of slavery." (*Memoirs of John Quincy Adams, Comprising Portions of His Diary from 1795 to 1848,* ed. Charles Francis Adams, 12 vols. [Philadelphia: J. B. Lippincott, 1874–77], 10: 123 [24 May 1839].) Clay expressed his fears in his letter to Francis Brooke, 3 Nov. 1838, *Works of Henry Clay,* 4: 429–31 (quotation 431).

33. Alvan Stewart to Myron Holley, 16 Dec. 1839, Myron Holley Papers, New-York Historical Society; William Jay to Messrs. I. J. Norton, A. H. Williams, and S. S. Cowles, com[mittee] of arrangements, Connecticut Anti-Slavery Society, 17 Apr. 1840, draft copy, Jay Family Papers, Rare Book and Manuscript Library, Columbia University. For an insightful discussion of the abolitionist schism, which involved the issues of women's rights and anticlericalism as well as political action, and which was more complex than a simple division between pro- and anti-Garrisonian forces, see Richard O. Curry and Lawrence B. Goodheart, "The Complexities of Factionalism: Letters of Elizur Wright, Jr. on the Abolitionist Schism, 1837–1840," *Civil War History* 29 (Sept. 1983), 245–59.

34. Alvan Stewart to Editor, Jan. 1840, *Massachusetts Abolitionist,* 20 Feb. 1840, p. 1, copying *Emancipator* (in the original, the word "put" is misprinted as "but").

35. These are the leading individuals as named in Curry and Goodheart, "Complexities of Factionalism," 248. All but Goodell and Leavitt have already been discussed. On Goodell, see "'The Hard Times! The Hard Times!' Remarks of William Goodell on the Adoption of Resolutions Reported by the Business Committee of the N.Y. State Anti-Slavery Society, Sept. 17, 1840," *Massachusetts Abolitionist,* 24 Dec. 1840, pp. 177–78, copying *Friend of Man,* wherein Goodell ridicules the notion that the interstate slave trade is constitutionally sacrosanct. Goodell later presented detailed arguments defending congressional power to abolish the interstate slave trade in his books *Views of American Constitutional Law, in Its Bearing upon American Slavery,* 2d ed. rev. (Utica: Lawson & Chaplin, 1845), 28–30, 43–46, and *Slavery and Anti-Slavery: A History of the Great Struggle in Both Hemispheres; With a View of the Slavery Question in the United States* (New York: Wm. Harned, 1852; reprinted New York: Negro Universities Press, 1968), 247–52. On Leavitt, see his editorial in *New York Emancipator,* 15 July 1841, quoted in Alan M. Kraut, "The Liberty Men of New York: Political Abolitionism in New York State, 1840–1848" (Ph.D. diss., Cornell University, 1975), 2n, wherein Leavitt says that political abolitionists "must suppress slavery in the District of Columbia and the domestic slave-trade."

36. Wright to Garrison, 6 Nov. 1837, in Curry and Goodheart, "Complexities of Factionalism," pp. 253–55 (quotation 254).

37. "Political Action," *Massachusetts Abolitionist,* 7 Feb. 1839, pp. 2–3.

Chapter 6. Little Will Remain to Be Done Except to Sing Te Deum

1. Alan M. Kraut, "The Liberty Men of New York: Political Abolitionism in New York State, 1840–1848" (Ph.D. diss., Cornell University, 1975), 66, citing *Friend of Man,*

8 Apr. 1840; S[amuel] E. Sewall, Isaac Clark, and E[lizur] Wright, Jr., "Address to the Abolitionists of Massachusetts," 20 June 1840, authorized by Massachusetts Anti-Slavery Convention for Independent Nominations, Boston, 27 May 1840, *Massachusetts Abolitionist,* 25 June 1840, p. 73; *Slavery and the Internal Slave Trade in the United States of North America; Being Replies to Questions Transmitted by the Committee of the British and Foreign Anti-slavery Society . . .* (London: Thomas Wand and Co., 1841), 276–77; H[arriet] M[artineau], *The Martyr Age of the United States of America* (Newcastle upon Tyne: Newcastle Upon Tyne Emancipation and Aborigines Protection Society, 1840), 43.

2. Austin Willey, *The History of the Antislavery Cause in State and Nation* (n.p.: Tribune Association, 1860; reprinted New York: Negro Universities Press, 1969), 176; Charles D. Cleveland, "Address of the Liberty Party of Pennsylvania to the People of the State," 22 Feb. 1844, *Anti-Slavery Addresses of 1844 and 1845, by Salmon Portland Chase and Charles Dexter Cleveland* (London: Sampson Low, Son, and Marston, 1867; reprinted New York: Negro Universities Press, 1969), 47; *The Address of the Southern and Western Liberty Convention held at Cincinnati, June 11 & 12, 1845, to the People of the United States* (Philadelphia: Office of the American Citizen, n.d.), 14; "North Western Liberty Convention, at Chicago, June 24, 1846," *The Liberty Almanac for 1847* (New York: William Harned, 1847); "Liberty State Committee of Massachusetts, address to the people of that State, in August, 1846," ibid.; *The Liberty Almanac for 1844* (Syracuse, N.Y.: I. A. Hopkins, 1844), 22; *The American Liberty Almanac for 1846* (Hartford: W. H. Burleigh, 1846), 28; *The Liberty Almanac for 1849* (New York: American and Foreign Anti-Slavery Society, 1849), 49.

3. Samuel Webb to Henry B. Stantan [*sic*], Chairman, Elizur Wright, Jr., Sec'y, 18 Sept. 1845, *Proceedings of the Great Convention of the Friends of Freedom in the Eastern and Middle States, Held in Boston, Oct. 1, 2, & 3, 1845* (Lowell, Mass.: Pillsbury and Knapp, 1845) [hereinafter cited as *Great Convention 1845*], 32–33; Joshua Leavitt, editorial in *New York Emancipator,* 15 July 1841, quoted in Kraut, "Liberty Men," 2n; Alvan Stewart, "Letter to Dr. Bailey," Apr. 1842, *Philanthropist,* reprinted in *Writings and Speeches of Alvan Stewart, on Slavery,* ed. Luther R. Marsh (New York: A. B. Burdick, 1860), 268; James G. Birney to Hartford Committee, 15 Aug. 1844, *Signal of Liberty,* 16 Sept. 1844, reprinted in *Letters of James Gillespie Birney, 1831–1857,* ed. Dwight L. Dumond, 2 vols. (New York: D. Appleton-Century, 1938), 2: 835; S. P. Chase to Messrs. H. B. Stanton, Chairman, and Elizur Wright Jr., Secretary, &c., 23 Sept. 1845, *Great Convention 1845,* 30–31.

4. [John G. Palfrey], "The Slave Power.—No. XXIII. What Can the Free States Do About It?" *Boston Daily Whig,* 19 Sept. 1846; John G. Palfrey, *Papers on the Slave Power, First Published in the "Boston Whig"* (Boston: Merrill, Cobb & Co., [1846]); Samuel May to John B. Estlin, 4 Dec. 1846, Rare Books Department, Boston Public Library, Courtesy of the Trustees; John G. Palfrey, *A Letter to a Friend* (Cambridge, Mass.: Metcalf and Company, 1850), 7–8; "Mr. Sumner's Speech at the Whig State Convention, Wednesday [23 Sept. 1846]," *Boston Daily Whig,* 25 Sept. 1846, copying *Boston Courier;* "Mr. Phillips's Resolutions," *Boston Daily Whig,* 25 Sept. 1846; "The Convention—No. 2 Facts," ibid., 1 Oct. 1846; Richard Sewell, *John P. Hale and the Politics of Abolition* (Cambridge: Harvard University Press, 1965), 84, citing *New Hampshire House Journal,* June sess. 1846, pp. 238–39, 376–79, 407; Wilbur H. Sie-

bert, *Vermont's Anti-Slavery and Underground Railroad Record* (Columbus, Ohio: Spahr and Glenn, 1937), 54–55, 57–58, citing Vermont *Acts and Resolves,* 1842, p. 97, and ibid., 1849, pp. 47–48.

In 1845 Adams, Sumner, and Palfrey had written a public statement protesting the admission of Texas as a state partly because it would legalize the slave trade between Texas and the existing states. (Charles Francis Adams, diary entry for 1 Nov. 1845, Adams Papers, Massachusetts Historical Society; "Preamble and resolutions of the Faneuil Hall meeting of November 4th, 1845," 8 pp. ms. and printed copy, John Gorham Palfrey Papers, Houghton Library, Harvard University.)

5. William Goodell, *Slavery and Anti-Slavery: A History of the Great Struggle in Both Hemispheres . . .* (New York: Wm. Harned, 1852; reprinted New York: Negro Universities Press, 1968), 478; Leonard L. Richards, *The Slave Power: The Free North and Southern Domination, 1780–1860* (Baton Rouge: Louisiana State University Press, 2000), 145–54.

It is sometimes asserted that Hale also thought that Congress could not abolish slavery in the District of Columbia, but that is not correct. Hale disagreed with Salmon Chase and others who believed that slavery in the federal district was and always had been unconstitutional. Hale accepted the southern view that the laws of Virginia and Maryland that sanctioned slavery had remained in effect in the district when it was ceded to the federal government. But in an 1848 letter to Chase, Hale acknowledged that Congress had the power to cancel the legal sanction for slavery in Washington. (John P. Hale to S. P. Chase, 8 June 1848, Chase Papers, Historical Society of Pennsylvania.) Hale ran for the presidency again in 1852 on the Free-Soil or, as it was then termed, Free Democratic ticket. Evidence on the Free Democrats is scant but there appears to have been no involvement in the interstate slave trade issue. For the party's platform, see Donald B. Johnson, comp., *National Party Platforms,* rev. ed., 2 vols. (Urbana: University of Illinois Press, 1978), 1: 18–20.

Van Buren was on record as opposing the abolition of slavery in the District of Columbia, but under pressure from Chase and others he finally stated that he would not deem it his duty to veto an act providing for it. In 1849 Van Buren's son John said that it was "desirable that the inter-state slave trade should cease" but doubtful that Congress had constitutional power to end it. (Martin Van Buren to Junius Amis et al., Washington, 6 Mar. 1836, *Emancipator* [Apr. 1836], p. 2, cols. 1–4; Salmon P. Chase to Martin Van Buren, 21 Aug. 1848, Van Buren Papers, Library of Congress; [Martin Van Buren] to [Benjamin Franklin Butler et al.], 22 Aug. 1848, ms. copy in Van Buren Papers, Library of Congress, printed in Oliver C. Gardiner, *The Great Issue: Or, The Three Presidential Candidates . . .* [New York: Wm. C. Bryant & Co., 1848; reprinted Westport, Conn.: Negro Universities Press, 1970], 142–50; *Inconsistency and Hypocrisy of Martin Van Buren on the Question of Slavery* [n.p., (1848?)]; *Evening Post Extra. Speech of John Van Buren, Delivered at Faneuil Hall, in Boston, Thursday evening, the 8th day of November, inst.* [n.p., (1849)], in Van Buren Papers, Library of Congress.)

6. Stanley Harrold, *Gamaliel Bailey and Antislavery Union* (Kent, Ohio: Kent State University Press, 1986), 118; Arthur Tappan et al., "To the Friends of Liberty," 1 July 1848, *National Era,* 6 July 1848, p. 106; Owen Lovejoy, open letter in response to political questions, Chicago, 15 July 1848, printed in Aurora *Guardian,* 18 July 1848,

reprinted in Owen Lovejoy, *His Brother's Blood: Speeches and Writings, 1838–64,* ed. William F. Moore and Jane Ann Moore (Urbana: University of Illinois Press, 2004), 83–84; Owen Lovejoy, open letter upon returning from the Free-Soil convention in Buffalo, *Western Citizen,* 22 Aug. 1848, reprinted ibid., 87; Richard Sewell, *Ballots for Freedom: Antislavery Politics in the United States, 1837–1860* (New York: Oxford University Press, 1976), 198, citing Henry Wilson in *Boston Daily Republican,* 29 Sept. 1849; Jacob Leisler [pseud. Vincent L. Bradford], *Letters to the People of Pennsylvania on the Political Principles of the Free Soil Party* (Philadelphia, 1850), 21. The last item is a pamphlet reprinting seven letters by Bradford originally published in the Philadelphia *Pennsylvanian* between September 1848 and February 1850.

7. *Disunion. Address of the American Anti-Slavery Society* [7 May 1844], Anti-Slavery Examiner, no. 12 (New York: American Anti-Slavery Society, 1845), 4, 6; Henry C. Wright, *The Dissolution of the American Union, Demanded By Justice and Humanity, As the Incurable Enemy of Liberty* (London: Chapman, Brothers, & Co., 1846), 10–11. On Garrisonian constitutionalism, see also Wendell Phillips, *The Constitution a Pro-Slavery Compact: Selections from the Madison Papers, &c.,* Anti-Slavery Examiner, no. 11 (New York: American Anti-Slavery Society, 1844); Wendell Phillips, *Review of Lysander Spooner's Essay on the Unconstitutionality of Slavery* (Boston: Andrews & Prentiss, 1847); [William I. Bowditch], *The United States Constitution,* Anti-Slavery Tracts, no. 1 (New York: American Anti-Slavery Society, [1855?]). The Garrisonians' stress upon the original intent of the framers makes them a notable exception to Paul Finkelman's suggestion that such an approach to the Constitution "may have been particularly Southern *before* the Civil War." (Paul Finkelman, "The Protection of Black Rights in Seward's New York," *Civil War History,* 34 [Sept. 1988]: 221n.)

8. Wendell Phillips to Charles Sumner, 17 Feb. 1845, Charles Sumner Correspondence, MS Am1 (4941), quoted by permission of the Houghton Library, Harvard University; Edmund Quincy, *An Examination of the Charges of Mr. John Scoble & Mr. Lewis Tappan Against the American Anti-Slavery Society,* 2d ed. (London: Whitfield, 1852), 7; Samuel J. May, "Slavery and the Constitution," *Quarterly Anti-Slavery Magazine,* 2 (Apr. 1837): 232; S[amuel] J. May, "The Liberty Bell Is Not of the Liberty Party," *The Liberty Bell. By Friends of Freedom,* ed. Maria Weston Chapman (Boston: Boston, Massachusetts, Anti-Slavery Fair, 1845), 160–61.

9. Lysander Spooner, *The Unconstitutionality of Slavery* (Boston: Bela Marsh, 1845), 81–86, 95–96; William Goodell, *Views of American Constitutional Law, in Its Bearing upon American Slavery* (Utica, N.Y.: Jackson & Chaplin, 1844), 43–46; William Goodell, "The Constitution and Slavery," *National Era,* 1 Apr. 1847, p. 1; Gerrit Smith to S[almon] P. Chase, 6 Aug. 1845, Salmon Chase Papers, Collection 121, Historical Society of Pennsylvania; Gerrit Smith to I. K. Ingalls, 15 Aug. 1848, quoted in Kraut, "Liberty Men of New York," 148.

Lewis Tappan to S[almon] P. Chase, 24 Feb. 1847, says that among abolitionists, views of the Constitution are varied "and some of them whimsical enough." In a follow-up letter, 10 June 1847, Tappan adds, "Spooner's views have been embraced by very many, probably because his doctrine is startling & people wish it to be true." (Both letters in Chase Papers, Collection 121, Historical Society of Pennsylvania.) For a succinct refutation by a Garrisonian of Spooner's interpretation of the 1808 clause, see Phillips, *Review of Lysander Spooner's Essay,* 60–62. In his 1852 book *Slavery and Anti-Slavery,* Goodell tried to describe fairly the constitutional positions of the Garrisonians, the moderates, and the radicals. For his pains, he found himself attacked from all sides. (Francis Jackson, "Goodell's Anti-Slavery History," *Liberator,* 2 Sept. 1853, p. 138, col. 2; William Goodell to Samuel May, Jr., Francis Jackson, et al., 3 Oct. 1853, Boston Public Library.) Eventually even some Garrisonians drifted toward the radical position. By 1860 Henry C. Wright was of the opinion that "a slaveholding State can have no rights which any individual, or any State, is bound to respect." (Henry C. Wright, *No Rights, No Duties: Or, Slaveholders, as Such, Have No Rights; Slaves, As Such, Owe No Duties . . .* [Boston: Printed for the author, 1860], 4.)

10. *Great Convention 1845,* 6; *American Anti-slavery Conventions: A Series of Extracts Illustrative of the Proceedings and Principles of the "Liberty Party" in the United States . . .* (Edinburgh: William Oliphant and Sons, 1846), 6; *Proceedings of the National Liberty* [radical rump] *Convention, Held at Buffalo, N.Y., June 14th & 15th, 1848 . . .* (Utica, 1848), 15–16 (quotation 15); *Substance of the Speech Made by Gerrit Smith in the Capitol of the State of New York, March 11th and 12th, 1850,* 2d ed. (Syracuse: V. W. Smith & Co., 1850); *Proceedings of the Convention of Radical Abolitionists, Held at Syracuse, N.Y., June 26th, 27th, and 28th, 1855* (New York: Central Abolition Board, 1856); Theodore Parker, *The Present Aspect of Slavery in America and the Immediate Duty of the North* (Boston: Bela Marsh, 1858); L[ewis] Tappan to Charles Sumner, 26 June 1860, Sumner Papers, Houghton Library, Harvard University.

John Greenleaf Whittier was to have written the 1848 radical rump convention's address, but when his health and morale faltered, Gerrit Smith took over the job. Henry Stanton praised Smith's document as "able, strong, calm, but quite elementary & A.B.C. like in its character." (H. B. Stanton to Salmon P. Chase, Boston, 6 Oct. 1845, in American Historical Association *Annual Report for 1902,* 2 vols. [Washington, D.C.: Government Printing Office, 1903], 2: 465–67 [quotation 466].)

In addition to the Liberty Party propaganda already mentioned, examples of abolitionist agitation of the interstate slave trade issue in the 1840s include *Letter of the Honorable William Jay, to Hon. Theo. Frelinghuysen* (New York, 1844), 6, and *The American Slavetrade,* tract no. 10 (Philadelphia: Pennsylvania Anti-Slavery Society, [1845?]). The latter item is an oddity in that it declares that anyone who swears allegiance to the U.S. Constitution is supporting slavery, yet also upholds the power of Congress to abolish the interstate slave trade.

11. Text of the Vermont revolutions of 19 Nov. 1849 as quoted by Jeremiah Clemens in *Congressional Globe,* 31 Cong., 1 sess. (10 Jan. 1850), appendix, p. 52.

12. Clemens's speech, ibid., 52–55 (quotations 52–53); John M. Martin, "The Senatorial Career of Jeremiah Clemens, 1849–1853," *Alabama Historical Quarterly* 43 (Fall 1981): 186–235; speech by Joseph E. Brown in the Georgia state senate as reported in *Federal Union,* 5 Feb. 1850, quoted in Ulrich B. Phillips, *The Life of Robert Toombs* (New York, 1913, reprinted New York: Burt Franklin, 1968), 92.

13. *Speech of the Hon. Henry Clay of Kentucky, On Presenting His Resolutions on the Subject of Slavery. Delivered in the Senate, Feb. 5th & 6th, 1850* (New York: Stringer & Townshend, 1850), 5. Horace Mann, *New Dangers to Freedom, and New Duties for Its Defenders* (Boston: Redding and Company, 1850), 11, charges that Clay aims at facilitating the movement of slaves into New Mexico.

14. "Union and Freedom Without Compromise," speech in Senate, 26–27 Mar. 1850, *Congressional Globe,* 31 Cong., 1 sess., appendix, 469–86 (quotations 476). A slightly less polished version of Chase's speech (and thus perhaps closer to what he actually said) is quoted in J. W. Schucker, ms. material on the life of Chase, Salmon Chase Papers, Historical Society of Pennsylvania.

15. Sewell, *John P. Hale,* 11, 35; *Congressional Globe,* 31 Cong., 1 sess., appendix (4 Apr. 1850), 536 (quotations).

16. *Congressional Globe,* 25 Cong., 3 sess. (11 Dec. 1838), 21–22; ibid., 31 Cong., 1 sess., appendix (3 Sept. 1850), 1630–33 (quotation 1630). Hunter's defense of the domestic slave trade probably was not made more persuasive by the fact that he also extolled at length the blessings of the external slave trade, insisting that "a christian slave upon the banks of the Mississippi" is far better off than "a Fetish worshipper upon the Niger." (Ibid., 1632.)

17. Ibid., 1634 (Clay), 1644 (Chase), 1645 (Foote).

18. "Letter of John Jay upon the Compromise Resolutions of Mr. Clay," *National Anti-Slavery Standard,* 21 Feb. 1850, p. 154, cols. 3–6, copying *New York Evening Post.* In the original, a bracketed exclamation point appears after the word "Republic."

19. *Resolutions and Address adopted by the Southern Convention. Held at Nashville, Tennessee, June 3d to 12th inclusive, in the year 1850* (Nashville: Harvey M. Watterson, 1850; reproduced on microfiche, Louisville: Lost Cause Press, 1977), 12; Thelma Jennings, *The Nashville Convention: Southern Movement for Unity, 1848–1851* (Memphis: Memphis State University Press, 1980), 36–39.

20. Clay had long remained optimistic. On 25 April he wrote, "My hopes are strong that we may settle the Slavery Questions; but all difficulties are not yet obviated." (Clay to "My dear Wife," 25 Apr. 1850, Henry Clay Papers, Library of Congress.)

21. William K. Boyd, "North Carolina on the Eve of Secession," American Historical Association *Annual Report for 1910* (Washington, D.C.: Government Printing Office, 1911), 171; *Speech of Hon. Langdon Cheves, in the Southern Convention, at Nashville, Tennessee, November 14, 1850* ([Charleston?]: Southern Rights Association, 1850), 15; *Journal of the State Convention, Held in Milledgeville, in* [10–14] *December, 1850* (Milledgeville, Ga.: R. M. Orme, State Printer, 1850), 19; *Journal of the State Convention of South Carolina* [26–30 Apr. 1852]; *Together with the Resolution and Ordinance* (Columbia, S.C.: Johnston & Cavis, 1852), 18–19, 24 (quotation); Jennings, *Nashville Convention,* 209; George W. Jones to Howell Cobb, Washington, D.C., 7 Dec. 1851, "The Correspondence of Robert Toombs, Alexander H. Stephens, and Howell Cobb," American Historical Association *Annual Report for 1911,* 2 vols. (Washington, D.C.: Government Printing Office, 1913), 2: 269–71.

22. *The Union, Past and Future: How It Works, and How to Save It. By a Citizen of Virginia,* 4th ed. (Charleston: Southern Rights Association, 1850), 7–8; Edward B. Bryan, *The Rightful Remedy. Addressed to the Slaveholders of the South* (Charleston: Southern Rights Association, 1850), 131; J.A.C. [almost certainly Jeremiah A. Clemens], *The Rights of the Slave States. By a Citizen of Alabama. From the Southern Quarterly Review, for Jan., 1851* (n.p.: Southern Rights Association, 1850), 29.

23. Frederick Douglass, *Narrative of the Life of Frederick Douglass, an American Slave, Written by Himself* (Boston: Anti-slavery Office, 1845; reprinted Cambridge: Belknap Press of Harvard University Press, 1960), ed. Benjamin Quarles, pp. 24, 26, 32,

42, 125; Dickson J. Preston, *Young Frederick Douglass: The Maryland Years* (Baltimore: Johns Hopkins University Press, 1980), 76; Frederick Douglass, "The Meaning of the Fourth of July for the Negro," speech at Rochester, N.Y., 5 July 1852, *The Life and Writings of Frederick Douglass,* ed. Philip S. Foner, 4 vols. (New York: International Publishers, 1950), 2: 181–204 (quotations 194–95).

24. [William Jay], *An Address to the Anti-slavery Christians of the United States* (New York: [American and Foreign Anti-Slavery Society], [1852]), 4–5; Joel Tiffany, *A Treatise on the Unconstitutionality of American Slavery: Together with the Powers and Duties of the Federal Government, in Relation to that Subject* ([Ohio?] [185?]; reprinted Miami: Mnemosyne Publishing, 1969), 134, 137; John G. Palfrey, *The Inter-state Slave Trade,* Anti-Slavery Tracts, no. 5 (n.p.: American Anti-Slavery Society, [1855?]). It is curious that Palfrey's tract was published by the Garrisonian-dominated AA-SS.

Some nonabolitionists also upheld the right of Congress to ban the slave trade. Leonard Marsh is believed to be author of the strange pamphlet *A Bake-Pan for the Dough-Faces* (Burlington, Vt.: C. Goodrich, 1854), which upholds such power and then says (p. 44), "*where the shoe pinches* is, that if slavery is circumscribed, you must get rid of your slaves *at any rate*. . . . Precisely so, gentlemen, voila, at last, the genuine cat let out of the bag! . . . If slavery is shut up, the fate awaits it which is said to happen to certain weeds; which are so noisome that, if there are many together, they presently stink themselves to death." See also the anonymous *Letter Addressed to the President of the United States on Slavery, Considered in Relation to the Constitutional Principles of Government in Great Britain and in the United States. By an American Citizen* (Boston: Redding and Company, 1855), 61–63, doubting the expediency of immediate emancipation but defending the right of Congress to end the interstate trade.

25. Moira Davison Reynolds, *Uncle Tom's Cabin and Mid-Nineteenth Century United States: Pen and Conscience* (Jefferson, N.C.: McFarland & Company, 1985), 9–12; Thomas F. Gossett, *Uncle Tom's Cabin and American Culture* (Dallas: Southern Methodist University Press, 1985), 51, 164; Harriet Beecher Stowe, *Uncle Tom's Cabin* (Boston: John P. Jewett & Co., 1852); reprinted New York: Washington Square Press, 1963), ch. 43, p. 440. Because Stowe's novel has appeared in many editions with varying pagination, I cite it by chapter as well as page.

26. Stowe, *Uncle Tom's Cabin,* ch. 20, p. 251; ch. 14, p. 150.

27. Ibid., ch. 1, p. 1; ch. 37, p. 396.

28. Forrest Wilson, *Crusader in Crinoline: The Life of Harriet Beecher Stowe* (Philadelphia: J. B. Lippincott, 1941; reprinted Westport, Conn.: Greenwood Press, 1972), 119–20, 115–16 (quotation), 129–37, 141–44; La Roy Sunderland, *Anti-Slavery Manual, Containing a Collection of Facts and Arguments on American Slavery* (New York: Piercy & Reed, 1837; reprinted New York: Negro Universities Press, 1969), 121–24, copying portions of Henry B. Stanton to "Brother [Joshua] Leavitt," 22 Apr. 1834, printed in *Liberator,* 17 May 1834, p. 77, and 24 May 1834, p. 83, copying *New York Evangelist;* Wilson, *Crusader in Crinoline,* 182–89.

29. Wilson, *Crusader in Crinoline,* 193–94; Harriet Beecher Stowe, *A Key to Uncle Tom's Cabin; Presenting the Original Facts and Documents upon Which the Story Is Founded. Together with Corroborative Statements Verifying the Truth of the Work* (Boston: John P. Jewett & Co., 1853), 5–6; Wilson, *Crusader in Crinoline,* 198, 218.

30. Gossett, *Uncle Tom's Cabin and American Culture,* 61–62; Stowe, *Uncle Tom's*

Cabin, ch. 30, pp. 334, 337; Charles Nichols, "The Origins of Uncle Tom's Cabin," *Phylon* 19 (Fall 1958): 328–34; Stowe, *Uncle Tom's Cabin,* ch. 5, p. 40; ch. 7, p. 51; ch. 45, p. 453.

31. Stowe, *Uncle Tom's Cabin,* ch. 1, p. 4; ch. 8, p. 72; ch. 17, p. 193; ch. 34, p. 371; ch. 43, p. 439.

32. Ibid., ch. 1, p. 7; ch. 12, pp. 135–36; ch. 10, p. 104. Stowe later acknowledged that her novel portrayed "only one class of the negro-traders" whereas some of the larger trading firms were run by men who were "gentlemanly in manners" and occasionally even moderately antislavery in sentiment. See Stowe, *Key to Uncle Tom's Cabin,* 8.

33. Stowe, *Uncle Tom's Cabin,* ch. 1, p. 9; Gossett, *Uncle Tom's Cabin and American Culture,* 198.

34. Gossett, *Uncle Tom's Cabin and American Culture,* 260–73, 164.

35. Stowe, *Uncle Tom's Cabin,* ch. 45, p. 452.

36. James B. Stewart, *Joshua R. Giddings and the Tactics of Radical Politics* (Cleveland: Press of Case Western Reserve University, 1970), 47, 69–78; [Joshua R. Giddings], *Pacificus: The Rights and Privileges of the several states in regard to slavery* ([Warren, Ohio?] [1843?]); [Joshua R. Giddings], *The Rights of the Free States Subverted, Or, An enumeration of some of the most prominent instances in which the Federal Constitution has been violated by our National Government, for the benefit of Slavery* (n.p., [1845?]), 15 (quotation); *A Letter from Hon. J. R. Giddings, Upon the Duty of Anti-Slavery Men in the Present Crisis* (Ravenna, Ohio: William Wadsworth, 1844), 14 (quotation).

37. Charles Sumner to Richard Cobden, 9 July 1850, *Memoir and Letters of Charles Sumner,* ed. Edward L. Pierce, 4 vols. (Boston: Roberts Brothers, 1877–93), 3: 217 (quotation); Charles Sumner, "Freedom National; Slavery Sectional: Speech in the Senate of the United States, 26th August, 1852, on his Motion to Repeal the Fugitive Slave Bill," *Recent Speeches and Addresses by Charles Sumner* (Boston: Higgins and Bradley, 1856), 92–93; S[almon] P. Chase to Theodore Parker, 12 Mar. 1854, Theodore Parker Papers, Massachusetts Historical Society; Charles Sumner, *Duties of Massachusetts at This Crisis. A Speech . . . delivered at the Republican Convention at Worcester, Sept. 7, 1854* (n.p., n.d.), 4; Charles Sumner, *The Anti-Slavery Enterprise: Its Necessity, Practicability, and Dignity . . . An Address before the People of New York, at the Metropolitan Theatre, May 9, 1855* (Boston: Ticknor and Fields, 1855), 24, 32; *Argument of Robert J. Walker, Esq. before the Supreme Court of the United States, on the Mississippi Slave Question* (Philadelphia: John C. Clark, 1841), 58 (quotation).

Sumner apparently tried to expunge from the record his earlier support for a ban on the interstate slave trade, inserting the words "on the high seas" so as to convert his 1846 statement upholding the power of Congress to ban the "slave-trade between the States" into a more moderate call for prohibition of the "slave-trade on the high seas between the States." (Compare the version of Sumner's speech at the Whig State Convention of Massachusetts, 23 Sept. 1846, as printed in *Boston Daily Whig,* 25 Sept. 1846, with the altered version that appears in *Charles Sumner: His Complete Works,* "Statesman Edition," 20 vols. [Boston: Lee and Shepard, 1900], 1: 310.) Gamaliel Bailey appears to have followed a course similar to that of Chase and Sumner; in 1854 Bailey called for termination of the coastal slave trade, not the entire interstate trade. (Harrold, *Gamaliel Bailey,* 163, citing *National Era,* 30 Mar. 1854.)

Gideon Welles used an argument rather like Robert Walker's, but for the purpose of condemning the 1850 Fugitive Slave Act. Welles said, "The South will themselves be convinced, at no distant day, that the results of this amplification of the powers of the general government will be fatal to themselves, for if that government can override the state jurisdictions and seize persons in the free states to carry into slavery, that same government will . . . strech [*sic*] its power into slave states for the purposes of emancipation." (Welles to [?], 19 Apr. 1851, 16 Oct. 1851, quoted in Sewell, *Ballots for Freedom,* 237.)

38. Paul Finkelman, *An Imperfect Union: Slavery, Federalism, and Comity* (Chapel Hill: University of North Carolina Press, 1981), 296–315.

39. *Speech of R[ichard] W. Thompson Upon the Political Aspects of the Slavery Question, Made at a Public Meeting of the People in Terre-Haute, Indiana, on the 11th day of August, 1855* (Terre Haute, Ind.: Express Power-Press Print, 1855); William Kauffman, *Masters of the Big House: Elite Slaveholders of the Mid-Nineteenth-Century South* (Baton Rouge: Louisiana State University Press, 2003), 281, quoting from a printed broadside, 28 Sept. 1856, John Perkins Papers, Southern Historical Collection, University of South Carolina; Edmund Ruffin, "Consequences of Abolition Agitation," *De Bow's Review* 22 (June 1857): 588. Richard Thompson later became a Republican (*Dictionary of American Biography,* 18: 468–69).

40. Robert W. Johannsen, ed., *The Lincoln-Douglas Debates of 1858* (New York: Oxford University Press, 1965), 41 (quotation), 76–77, 78 (quotation).

41. Ibid., 138, 139; Speech on the Sub-Treasury, [26] Dec. 1839, *The Collected Works of Abraham Lincoln,* ed. Roy P. Basler, 9 vols. (New Brunswick, N.J.: Rutgers University Press, 1953–55), 1: 159–79; Speech in U.S. House of Representatives on Internal Improvements, 20 June 1848, ibid., 480–90. I first drew attention to this matter in my article "Abraham Lincoln and the Ideal of Equality," *Journal of the Illinois State Historical Society,* 75 (Winter 1982): 289–308.

42. Frederick Douglass, "What Is My Duty as an Anti-slavery Voter?" *Frederick Douglass' Paper,* 25 Apr. 1856, reprinted in Foner, *Life and Writings of Frederick Douglass,* 2: 392; "Speech of Wendell Phillips, Esq., at the New England Anti Slavery Convention, Wednesday, May 30, 1860," *Liberator,* 8 June 1860, p. 89.

Chapter 7. Great and Terrible Realities

1. A member of the South Carolina legislature described the situation succinctly: "By reference to the census returns of 1808 [*sic* 1810?], it will be seen that the slave and hireling States were equal in number and nearly equal in population. Since that time no slaves have come to the South, but since that time five millions of foreigners have come to the North, and while therefore the South at present have but fifteen States and ten millions of people, the North has seventeen States and sixteen millions of people. . . . In view of these facts it would seem certain that the South has come to be at the mercy of the North in legislation, and that these restrictions have been the cause of it." *Speech upon the Foreign Slave Trade, before the Legislature of South Carolina [4 Dec. 1858], by L. W. Spratt, Esq., of Charleston* (Columbia, S.C.: Steam-power Press Southern Guardian, 1858), 5.

2. *Abraham Lincoln's Record on the Slavery Question. His Doctrines Condemned by*

Henry Clay. The Mass of Lincoln's Supporters Hostile to the Constitution . . . (Baltimore: Murphy & Co., [1860]).

3. "Substance of a Speech delivered by Hon. John C. Breckinridge in the Hall of the House of Representatives at Frankfort, Dec. 21st, 1859," in John Townsend, *The South Alone Should Govern the South. And African Slavery Should Be Controlled By Those Only, Who Are Friendly To It,* 1860 Association tract no. 1 (Charleston: Evans & Cogswell, 1860), 34–40. Another southern spokesman appears to have borrowed from this speech later on; see Henry A. Wise, "Overt Acts of Northern Aggression," *De Bow's Review* 30 (Jan. 1861): 116–18.

4. Ollinger Crenshaw, *The Slave States in the Presidential Election of 1860* (Baltimore: Johns Hopkins Press, 1945), 186–87, citing remarks by William W. Holden in *North Carolina Semi-Weekly Standard* (Raleigh), 7 Jan. 1860; L[ucius] J[eremiah] Gartrell, *The Dangers of Black-Republicanism, and the Duty of the South. Speech of Hon. L. J. Gartrell, of Georgia, in the House of Representatives, January 10, 1860* (n.p.: Lemuel Towers, n.d.), 15; Steven A. Channing, *Crisis of Fear: Secession in South Carolina* (New York: Simon and Schuster, 1970), 176, quoting James Farrow to James Johnston Pettigrew, 15 Feb. 1860, Pettigrew Family Papers, North Carolina Department of Archives and History, Raleigh; John Townsend, 7 June 1860, in Townsend, *South Alone,* 34; Reverdy Johnson, speech at Faneuil Hall, Boston, June 1860, quoted in *The "Southern Rights" and "Union" Parties in Maryland Contrasted* (Baltimore: W. M. Innes, 1863), 6–7.

Gartrell was addressing John Hickman of Pennsylvania, a Democrat who had sided with Douglas against Buchanan and now was defecting to the Republicans. Not all southern spokesmen were so apprehensive about Lincoln and his party. Even in South Carolina, Douglas Democrat Benjamin F. Perry declared that southerners had only themselves to blame for creating the situation that made a Lincoln presidency likely. Perry thought the South should simply wait and see what happened after the election. "It may be," he said, "that 'Old Abe' will go out of office quite a favorite with the Southern people." (Crenshaw, *Slave States,* 220, quoting letter by B. F. Perry, Greenville Court House, 13 Aug. 1860, printed in *Charleston Courier,* copied in *New York Herald,* 24 Aug. 1860.)

5. "The Montgomery Address of Stephen A. Douglas [2 Nov. 1860]," ed. David R. Barbee and L. Bonham Milledge, Jr., *Journal of Southern History* 5 (Nov. 1939): 527–52; Charles Sumner, "The Barbarism of Slavery," speech in Senate, 4 June 1860, *Charles Sumner: His Complete Works,* 20 vols. (Boston: Lee and Shepard, 1900): 6: 232; *Speech of William M. Evarts, of New York City, at Auburn, Tuesday, Oct. 16, 1860,* Evening Journal tracts, no. 18 (n.p., n.d.), 9.

6. Republican Platform, 1860, appendix A (pp. 237–43) in Emerson David Fite, *The Presidential Campaign of 1860* (New York: Macmillan, 1911; reprinted Port Washington, N.Y.: Kennikat Press, 1967), 238; Don E. Fehrenbacher, "Lincoln and the Mayor of Chicago," chap. 4 (pp. 33–43) of Don E. Fehrenbacher, *Lincoln in Text and Context: Selected Essays* (Stanford, Calif.: Stanford University Press, 1987), 43, quoting Wentworth editorial in *Chicago Democrat,* 30 Oct. 1860; Carl Schurz, *Slavery at War with the Moral Sentiment of the World: A Speech by Carl Schurz, of Wisconsin. Delivered in St. Louis, Aug. 1, 1860,* Evening Journal tracts, no. 11 ([Albany, N.Y.]: Albany Evening Journal, [1860]), 5; John Jay, *The Rise and Fall of the Pro-Slavery Democracy, and the Rise and Duties of the Republican Party. An Address to the Citizens of Westchester*

County, New York. Delivered at the Court-House at Bedford on the Eve of the Presidential Election, Nov. 5, 1860 (New York: Roe Lockwood & Co., 1861), 41–42.

James B. De Bow later reprinted Jay's speech as evidence that southern secession was justified. ("Why We Resist and What We Resist," *Debow's Review* 30 [Feb. 1861]: 236–46.) De Bow reproduced Jay's text accurately but inserted inflammatory subheadings. For the section of the speech that mentions banning the interstate slave trade, De Bow used the heading "Tender Mercies of The Abolition Wolf Toward the Southern Lamb, and What Father Lincoln Is to Do for His Children." (Ibid., 244.)

7. "Breckinridge Campaign Speech by William L. Yancey, New York, New York, October 10, 1860," appendix D (pp. 301–29) in Fite, *Presidential Campaign,* 316–17. See also William L. Barney, *The Secessionist Impulse: Alabama and Mississippi in 1860* (Princeton, N.J.: Princeton University Press, 1974), 101, citing newspaper sources for similar arguments by other Breckinridge Democrats.

8. Roane, "The South, in the Union, or out of It," *De Bow's Review* 29 (Oct. 1860): 448–65 (quotations 452, 453, 454).

9. William Gannanway Brownlow, *Sketches of the Rise, Progress, and Decline of Secession; with a Narrative of Personal Adventures among the Rebels* (Philadelphia: George W. Childs, 1862; reprinted New York: Da Capo Press, 1968), 67, 69.

10. Henry Winter Davis, speech at Baltimore, 27 Sept. 1860, *New York Times,* 29 Sept. 1860, p. 1. According to the *Times,* this speech was delivered "at a meeting of the old American Party, which was very numerously attended." See also Crenshaw, *Slave States,* 115–17.

11. Crenshaw, *Slave States,* 137–38, citing (1) *Lynchburg Virginian,* copied in Washington *National Intelligencer,* 1 Nov. 1860, (2) *Lexington Valley Star,* 13 Sept. 1860 and 11 Oct. 1860, and (3) *Lynchburg Daily Virginian,* 23 Oct. 1860; John M. Botts, *Union or Disunion. The Union cannot and shall not be dissolved. Mr. Lincoln not an abolitionist. Speech of the Hon. John M. Botts, at Holcombe Hall, in Lynchburg, Virginia, on Thursday evening, October 18 [1860]* (n.p., [1860?]), 18–19 (quotation 18); Illinois General Assembly, House of Representatives, *Journal,* 10th General Assembly, 1st sess. (1837), 241–44, 817–18; *The Collected Works of Abraham Lincoln,* ed. Roy P. Basler, 9 vols. (New Brunswick, N.J.: Rutgers University Press, 1953–55), 1: 74–76.

12. J. G. Nicolay to "Dear Sir" (form reply to requests for political opinions), Springfield, [June?] 1860, Basler, *Collected Works,* 4: 60; Lincoln to Samuel Galloway, Springfield, 19 June 1860, ibid., 79–80; Lincoln to George T. M. Davis, Springfield, 27 Oct. 1860, ibid., 132–33; Lincoln to George D. Prentice, Springfield, 29 Oct. 1860, ibid., 134–35; Lincoln to William S. Speer, Springfield, 23 Oct. 1860, ibid., 130; Lincoln to John Hill, Springfield, Sept. 1860, ibid., 104–8.

13. Although by 1860 most southern newspapers as well as leading periodicals like *De Bow's Review,* the *Southern Literary Messenger,* and the *Southern Quarterly Review* were dominated by secessionists, southern public opinion remained ambivalent. Even among the delegates to the February 1861 Montgomery convention that created the Confederacy, about forty percent had not in the past been radical secessionists. (Emory M. Thomas, *The Confederacy as a Revolutionary Experience* [Englewood Cliffs, N.J.: Prentice-Hall, 1971], 33–34; Charles Robert Lee, Jr., *The Confederate Constitutions* [Chapel Hill: University of North Carolina Press, 1963], 39.)

14. *Remarks Made by Thomas R. R. Cobb, Esq., In the Hall of the House of Represen-*

tatives [Milledgeville, Ga.], *Monday Evening, November 12, 1860* (Atlanta, 1860), reprinted in William W. Freehling and Craig M. Simpson, eds., *Secession Debated: Georgia's Showdown in 1860* (New York: Oxford University Press, 1992), 15; Joseph E. Brown, public letter, 7 Dec. 1860, *Federal Union* (Milledgeville), 11 Dec. 1860, reprinted ibid., 148–49 (quotation 149).

15. Jabez L. M. Curry, *Perils and Duty of the South. Substance of a Speech delivered by Jabez L. M. Curry, in Talladega, Alabama, November 26, 1860* (n.p.: Lemuel Towers, n.d.), 6, 9, 7.

16. M[adison] S[tarke] Perry, *Governor's Message, Transmitted to the Legislature of Florida, November 26, 1860* (n.p., n.d.), 3–4.

17. Charles Anderson, *Speech of Charles Anderson, Esq., on the State of the Country, at a Meeting of the People of Bexar County, at San Antonio, Texas, November 24, 1860* (Washington, D.C.: Lemuel Towers, 1860), 7, 12, 13; Extract from Journal of the Georgia Convention, 18 Jan. 1861, in *The War of the Rebellion: A Compilation of the Official Records of the Union and Confederate Armies,* 70 vols. (Washington, D.C., 1880–1901), series 4, 1: 57–60 (quotation 59); Alabama secession ordinance, minority report by the committee of thirteen, ibid., 44–45.

18. Joel Parker, "To the Editor of the Boston Journal," 25 Dec. 1860, in Joel Parker, *Personal Liberty Laws, (Statutes of Massachusetts,) and Slavery in the Territories, (Case of Dred Scott.)* (Boston: Wright & Potter, 1861), 11, 12; *Concessions and Compromises* (Philadelphia, 8 Dec. 1860); 8; Henry J. Raymond to Hon. W. L. Yancey, 25 Dec. 1860, in Henry J. Raymond, *Disunion and Slavery: A Series of Letters to Hon. W. L. Yancey of Alabama* (n.p., n.d.), 32. Raymond's immediate concern was a false story that Lincoln had endorsed Negro suffrage. Despite Raymond's effort to scotch it, the story was repeated by T. J. Wharton, commissioner from Mississippi, in his speech to a joint session of the Tennessee legislature on 8 January 1861. (A. Lincoln to Henry J. Raymond, Springfield, 18 Dec. 1860, Basler, *Collected Works,* 4: 156; "Document A" [pp. 149–63], *Journal of the* [Mississippi] *State Convention and Ordinances Adopted in January, 1861, with an Appendix* [Jackson, Miss.: E. Barksdale, State Printer, 1861], 156.)

19. "A Declaration of the Immediate Causes which Induce and Justify the Secession of the State of Mississippi from the Federal Union," 26 Jan. 1861, *Journal of the* [Mississippi] *State Convention,* 86–88; report from committee of seventeen to report the ordinance of secession, Journal of the Georgia Convention, *War of the Rebellion,* series 4, 1: 84; *Ordinances and Resolutions of the Convention Held in the City of Austin 28th of January, 1861, February 24th, 1861* (Austin, Texas, 1861), 4.

20. J. L. M. Curry, Alabama Commissioner to Maryland, to Thomas H. Hicks, Governor of Maryland, 28 Dec. 1860, *War of the Rebellion,* series 4, 1: 40; Alexander H. Handy, *Speech of the Hon. A. H. Handy, Commissioner to Maryland, from the State of Mississippi. Delivered at Princess Anne, on the First Day of January, A.D. 1861* (Jackson: Mississippian Book and Job Printing Office, 1861), 8; Fulton Anderson, "Address of Hon. Fulton Anderson, of Mississippi," 18 Feb. 1861, *Addresses Delivered before the Virginia State Convention by Hon. Fulton Anderson, Commissioner from Mississippi, Hon. Henry L. Benning, Commissioner from Georgia, and Hon. John S. Preston, Commissioner from South Carolina, February 1861* (Richmond: Wyatt M. Elliott, 1861), 10.

Mississippi appointed the first commissioners within a few weeks of Lincoln's election. The other deep South states followed its example. Some fifty-two individuals served as secession commissioners from December 1860 through April 1861. (Charles B. Dew, *Apostles of Disunion: Southern Secession Commissioners and the Causes of the Civil War* [Charlottesville: University Press of Virginia, 2001], 18–19. 23.)

21. Reverdy Johnson, "Speech of Hon. Reverdy Johnson," *Proceedings and Speeches at a Public Meeting of the Friends of the Union, in the City of Baltimore, Held at the Maryland Institute, On Thursday Evening, January 10, 1861* (Baltimore: John D. Toy, 1861), 46–48; John S. Carlisle, *Speech of John S. Carlisle, of Harrison, in the Virginia State Convention, Delivered Thursday, March 7, 1861* (Richmond: Whig Book and Job Office, 1861), 11; George W. Richardson, *Speech of George W. Richardson, of Hanover, in Committee of the Whole, on the Report of the Committee on Federal Relations, in the Convention of Virginia, April 4, 1861* (Richmond: Whig Book and Job Office, 1862), 9–10.

22. Passage written for Lyman Trumbull's speech at Springfield, Ill., 20 Nov. 1860, Basler, *Collected Works,* 4: 141–42; Lincoln to Henry Raymond, Springfield, 28 Nov. 1860, ibid., 145–46; John A. Gilmer to Lincoln, House of Reps., 10 Dec. 1860, Abraham Lincoln Papers, Library of Congress microfilm; Lincoln to Gilmer, Springfield, 15 Dec. 1860, Basler, *Collected Works,* 4: 151–53; Lincoln to Alexander H. Stephens, Springfield, 22 Dec. 1860, ibid., 160–61.

23. Ronald T. Takaki, *A Pro-Slavery Crusade: The Agitation to Reopen the African Slave Trade* (New York: Free Press, 1971); "What Slave States May Secede, and What 'Niggers for the Niggerless' May Have to Do With It," *Cleveland Daily Plain Dealer,* 15 Dec. 1860, reprinted in Howard C. Perkins, ed., *Northern Editorials on Secession,* 2 vols. (New York: D. Appleton-Century, 1942): 2: 853–54.

24. Dew, *Apostles of Disunion,* 35, quoting William R. Smith, *The History and Debates of the Convention of the People of Alabama . . . 1861* (Montgomery, 1861), 432–36; B[eriah] Magoffin, Governor of Kentucky, to S[tephen] F. Hale, Commissioner from the State of Alabama to the Commonwealth of Kentucky, 28 Dec. 1860, *War of the Rebellion,* series 4, 1: 11–15 (quotation 15); J. L. M. Curry to Thomas H. Hicks, 28 Dec. 1860, ibid., 38–42.

25. Constitution of the Provisional Government of the Confederate States of America, *War of the Rebellion,* series 4, 1: 92–99 (quotation 94).

26. Samuel Hall, "Remarks of Samuel Hall, Esq., Commissioner from Georgia, before the General Assembly of North Carolina, on February 13th, 1861," appendix (pp. 348–65) to *Journal of the Public and Secret Proceedings of the Convention of the People of Georgia, Held in Milledgeville and Savannah in 1861. Together with the Ordinances Adopted* (Milledgeville, Ga.: Boughton, Nisbet & Barnes, State Printers, 1861), 363–64.

27. Henry L. Benning, "Address of Hon. Henry L. Benning of Georgia," *Addresses Delivered before the Virginia State Convention,* 21–42 (quotation 41).

Despite their desire to win over the upper South, some lower South extremists still clung to their dream of resuming the Africa trade. The South Carolina convention that met 26 March through 5 April 1861 actually passed a resolution proposing that the Confederate constitution be amended so as to give the Confederate Congress complete control over slave imports, thus removing the absolute constitutional prohibition against the Africa trade and opening the way to its possible resumption. The resolution is printed in *War of the Rebellion,* series 4, 1: 208.

28. *U.S. Congressional Globe,* 36 Cong., 2 sess., 76–79 (House, 12 Dec. 1860); ibid., 1:82–83 (Senate, 13 Dec. 1860).

29. "Report of the Committee of Thirty-three," *House Reports,* 36 Cong., 2 sess., Report No. 31, pp. 3, 5; *Globe,* 36 Cong., 2 sess., 114 (Senate, 18 Dec. 1860).

30. "Report of the Committee of Thirty-three," 16, 25–26, 10 (quotation); "Report of the Committee of Thirteen," *Senate Reports,* 36 Cong., 2 sess., Report No. 288; *Globe,* 36 Cong., 2 sess., 279–81, 404–9.

31. *Globe,* 36 Cong., 2 sess., appendix, 41–42 (Senate, 3 Jan. 1861).

32. "Joint Resolutions inviting the other States to send commissioners to meet commissioners on the part of Virginia, and providing for the appointment of the same," 19 Jan. 1861, *War of the Rebellion,* series 4, 1: 90–91; "Resolutions of the Legislature of the State of Tennessee, relative to the present condition of national affairs, and suggesting certain amendments to the Constitution," [21 Jan. 1861], *House Misc. Documents,* 36 Cong., 2 sess., Misc. Doc. no. 27, p. 2.

33. "Proceedings of the Conference Convention," 4–27 February 1861, in *Report of the Kentucky Commissioners to the Late Peace Conference Held at Washington City, Made to the Legislature of Kentucky* (Frankfort: Jno. B. Major, State Printer, 1861), 84, 8 (quotation), 46, 72.

34. Lincoln to Seward ("private and confidential"), Springfield, 1 Feb. 1861, Basler, *Collected Works,* 4: 183; *Globe,* 36 Cong., 2 sess., 1269–70.

35. John C. Breckinridge, *Forts in the Seceding States: Speech of Hon. John C. Breckinridge, of Kentucky, in the Senate of the United States, March 18, 1861* (n.p., n.d.), 5–6; *American National Biography,* s.v. John C. Breckinridge.

36. The classic essay arguing that the election of Lincoln offered no immediate threat to slavery is Arthur C. Cole, "Lincoln's Election an Immediate Menace to the States?" *American Historical Review* 36 (July 1931): 740–67. Lincoln had expressed fears of southern territorial aggression as far back as the 1858 debates. That they were not just political rhetoric is evident from the fact that he continued to make them in private. He told the chairman of the Indiana State Republican Committee that if popular sovereignty became "settled policy," then "filibustering for all South of us, and making slave states of it, follows in spite of us, with an early Supreme court decision, holding our free-state constitutions to be unconstitutional." (Lincoln to John D. Defrees, Springfield, 18 Dec. 1860, Basler, *Collected Works,* 4: 155.)

The secessionists' rational assessment of the Republican threat was put well by John Townsend: "The popular vote of the South is now greater and stronger in relation to that party, than it will ever be again; and we have greater power to resist them, than we shall ever again have; especially with the aid of such large minorities, now against them, in their own States." Townsend was confident also that the importance of cotton would preclude any British "meddling with our Institution" of slavery. (Townsend, *South Alone,* 50, 59.)

37. Lincoln to Stephens, 22 Dec. 1860, Basler, *Collected Works,* 4: 160–61.

Chapter 8. The Friction and Abrasion of War

1. Lincoln to Horace Greeley, 22 Aug. 1862, *The Collected Works of Abraham Lincoln,* ed. Roy P. Basler, 9 vols. (New Brunswick, N.J.: Rutgers University Press, 1953–55), 5: 388–89.

2. Appeal to Border State Representatives to Favor Compensated Emancipation, 12 July 1862, ibid., 317–19 (quotation 318).

3. *Douglass's Monthly* 4 (October 1861): 543.

4. Henry Wilson, *History of the Antislavery Measures of the Thirty-seventh and Thirty-eighth Congresses, 1861–1864* (Boston: Walker, Wise, and Company, 1864; reprinted New York: Negro Universities Press, 1969), 93–95 (quotation 93), 106.

5. "Constitution of the Confederate States of America," appendix C (pp. 171–200) of Charles Robert Lee, Jr., *The Confederate Constitutions* (Chapel Hill: University of North Carolina Press, 1963), 179, 194. The commerce power was granted in Article I, Section 8, Clause 3. The right of transit and sojourn was tacked onto the privileges and immunities guarantee in Article IV, Section 2, Clause 1. The provision regarding slaves carried as well as escaping across state lines was in Article IV, Section 2, Clause 3.

6. Robert H. Gudmestad, *A Troublesome Commerce: The Transformation of the Interstate Slave Trade* (Baton Rouge: Louisiana State University Press, 2003), chap. 5; Eugene D. Genovese, *A Consuming Fire: The Fall of the Confederacy in the Mind of the White Christian South* (Athens: University of Georgia Press, 1998), 5, 11 (Dabney quotation), 110, 19–21; Thomas R. R. Cobb, *An Inquiry into the Law of Negro Slavery in the United States of America* (n.p.: T. & J. W. Johnson & Co., 1858; reprinted New York: Negro Universities Press, [1968]), 245–46.

7. Genovese, *Consuming Fire,* 22 (Lindsley quotation), 52, 54 (Verot quotation), 57, 58 (Tichnor quotation), 59 (Lyon quotations); Bell Irvin Wiley, "The Movement to Humanize the Institution of Slavery During the Confederacy," *Emory University Quarterly* 5 (1949): 219 (quoted title of Lyon's bill).

8. May Spencer Ringold, *The Role of the State Legislatures in the Confederacy* (Athens: University of Georgia Press, 1966), 59 (Lyon quotation). Bell Wiley speculated that reformers would have carried on with "renewed zeal" if the Confederacy had won the war. That may be, but no amount of zeal would have brought success. Eugene Genovese is surely right when he argues that slaveholders could not accept what amounted to a social revolution. (Wiley, "Movement to Humanize," 220; Genovese, *Consuming Fire,* 111.)

9. While historians once believed that the aristocracy favored the Confederacy while the middle and working classes backed the Union, more recent scholarship has demonstrated that the division cut across class lines. See especially Duncan Andrew Campbell, *English Public Opinion and the American Civil War* (Suffolk, U.K.: Boydell, 2003).

10. Harriet Martineau, "The Brewing of the American Storm," *Macmillan's Magazine* 6 (June 1862): 97–107 (quotations 98).

11. James Spence, *The American Union; Its Effect on National Character and Policy, with an Inquiry into Secession as a Constitutional Right, and the Causes of the Disruption,* 3d ed. (London: Richard Bentley, 1862), vii; J. E. Cairnes, *The Slave Power: Its Character, Career, and Probable Designs; Being an Attempt to Explain the Real Issues Involved in the American Contest,* 2d ed. (London: Macmillan and Co., 1863), quotations 121, 120–21.

12. Cairnes, *Slave Power,* 121–35 (first three quotations 121, others 127–28, 128, 134–35), 282–98.

13. Abraham Lincoln to John E. Cairnes, Washington, 1 Aug. 1862, *The Collected Works of Abraham Lincoln: Supplement, 1832–1865,* ed. Roy P. Basler (Westport, Conn.: Greenwood Press, 1974), 144; George McHenry, *The Position and Duty of Pennsylvania: A Letter Addressed to the President of the Philadelphia Board of Trade* (Lon-

don: Henry F. Mackintosh, 1863), 9; J. E. Cairnes and George McHenry, *The Southern Confederacy and the African Slave Trade* (Dublin: McGlashan & Gill, 1863), 51.

14. Francis Fedric, *Slave Life in Virginia and Kentucky; or, Fifty Years of Slavery in the Southern States of America* (London: Wertheim, Macintosh, and Hunt, 1863), 43–44. Throughout the original, the word "trader" is enclosed in quotation marks.

15. John Hawkins Simpson, *Horrors of the Virginian Slave Trade and of the Slave-Rearing Plantations. The True Story of Dinah, an Escaped Virginian Slave, Now in London, on Whose Body are Eleven Scars Left by Tortures which were Inflicted by Her Master, Her Own Father* (London: A. W. Bennett, 1863), vi, 61.

16. Campbell, *English Public Opinion,* 10, 195; John Bright, speech at Rochdale, Lancashire, 3 Feb. 1863, *Speeches of John Bright, M.P., on the American Question* (Boston: Little, Brown, and Company, 1865), 150–51. A photograph of Bright was the only conspicuous decoration in Lincoln's austere office. (Joseph E. Suppiger, *The Intimate Lincoln* [Lanham, Md.: University Press of America, 1985], 228, 235.)

17. Howard Jones, *Abraham Lincoln and a New Birth of Freedom: The Union and Slavery in the Diplomacy of the Civil War* (Lincoln: University of Nebraska Press, 1999), 105–9, 137, 147, 156, 162.

18. Israel Washburn, Jr., "The Logic and End of the Rebellion," *Universalist Quarterly* 21 (Jan. 1864): 5–25 (quotations 21, 22.)

19. Israel Washburn, Jr., to Abraham Lincoln, Portland, 22 Jan. 1864, Abraham Lincoln Papers, Library of Congress microfilm. On Lincoln's keen interest in Washburn's election to the governorship and his later appointment of him to the collectorship at Portland, see Abraham Lincoln to Hannibal Hamlin, Springfield, Ill., 4 Sept. 1860, Basler, *Collected Works,* 4: 110; Abraham Lincoln to Elihu B. Washburne, Springfield, 9 Sept. 1860, ibid., 113–14; Abraham Lincoln to Elihu B. Washburne, Executive Mansion, Washington, 26 Oct., 1863, ibid., 6: 540–41. Elihu, an Illinois congressman with whom Lincoln was well acquainted, was Israel's brother but chose to use an "e" at the end of his surname.

20. Lincoln to "Gentlemen of the Committee," 9 June 1864, Basler, *Collected Works,* 7: 380; Wilson, *History of the Antislavery Measures,* chap. 21 (pp. 362–66), "The Coastwise Slave-Trade," quotations, 363, 366; Edward McPherson, *The Political History of the United States of America During the Great Rebellion,* 2d ed. (Washington, D.C.: Philip & Solomons, 1865), 243 (quotation).

21. Bell Irvin Wiley, *Southern Negroes, 1861–1865,* 2d ed. (New York: Rinehart, 1953), chap. 5 (pp. 85–97), "The Slave Trade," quotations 88, 91.

22. Edmund L. Drago, ed., *"Broke by the War": Letters of a Slave Trader* (Columbia: University of South Carolina Press, 1991), 1–3; Charles Carleton Coffin, *The Boys of '61; Or, Four Years of Fighting. Personal Observations with the Army and Navy, from the First Battle of Bull Run to the Fall of Richmond* (Boston: Estes and Lauriat, 1884), 500–503.

Index